The Free-Living Lower Invertebrates

Frederick M. Bayer and Harding B. Owre
INSTITUTE OF MARINE SCIENCE, UNIVERSITY OF MIAMI

The Macmillan Company, New York

Collier-Macmillan Limited, London

Library of Congress
catalog card number: 67–13600

The Macmillan Company,
New York
Collier-Macmillan Canada, Ltd.,
Toronto, Ontario

Printed in
the United States of America

259856

Porifera

Coelenterata

Ctenophora

Platyhelminthes

Nemertea

Preface

BECAUSE of its complexity, the field of invertebrate biology has never been noted for outstanding textbooks, particularly in the English language. In the past thirty years, the massive accumulation of information on the lower invertebrates has been made available to students to a variable extent —but only in two forms: the textbook, in which coverage must be superficial if the major aspects of invertebrate life are to be treated; and the treatise. The treatise contains so much detail that it often fills several volumes and is unsuitable for use at the introductory and intermediate levels of instruction. We have attempted to bridge the gap between textbook and treatise with a volume of moderate complexity—a broad survey, amply illustrated, of the five acoelomate phyla. Parasites were omitted, inasmuch as they constitute a separate field which, if accorded the attention commensurate with that given the free-living forms, would make the volume unwieldy.

Several of the coelomate phyla have been given concise treatment by other biologists—the annelids, by R. P. Dales; the mollusks, by J. E. Morton; and the echinoderms, by David Nichols. These books are all in the Hutchinson University Library. Used in conjunction with these works, our volume on the lower Metazoa provides a comprehensive but not exhaustive coverage of the major invertebrate phyla, with the important exception of the Arthropoda.

Our book is written for a wide audience. It contains adequate information for use at the advanced undergraduate level; and at the introductory level, material appropriate to the syllabus can be selected by the instructor. Graduate students and professional biologists interested in marine problems will find the book to contain a distillation of material that would fill several volumes if treated *in extenso*. We drew heavily upon the original literature in compiling this book, and we certainly could not have written it without reference to such classic treatises as Bronn's *Klassen und Ordnungen des Tierreichs*, Grassé's *Traité de Zoologie*, and Hyman's *The Invertebrates*. We owe an enormous professional debt to all three works. In planning illustrations to demonstrate the features discussed, we selected from original sources or made new drawings and photographs from our own material. In most cases we chose naturalistic rather than diagrammatic representations, so the student will see illustrations that are reasonably similar to the demonstrations he will study in laboratory exercises. We especially wish to acknowledge the excellence of the many new drawings by Mr. Peter Loewer as a major contribution to this book.

F. M. B.
H. B. O.

Contents

INTRODUCTION   1

MORPHOLOGY AND CLASSIFICATION   5
Introduction / Structure / Histology / Skeleton / Classification,
Phylum Porifera

REPRODUCTION AND EMBRYOLOGY   15
Asexual Reproduction / Sexual Reproduction

PHYSIOLOGY   20

ECOLOGY AND DISTRIBUTION   21

PHYLOGENY   23

1
Phylum
Porifera
1

INTRODUCTION   25
General Features / Histology

MORPHOLOGY AND CLASSIFICATION   37
Class Hydrozoa / Class Scyphozoa / Class Anthozoa /
Classification, Phylum Coelenterata

REPRODUCTION AND EMBRYOLOGY   94
Asexual Reproduction / Sexual Reproduction

PHYSIOLOGY   107
Respiration / Nervous system and behavior / Digestion

ECOLOGY AND DISTRIBUTION   113
Reefs / Biological Relationships

2
Phylum
Coelenterata
25

3
**Phylum
Ctenophora
124**

INTRODUCTION   124

MORPHOLOGY AND CLASSIFICATON   125
General Features / Structure / Histology / Classification,
Phylum Ctenophora

REPRODUCTION AND EMBRYOLOGY   137
Asexual Reproduction / Sexual Reproduction

PHYSIOLOGY   140
Respiration / Nervous Reactions / Digestion / Behavior

ECOLOGY AND DISTRIBUTION   142
Ecology / Distribution

4
**Phylum
Platyhelminthes
144**

INTRODUCTION   144

MORPHOLOGY AND CLASSIFICATION   145
General Features / Histology and Structure / Classification,
Phylum Platyhelminthes

REPRODUCTION AND EMBRYOLOGY   168
Asexual Reproduction / Sexual Reproduction

PHYSIOLOGY   171
Respiration / Osmoregulation / Nervous and Sensory Reactions
/ Locomotion / Feeding and Digestion

ECOLOGY AND DISTRIBUTION   176

5
**Phylum
Nemertea
178**

INTRODUCTION   178

MORPHOLOGY AND CLASSIFICATION   184
Morphology / Classification, Phylum Nemertea

REPRODUCTION AND EMBRYOLOGY   197
Asexual Reproduction / Sexual Reproduction

PHYSIOLOGY   200
Respiration / Nervous and Sensory Reactions / Feeding and
Digestion

ECOLOGY AND DISTRIBUTION   203

Selected References   205

Sources of Illustrations   207

Index   219

[viii]

Phylum Porifera

Introduction

The sponges are an ancient group of aquatic animals whose life processes depend on a flow of water through their bodies. These creatures, and some coelenterates, among other lower invertebrates, were called zoophytes ("animal-plants") by Renaissance and later scholars, such as Linnaeus, who questioned their position in the realm of nature. Their animal organization was finally accepted in the mid-nineteenth century, although John Ellis had reported water currents and movements of the osculum in 1765. As late as 1846, James Dana, scientific leader of our first oceanographic voyage, the United States Exploring Expedition, expressed doubt that they are animals. The name Porifera (from the Latin *porus*, pore, and *ferre*, to bear) was created in 1836 by R. E. Grant.

It is easy to understand the confusion of the early naturalists because sponges have no organs and, to the unaided eye, no external animal characteristics. There is a huge range in size, from organisms a few millimeters high to massive growths as big as large hassocks. Most sponges are sessile as adults, growing attached to submerged objects such as rocks and pilings or anchoring themselves in the bottom, but some species normally lie free. Colored yellow, green, blue, red, violet, as well as drab browns and grays, these are conspicuous inhabitants of shallow marine waters from Arctic and Antarctic areas to the equator, and they

Phylum Porifera

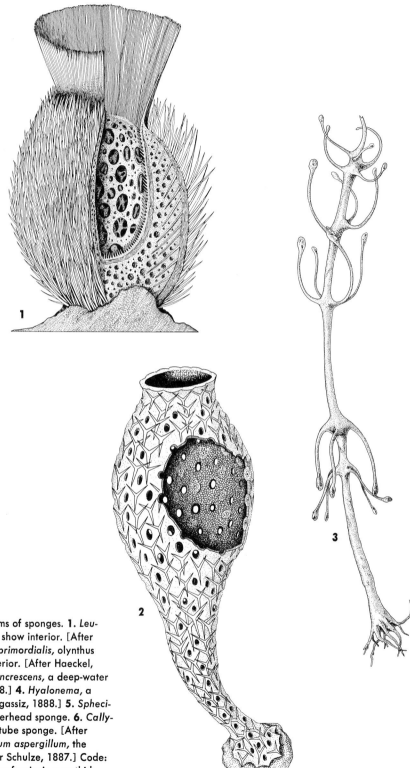

Figures 1 to 7. Growth forms of sponges. **1.** *Leucandra aspera,* cut away to show interior. [After Haeckel, 1872.] **2.** *Ascetta primordialis,* olynthus stage, cut away to show interior. [After Haeckel, 1872.] **3.** *Chondrocladia concrescens,* a deep-water sponge. [After Agassiz, 1888.] **4.** *Hyalonema,* a glass-rope sponge. [After Agassiz, 1888.] **5.** *Spheciospongia vesparia,* the loggerhead sponge. **6.** *Callyspongia vaginalis,* common tube sponge. [After Dendy, 1890.] **7.** *Euplectellum aspergillum,* the Venus's flower basket. [After Schulze, 1887.] Code: A, anchor spicules; B, colony of epizoic zoanthids.

1

2

3

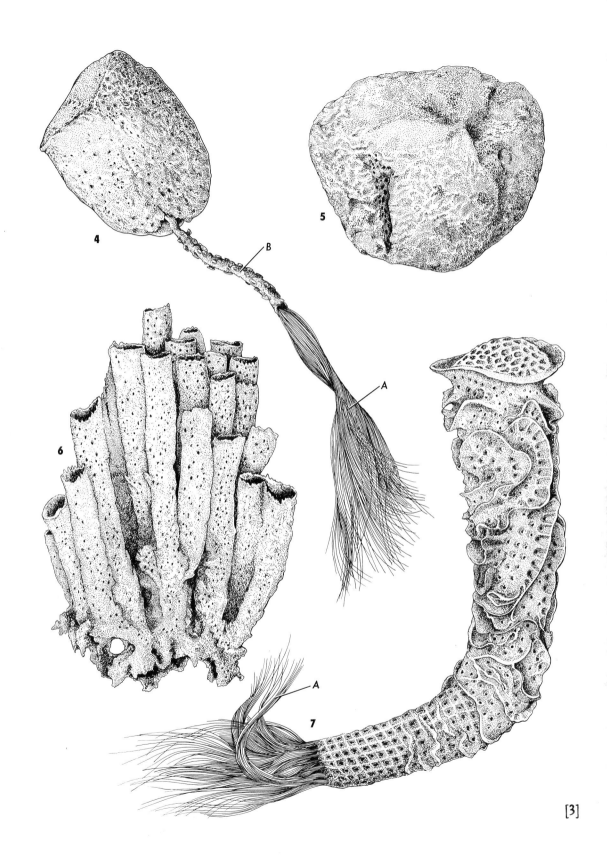

also occur in great depths. Only one small family lives in fresh water. Their form may be regular—that is, cylindrical or vase- or fan-shaped (Figures 1, 2, 6)—but most sponges are asymmetrical growths whose shape may depend on the environment (Figure 5). Because of the structure of their siliceous skeleton, the glass sponges (Hexactinellida) have the most elegant form of all (Figure 7).

Fundamentally, the body design of all sponges is the same, consisting of a *dermal layer*, perforated by many small pores through which water enters, and a *gastral layer* of flagellated collar cells, *choanocytes*. These line an internal cavity and ingest water-borne food. The beating of their flagella originates and maintains the movement of water from the exterior to the internal cavity and then out through the *osculum*, the largest body aperture. The term osculum thus is a misnomer since the opening regularly serves for the ejection of water and wastes rather than for ingestion. The simplest sponges are small, with a single choanocyte-lined internal cavity and one osculum, but most are much larger aggregates of choanocyte-lined chambers and may have many oscula (Figures 5, 6, and 11). Commonly the body is strengthened by an internal skeleton of calcareous or siliceous elements termed *spicules* or by a network of horny fibers (*spongin*—Figure 27). Some species contain both siliceous spicules and spongin and a few have no skeleton at all. The commercial sponges are among those whose skeleton is constructed of spongin alone, and it is this nonliving material which forms the familiar bath sponge, all the cells having been removed by a curing process. The spongin of commercial species is an albuminoid protein related to the keratins of hair, nails, and horn.

Since pre-Christian times when man first discovered the special qualities of the spongin skeleton, sponges have been harvested by diving and used in commerce. The trade, mentioned in the works of Homer and other writers of ancient Greece, apparently was originated by inhabitants of the eastern Mediterranean. It became a widespread and lucrative fishery in the Mediterranean which produced the world supply of sponges until the nineteenth century. Development of the fishery in the western North Atlantic began in 1841 when a Frenchman who had been shipwrecked in the Bahama Islands sent a sample lot to Paris. The first Florida sponges were shipped from Key West to New York in 1849. Later, extensive beds of fine quality sponges were found in the eastern Gulf of Mexico, and about 1899 Tarpon Springs, Florida, supplanted Key West as the sponge center of the United States. By 1938, sponge production in the western North Atlantic far exceeded that in the Mediterranean (1,750,000 vs. 700,000 lbs), the primary producers being the United States and the Bahamas. Subsequently a fungal blight or "wasting disease" caused a precipitous decline in the fishery and recovery has been very slow.

Although synthetic sponges are now generally used in the household and for washing vehicles, natural sponges remain in demand in the arts and industry because of their special qualities of durability, softness, resiliency, and capacity for copious retention of fluid. Known by a variety of common names such as turkey cup, elephant ear, sheepswool, velvet, hardhead, and glove sponge, the majority of the commercial species belong to the genera *Euspongia*, *Hippiospongia*, and *Spongia*.

Sponges probably evolved in the Precambrian period more than 600 million years ago. Over 1,000 fossil genera have been described and of these only about 20 seem to be identical with Recent genera. Living today are approximately 10,000 species in 1,400 genera.

Morphology and Classification

INTRODUCTION

Because sponges have no organ systems and are unique among animals in the porous structure of their bodies and in having internal cavities lined with choanocytes, the phylum Porifera is often placed alone in a special subkingdom, Parazoa, of the kingdom Animalia. However, many modern experts prefer to classify the Porifera at the base of the subkingdom Metazoa in consideration of their many metazoan characteristics. Among these are similarities in types of cells, such as eosinophilic amoebocytes and collar cells, in spermatogenesis and oogenesis, and in the presence of a tetraradial symmetry in some sponge larvae. Biochemical studies have shown that sponges differ considerably from other animals in their lipoid substances and, in fact, a number of new sterols and fatty acids have been discovered in them. On the other hand, the nucleic and amino acids are essentially the same as those found in higher animals. Interestingly enough, spongin fibers and mammalian collagen are generally comparable in the amounts and pattern of amino acids. We adopt the view that the phylum Porifera is the simplest and most primitive group in the subkingdom Metazoa.

STRUCTURE

The loosely organized tissues of sponges are arranged in three basic designs: *asconoid structure*, the simplest (Figure 8); *syco-*

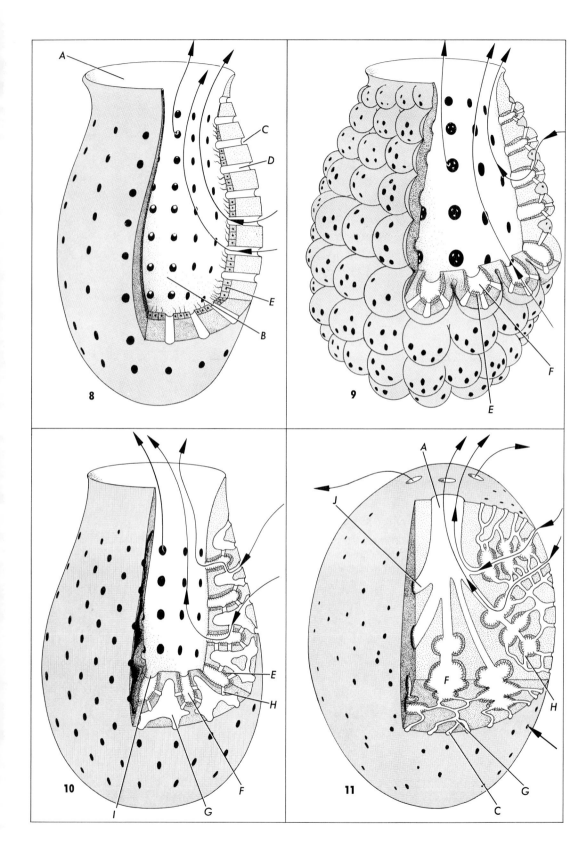

noid, of intermediate complexity (Figures 9, 10); and *leuconoid*, the most involved (Figure 11). In the vase-shaped asconoid type, a thin body wall surrounds a spacious cavity, the *spongocoel*. The wall consists of a one-layered *epidermis* (dermal layer), a relatively thick *mesenchyme* of cells and spicules embedded in a colloidal gel (gelatinous matrix) and, internally, the gastral layer of choanocytes which lines the spongocoel except for the region immediately surrounding the osculum. The wall is perforated by numerous minute *incurrent ostia* (Figure 8). These are the outer openings of tiny canals which perforate epidermal cells called *porocytes*. The elongate porocytes, with their *intracellular canals*, extend from the epidermis through the mesenchyme to the spongocoel, thus forming the incurrent path for the flow of water impelled by the beating of flagella of the choanocytes within.

The next level of structural complexity is the syconoid type, which is also vase-shaped, with a single osculum. The major difference from asconoid sponges is that the body wall grows outward in numerous finger-like projections at more or less regular intervals and the choanocytes line the projections, not the spongocoel. The choanocyte-lined cavities within the projections are called *radial canals* (Figure 9). Externally, between the projections are spaces, *incurrent canals*, the walls of which are pierced by many openings, *prosopyles*. The prosopyles are the functional and perhaps morphological equivalent of the asconoid porocyte. Thus, in the simplest syconoid sponges, water is pulled into the incurrent canals, through the prosopyles to the radial canals, and passes thence into the spongocoel via inner openings of the radial canals, *internal ostia*. It flows out of the body through the osculum.

In most syconoid sponges, however, the incurrent and radial canals are enclosed within the wall, the epidermal and mesenchymal tissues having formed a *cortex*, an outer layer shielding the canal system. The cortex, too, is perforated, by *dermal ostia* through which water flows into the incurrent canals. The lining of the incurrent canals corresponds to the outer surface of the asconoid type and is thus epidermal, just as the gastral layer of choanocytes which lines the spongocoel of asconoid sponges is here restricted to the radial canals. An epithelium derived from epidermal tissue lines the spongocoel. Whereas in asconoid

Figures 8 to 11. Structure of sponges. **8.** Ascon type. **9.** Sycon type. **10.** Sycon type with cortex. **11.** Leucon type. Arrows indicate course of water currents through the body. Code: *A*, osculum; *B*, spongocoel; *C*, ostium; *D*, intracellular canal; *E*, gastral layer; *F*, radial canal; *G*, incurrent canal; *H*, prosopyle; *I*, internal ostium; *J*, excurrent canal.

sponges water flows through porocytes directly to the spongocoel and out through the osculum, in the most complex syconoid sponges it has a more circuitous route through these apertures and internal spaces: dermal ostia, incurrent canals, prosopyles, radial canals, internal ostia, spongocoel, osculum.

The glass sponges, class Hexactinellida, have a peculiar structure, different from all others. The body consists of a network, the *trabecular net*, in which the flagellated chambers are located. Apparently there is no epidermis. The trabecular net is said to be formed by the union of pseudopodia of various types of amoebocytes. The appearance is that of a relatively coarse mesh enclosing large spaces. The trabecular net extends from the external surface through to the spongocoel. Within it lie elongated flagellated chambers which have been likened to the radial canals of syconoid sponges. This delicate cellular structure is supported by unique siliceous spicules, often united in an elaborate and beautiful glassy framework (Figures 21, 22).

The structure of most sponges is the leuconoid type in which the body wall is very thick, and usually a true spongocoel is lacking (Figure 11). Mesenchyme forms the bulk, and the cortex may be so extensive that subdermal spaces are formed between the dermal ostia and the incurrent canals. Those essential cells, the choanocytes, line multiple tiny, round or oval pockets in contrast to the relatively large, elongate radial canals of syconoid sponges. Many oscula may be present, each serving as an exit for the fluid pulled into a particular system of apertures, canals, and spaces. Water, impelled as in all sponges by the beating of innumerable choanocytic flagella, enters dermal ostia, flows into subdermal spaces and incurrent canals, through prosopyles into canals leading to the flagellated chambers, out canals to excurrent channels, and thence through oscula to the exterior. Sponges grow large and solid with the development of this intricate system whereby many units of intake and output are grouped. The ratio of water-exposed internal surface to external surface is obviously far greater in leuconoid than in syconoid and asconoid sponges. The efficiency of this more complex structure is demonstrated by the abundance in numbers of species as well as of individuals of leuconoids compared with other sponges, and the great size that some species of leuconoids attain.

HISTOLOGY

The epidermis (dermal layer) is formed of *pinacocytes*, flat polygonal cells thickened in the nuclear area (Figure 12). These cells also line all the internal canals and spaces of syconoid and leuconoid sponges except, of course, for the flagellated chambers. By contracting the thin peripheral areas toward the central part of the cell, pinacocytes can produce a slight reduction of surface area. This is apparently a labile type of cell; the tubular *porocytes* (Figure 12) are modified pinacocytes, and "nervous type" cells as well may be derived from them. The highly contractile porocyte closes and opens the outer aperture of its intracellular canal by means of a cytoplasmic diaphragm which it can advance and retract. Porocytes, once considered characteristic of and restricted to asconoid calcareous sponges, have been found in some siliceous species (the fresh-water family Spongillidae) and are thought to be present generally in siliceous sponges.

Beneath the thin epidermis lies the *mesenchyme* (Figure 12), a colloidal gel containing free amoeboid cells and the skeletal elements, spicules or spongin or both. Hexactinellid sponges apparently lack the gelatinous matrix. The *amoebocytes* have received numerous special names according to structure or supposed function; because the validity of some of these names is doubted, only a few will be mentioned. Some are eosinophilic cells, others hyaline. The *archaeocytes,* a type of amoebocyte with a large nucleus and conspicuous nucleolus and blunt pseudopodia, have long been considered generalized, totipotent cells, that is, capable of differentiating into any of the other kinds, including the reproductive cells. However, there is evidence that, in some sponges at least, the oocytes and spermatocytes are derived from choanocytes. *Scleroblast* is the term applied to those amoebocytes which secrete spicules (Figure 14), and *spongioblast* to those forming spongin fibers. An unusual amoeboid cell, the *lophocyte* (Figure 15), has been found in fresh-water and marine siliceous sponges. This bears one or, rarely, two tufts of long fibrils and may function in excretion or in the secretion of spongin fibers. Other mesenchymal cells are the fusiform, contractile *myocytes,* which resemble invertebrate smooth muscle cells and are circularly oriented around the osculum and other apertures whose size they regulate (Figure 13). It has been generally accepted that sponges lack sensory and nerve cells, but in recent years specialists have described bipolar and multipolar "nervous type" cells with long processes which connect parts of the anatomy such as dermal and gastral layers, and gastral layer and canal (Figure 15). Indeed, Tuzet (in Dougherty, 1963) reported having observed the movement of pinacocytes from the epidermis into the mesenchyme, where they developed into nerve cells, and she believes that the sensitive cells of sponges are all derived from the epidermis. However, in the opinion of most specialists, the histological evidence

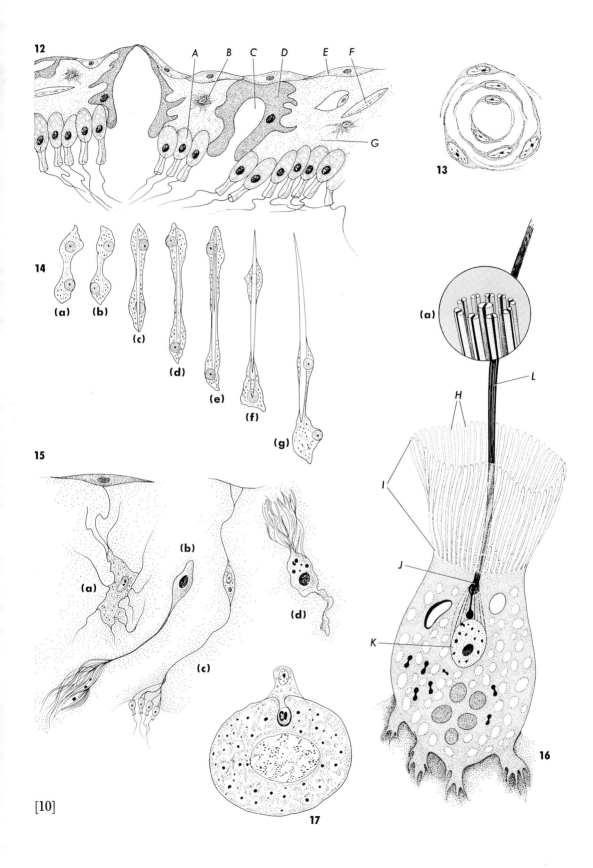

presented so far, based largely on silver-impregnated tissues viewed by light microscopy, is insufficient to demonstrate the existence of nerve cells according to accepted standards in the other phyla.

The choanocytes (collar cells—Figures 12, 16), which line the spongocoel of the asconoids, the radial canals of the syconoids, and the numerous, tiny chambers of the leuconoid forms, are round or oval, sometimes very elongate, with a large nucleus. From the free end extends one long flagellum surrounded by a contractile extension, the *collar*. These cells are structurally similar to protozoans of the family Craspedomonadidae, commonly called choanoflagellates. The similarities between choanocyte and choanoflagellate usually cited are the presence of the collar and the single flagellum, which in both arise from a blepharoplast (basal body) to which a parabasal body is attached. By examination with electron microscope, the ultrastructure of the collars of some choanocytes has been found to resemble that of choanoflagellates in that both consist of contiguous extensions from the cell body. The choanocyte has long been recorded as a type of cell restricted among multicellular animals to the Porifera. However, collared cells with one flagellum form the flagellated epithelia of certain common reef corals and also occur in the larvae of some Echinodermata and in the oviducal epithelium of the sea cucumber *Caudina*.

Choanocytes form a gastral layer one cell thick, with their bases appressed to the mesenchyme and their flagella and collars extending freely into the water-filled cavities. This arrangement is not static, for the choanocytes may also move into the mesenchyme. There is evidence that, in addition to their other functions, the choanocytes of some species play an important role in reproduction. This will be discussed in more detail in the section on reproduction.

Figures 12 to 17. Histology of sponges. **12.** Cross-section of asconoid sponge wall. [Redrawn from Prenant, 1925.] **13.** Myocytes surrounding prosopyle. [Redrawn from Dendy, 1893.] **14** (a) to (g). Stages in development of a monaxon spicule. [Redrawn from Minchin, 1908.] **15.** Lophocytes (b) and (d), and nervous-type cells (a) and (c). [Redrawn from Tuzet and Pavans de Ceccaty, 1953.] **16.** Choanocyte, diagrammatic, based on electron microscopy. [Adapted from Rasmont, 1959, and others.] **17.** Sperm carrier cell fertilizing ovum. [Redrawn from Dubosc and Tuzet, 1937.] Code: A, choanocytes; B, amoebocytes; C, pore of porocyte; D, porocyte; E, pinacocyte; F, spicule; G, mesenchyme; H, microvilli forming the collar I; J, basal granule of flagellum; K, nucleus; L, flagellum, with arrangement of component fibrils shown in inset (a).

Phylum Porifera

SKELETON

Spicules are variously shaped structures composed either of calcium carbonate or silicon compounds secreted by scleroblasts in the mesenchyme. Large spicules called *megascleres* may extend through the epidermis to the outside and are often found in protective arrangements around the oscula and other apertures. *Microscleres* are small spicules in the mesenchyme. The types, location, and relative numbers of megascleres and microscleres are important characteristics in the classification of sponges. There is a large terminology based on the number of axes and rays and other aspects of the spicular form. We will discuss only the major types as follows:

1. *Monaxon* spicules (Figure 18), which have a single straight or curved axis and may be spiny or smooth, pointed at both ends, rounded or knobbed at both ends or pointed at one end and rounded at the other. Some monaxons terminate in plates or anchor-shaped hooks.

2. *Triradiates*, with three rays (Figure 19), common in calcareous sponges.

3. *Tetraxon* spicules, which are four-rayed with the rays extending out from a central point, not in the same plane. The four rays may be approximately equal in length, but more often one is longer than the other three, producing the forms called *triaenes* (Figure 20).

4. *Hexactinal* or *triaxon* spicules, which have three axes arranged at right angles to one another so that six rays extend outward from a central point. The name of the glass sponges, class Hexactinellida, is derived from the structure of these spicules, which are found only in that class. The basic hexactinal form may be modified and decorated in many ways (Figure 21). Glass sponges also contain other types of spicules such as monaxons and tetraxons, and in many species bundles of long glassy spicules protrude from the base of the body, anchoring it in the substrate.

Figures 18 to 29. Skeletal structures of sponges. **18.** Monaxial spicules. [After Dendy, 1916.] **19.** Triradiate spicules. [After Dendy, 1918.] **20.** Triaene type of tetraxon spicules. [After Dendy, 1915.] **21.** Various ornate types of hexactinellid spicules: (a) oxyhexaster; (b) hexact; (c) pinulated pentact; (d) amphidisc; (e) scopula; (f) floricome; (g) discohexaster. [Redrawn from Schulze, 1887.] **22.** Siliceous network of fused hexactinellid spicules. [Redrawn from Schulze, 1887.] **23.** Anisochelas. [After Dendy, 1915.] **24.** Sigmas. [After Dendy, 1915.] **25.** Desmas. [After Sollas, 1888.] **26.** Spherasters and sterrasters. [After Dendy, 1916.] **27.** Pure spongin fibers. **28.** Spongin fibers with core of spicules. [Redrawn from Dendy, 1890.] **29.** Spongin fibers containing projecting spicules—echinated fibers. [Redrawn from Dendy, 1890.]

5. *Polyaxon* spicules or, generally, *asters* (Figure 26), which are spicules consisting of many axes crossing at a central point. Usually these are microscleres.

6. *Spheres*, which are nonradiate concretions.

7. *Desmas* (Figure 25), which are irregularly branching forms.

The process of secretion of spicules by the scleroblasts is not well understood. A binucleate or multinucleate cell commences formation of the spicule by secreting a sliver within the cell body. As the mineral structure grows, the scleroblast divides and the daughter cells move outward from the center to complete the specific form (Figure 14). Apparently all of the minerals deposited in such intricate fashion are derived from the fresh or salt water which the animals pass through their bodies. Spongioblasts in series secrete spongin fibers. The little-known lophocytes are also said to form spongin. It is known that the skeletal elements of sponges are secreted by mesenchymal cells, but the mechanisms whereby these structures are formed are poorly understood.

CLASSIFICATION, PHYLUM PORIFERA *

I. Class Calcarea. Skeleton composed entirely of calcareous spicules (monaxon, tetraxon).
  A. Order Homocoela (*Leucosolenia*). Asconoid structure.
  B. Order Heterocoela (*Sycon, Scypha*). Syconoid or leuconoid structure.

II. Class Hexactinellida. With six-rayed (triaxon) or modified six-rayed siliceous spicules; no well-defined dermal layer.
  A. Order Hexasterophora (*Euplectella*, Figure 7). With hexasters, without amphidiscs (Figure 21d).
  B. Order Amphidiscophora (*Hyalonema*, Figure 4). With amphidiscs, without hexasters (Figure 21g).

III. Class Demospongiae. Skeleton composed of siliceous spicules or spongin fibers or both. Spicules never triaxon, usually differentiated into megascleres and microscleres; rarely, skeleton is absent.

IIIa. Subclass Tetractinellida. With tetraxon spicules, or in some cases, no spicules; without spongin.
  A. Order Myxospongida (*Halisarca*). Without spicules.
  B. Order Carnosa (*Chondrilla*, chicken-liver sponge). Megascleres and microscleres not sharply differentiated; triaenes (Figure 20) usually lacking.
  C. Order Choristida (*Geodia; Craniella*). Megascleres and microscleres distinct; triaenes present.

* After Hyman (1940) and Rothschild (1961).

IIIb. Subclass Monaxonida. With monaxon megascleres; spongin may or may not be present.

    A. Order Hadromerina (boring sponges, *Cliona*; loggerhead sponge, *Spheciospongia*). Megascleres mostly monaxon, pointed at one end and knobbed at other (tylostyles, Figure 18); microscleres, if present, asters (Figure 26); without spongin.

    B. Order Halichondrina (*Halichondria*). Generally with two or more types of megascleres intermingled, not localized, and without microscleres; with little spongin.

    C. Order Poecilosclerina (*Adocia*; fire sponge, *Tedania ignis*; *Mycale*; *Microciona*; *Chondrocladia*). With two or more kinds of megascleres, localized in distribution—for example, one type may be found only in cortex and another in area of flagellated chambers; spicules generally united by spongin into a network (Figure 28, 29); microscleres of various types. Includes majority of Demospongiae.

    D. Order Haplosclerina (*Haliclona*; fresh-water sponges, family Spongillidae, *Spongilla*, *Ephydatia*, etc.). With one kind of megasclere, pointed at both ends (oxea), not localized, with or without microscleres; spongin usually present.

IIIc. Subclass Keratosa (the horny sponges, *Spongia*, *Hircinia*, *Verongia*). Without siliceous spicules; skeleton composed of spongin fibers (Figure 27).

Reproduction and Embryology

ASEXUAL REPRODUCTION

Sponges have a high capacity for regeneration of wounded or lost tissues. The classical experiments of H. V. Wilson, who forced sponge tissue through fine silk cloth, showed that even when the cells which normally form epithelium, mesenchyme, and gastral layer are completely jumbled, they will reassemble and develop into a new animal. Such clumps of cells are called *reunition masses*. Sponge fishermen know the trick of cutting commercial species into pieces and then waiting until they grow to marketable size. Disease and predators may wreck these efforts, but healthy sponge tissue is apparently indestructible in a favorable habitat. The various amoebocytes in the mesenchyme are those which build the new structures.

When environmental conditions such as quality of the water, amount of food available, temperature, depth, and substrate are favorable, a sponge will grow to the size limit of its particular species. If, however, some conditions become unfavorable, sponges can reproduce asexually and thereby insure the survival of their kind. One asexual process is the formation of *reduction bodies* within the deteriorating sponge. Amoebocytes clump together and epithelial cells surround them. When the original sponge body falls apart, each group of cells can grow into a new animal.

Similar to reduction bodies are the *gemmules* (Figures 30 to 32) which are well known among fresh-water sponges and less known but apparently common in the abundant marine species. In fresh-water forms, these structures commence as aggregations of amoebocytes (archaeocytes), surrounded by amoebocytes which differentiate into columnar cells. These secrete a hard covering over the sphere of amoebocytes within and may also secrete an outer encasement. In the most elegant gemmules, scleroblasts secrete spicules to make a radial armature between outer and inner coverings (Figure 32). The cells inside this complicated housing can emerge when external conditions are suitable through a special aperture, the *micropyle* (Figure 32). This opens because of biochemical activity within. The freed cells remain associated and develop into a new sponge. In marine species, the structure of gemmules is not as elaborate, so far as we know.

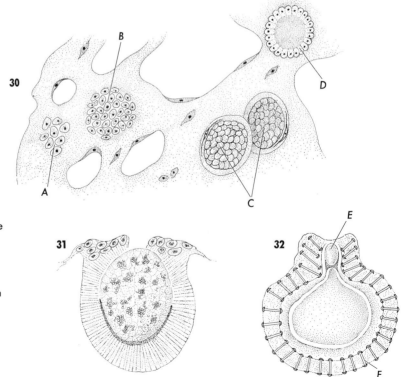

Figures 30 to 32. Reproduction in sponges. **30.** Formation of gemmules in marine sponge. [Redrawn from Wilson, 1894.]
31 and 32. Early and final stages of gemmule in fresh-water sponge. [Redrawn from Evans, 1900.] Code: A and B, archaeocytes clustering; C, later stage in formation; D, fully formed gemmule; E, micropyle; F, layer of spicules.

Amoebocytes clump and are surrounded by a thin membrane of flat cells which later become columnar and flagellated except at the posterior pole. These gemmules resemble the larvae which develop from the zygote in sexual reproduction. They, too, develop into sponges, given proper substrate and physicochemical conditions.

Sexual Reproduction

Some species are dioecious, but most are hermaphrodites which may produce ova and sperm at different times. Both archaeocytes and choanocytes have been observed to differentiate into gametes, the maturation divisions being similar to those which occur in higher animals. The ova are retained by the parent while the mature sperm may be carried out of the body by the exhalant current. It is assumed that the ova are fertilized by sperm which enter with the inhalant current. It is not known if self-fertilization or cross-fertilization is most frequent. In any case, fertilization of the ovum, located in the mesenchyme, is effected by a *carrier cell*, an amoebocyte, or a differentiated choanocyte which the sperm enters. When carrier cell with sperm reaches the ovum, the ovum forms a cytostome, as amoebae may, to engulf both carrier and male gamete (Figure 17). The entire zygote cleaves in a radial pattern into cells of equal or nearly equal size (radial holoblastic cleavage), and the embryo develops into a free-swimming larva before it leaves the parent. In the sponges, there are two major types of larva, the *amphiblastula* and the *parenchymella* (Figures 36, 41). The amphiblastula is commonest in the class Calcarea, and the parenchymella, in the Demospongiae.

An interesting series of events occurs in the development of the amphiblastula larva. At the 16-cell stage, the embryo is flat and it lies with one flat side just beneath a layer of choanocytes. Those eight "upper" cells, which are closest to the choanocytes, are larger than the rest and will eventually give rise to the epidermal cells of the adult. The "lower," smaller cells are the ones which later will form choanocytes. Within this group of cells, there is a cavity, the *blastocoel* (Figure 33). This first becomes evident at the 4- to 8-cell stage. The smaller cells (micromeres) develop flagella on the inside, so that the flagella project into the blastocoel (Figure 33). Meanwhile the larger cells (macromeres) on the opposite side have parted in the central area, leaving an opening ("mouth") through which other sponge cells can be ingested. This stage of development is called a *stomoblastula* (from *stomo*, mouth; *blastula*, a multicellular embryo) (Figure 33). Next occurs an astonishing developmental phenomenon in which the

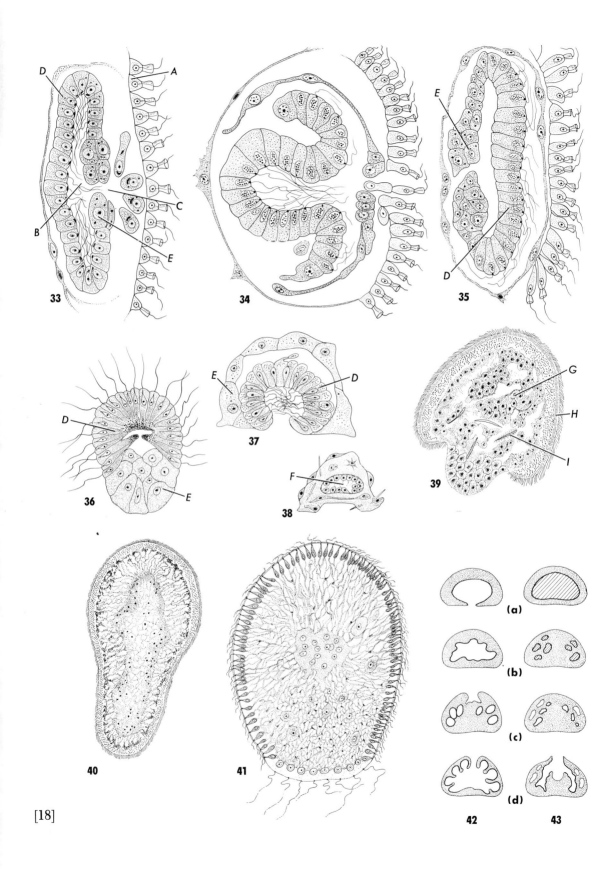

embryo turns inside out, via the "mouth" (Figure 34). Those cells (micromeres) which were flagellated at their inner ends move out so that the flagella are now located on the outside of a part of the larva (Figure 35). The macromeres which surrounded the embryonic "mouth" remain larger and nonflagellated. This *inversion* is similar to that which occurs in phases of the life cycle of the flagellate protozoan *Volvox* (Figure 44). No other similar phenomena are known; this similarity is thus considered another link between flagellate Protozoa and Porifera.

When inversion has occurred and there are numerous externally flagellated cells and fewer large, nonflagellated cells, the embryo is able to move from the mesenchyme into the exhalant current and commence independent life outside the parent. This free-swimming larva is the *amphiblastula* (Figure 36). It swims with the flagellated end foremost, continues to grow, and, after a brief planktonic life, settles onto a suitable substrate, flagellated end down. The flagellated cells move inward by a process termed *invagination* or *emboly* and are then surrounded by the macromeres (Figures 37, 38). The inner space which the flagellated cells encompass will become the spongocoel. The flagellated cells of the larva differentiate into choanocytes, archaeocytes, and other amoebocytes. The larval macromeres become pinacocytes, scleroblasts, and porocytes. In the calcareous sponges, an asconoid structure, the *olynthus* (Figure 2), is a stage recognized before the development of incurrent and radial canals.

The *parenchymella*, the characteristic larva of the Demospongiae, is also called a stereogastrula because it is solid (stereo) and two-layered (gastrula). The outer layer of cells is wholly or partially flagellated and it surrounds a solid inner mass (Figure 41). Just as the amphiblastula does, the parenchymella settles by its "anterior" end—that is, that which is foremost in swimming. At settlement, its flagellated cells are external. In some species, the external flagellated cells move inward to form choanocytes, and

Figures 33 to 43. Reproduction in sponges. 33. Developing larva of Grantia at stomoblastula stage. 34. Inversion of stomoblastula of Sycon. 35. Young amphiblastula of Sycon after inversion. [33, 34, and 35 redrawn from Dubosc and Tuzet, 1937.] 36. Amphiblastula of Sycon. 37 and 38. Settled young sponge after invagination of flagellated cells. [36, 37, and 38 redrawn from Hammer, 1908.] 39 to 41. Parenchymella larvae of demosponges. [Redrawn from Levi, 1956.] 42 and 43. Two types of development of canal systems in demosponges. [Redrawn from Levi, 1957.] Code: A, maternal choanocyte; B, blastocoel; C, mouth; D, flagellated cell (micromere); E, macromere; F, spongocoel; G, archaeocyte; H, flagellated layer; I, larval spicule.

Figure 44. Stages in the inversion of Volvox. [Redrawn from Zimmermann, 1925.]

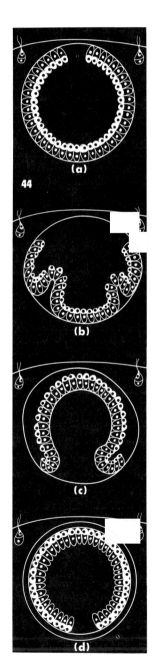

44

(a)

(b)

(c)

(d)

internal cells migrate outwards. In others, there is no such exchange but an histogenesis whereby the larval cells differentiate into adult tissues. Spaces form within the central mass. These are the beginnings of the system of canals and flagellated chambers. This is shown in Figures 42 and 43.

In cross sections through the flagellated portion of the larvae of certain Calcarea, workers have found four large cells symmetrically arranged around the animal–vegetal axis. They differ from neighboring cells in lacking flagella, having a large nucleus and being pigmented. Eventually they deteriorate. The arrangement of the cells has been interpreted by some workers as evidence of a primary tetraradial symmetry such as that found in hydrozoan medusae.

Physiology

Information on the physiology of sponges is scant, and generalizations are invariably based on observations, often fragmentary, of a very few species. All functions depend on the flow of water through the body, the current being created by the uncoordinated beating of flagella of the choanocytes. In leuconoid sponges (Figure 11) the choanocytes are located closer to the incurrent opening of the chambers than the excurrent, and they are oriented so that their collars are more or less directed toward the excurrent aperture. The flagella move in a spiral path from base to tip. The efficiency of these tiny propelling structures depends on the fact that the incurrent apertures and canals are smaller in diameter than the excurrent canals and osculum (oscula). Thus the asconoid sponge with its relatively huge spongocoel is a less effective water-moving unit than sponges of syconoid and, particularly, leuconoid structure.

The rate of flow has been studied in a small (10 cm high, 1 cm in diameter) leuconoid calcareous sponge, *Leuconia*. It has an estimated 81,000 incurrent canals, 2,250,000 flagellated chambers, 5,200 excurrent canals, and an osculum only 0.20 cm in diameter. The velocity was slowest (0.001 cm/sec) in the flagellated chambers, where the choanocytes capture particles of food, and fastest (8.5 cm/sec) at the osculum which ejects upwards a stream of waste-laden water at an estimated volume of 22.5 liters per day.

Sponges are thus filter-feeders. Their food consists of particles of organic detritus and minute zoo- and phytoplankton, including protozoans and bacteria. Digestion is intracellular and apparently does not usually take place within the choanocytes, which collect food, but in adjacent amoebocytes to which it is transferred. As in Protozoa, food is digested in vacuoles which first show an acid and, later, an alkaline reaction. Various proteolytic enzymes similar to trypsin, pepsin, rennin, erepsin, and others have been identified from sponge extracts, but it is not certain that these are all sponge products because of the numerous bacteria and other organisms which normally inhabit the canals and chambers. Digested food is stored in amoebocytes as glycogen, fat, and glyco- and lipoproteins. Indigestibles and wastes ejected by the amoebocytes and other cells are removed via the exhalant current. In a few studies of excretion, ammonia and complicated basic nitrogenous compounds have been found but not the common nitrogenous wastes such as urea and uric acid.

Response to chemical and mechanical stimuli and, in some cases, to light is a slow contraction. The commonest grossly observable reaction in sponges, particularly the Demospongiae, is closure of the osculum, which may occur in response to high temperatures, impurities in the water, CO_2, lack of oxygen, removal from water, injury, and other tactile stimulation. The effector is a sphincter of myocytes surrounding the osculum; in one species, closure in response to touch occurred in about three minutes. Such stimuli can also cause closure of porocytes and rounding up of the pinacocytes so that the epidermis shrinks. The excitation moves short distances (1 to 2 cm) but usually not as far as another osculum. Spatial summation and the greatest distance of spread of excitation known so far has been reported to result from pricking the base of a colony of *Tethya*. A pronounced general contraction of the body was accompanied by closure of the most distant oscula, 4 to 8 cm away from the base, all of this beginning several seconds after stimulation and completed after some minutes. Sponges presumably lack nervous elements altogether and excitation is a matter of transmission from cell to cell (neuroid transmission) at a rate of a few millimeters per minute.

Very little can be said about respiration except that it is aerobic. Any condition which causes severe reduction in the supply of oxygen will cause a sponge to deteriorate. Evidence of a physiological gradient was found in studies of an asconoid sponge, the upper half of which used 10 to 50 per cent more oxygen per gram per hour than the basal half.

Ecology and Distribution

Sponges are widely distributed in marine habitats, but the great majority, both of species and individuals, occurs in the upper sublittoral zone—that is, from the low-tide mark down to about

50 meters. Apparently salinity is a limiting factor in distribution, for sponges are uncommon in brackish water. The relatively few fresh-water species (class Demospongiae, order Haplosclerina, family Spongillidae) live around the world in ponds, lakes, and streams where they form encrusting growths on submerged objects.

Generally, species with calcareous and siliceous skeletons are more abundant in temperate and boreal waters and in the depths than in subtropical waters, and the reverse is true of those with spongin skeletons. Most of the Calcarea inhabit the shallow salt waters of the littoral (intertidal) and sublittoral zones. The Hex-actinellida occur in all the oceans from polar latitudes to the equator but are most abundant in the deep waters of the tropics. Although some species live in relatively shallow waters, above 100 meters, and others at great depths (glass sponges were collected from 6,770 meters on the Galathea expedition), the majority are found between approximately 500 and 1,000 meters. The root spicules (Figure 4) serve to anchor the body on the soft, oozy bottom. Other adaptations for life in the quiet deep waters where conditions change slowly or not at all are the rigid siliceous skeleton (Figure 22), the open construction without a dermal layer, and the apparent lack of contractility. Members of the class Demospongiae, in which the majority of species is classified, are widespread and abundant in shallow water. A few species were collected on the Galathea expedition at the great depth of 7,000 meters. Deep-water demosponges often have long basal "stalks" and unusual form, for example, *Chondrocladia* (Figure 3).

Associated with sponges live many other organisms—bacteria, uni- and multicellular algae, protozoans, and numerous metazoans such as platyhelminth and annelid worms, mollusks, and crustaceans. Usually they grow on the surface or inhabit the canal system and flagellated chambers, but some actually live in the tissues of the sponge. The guest organism always gains some benefit from the association. If the host is neither harmed nor benefited, the relationship is called *commensalism*. Many kinds of sessile organisms—for example, coelenterates, bryozoans, and barnacles—may use sponge surfaces as substrata, but most of these relationships are purely accidental. An example of an association which may be obligate is the regular occurrence of zoanthid coelenterates on the root tuft of the glass sponge *Hyalonema*. *Inquilinism* is a commensal relationship in which one species lives within the body of another. The canal systems routinely house inquiline species of annelids, mollusks, crustaceans, and many other groups which gain shelter and the multiple advantages of circulating water but apparently do not harm their host. The commensals may be astonishingly numerous. Dr. A. S. Pearse once took the trouble to count all the snapping shrimps (*Synalpheus*) that he could find in a large loggerhead sponge (*Spheciospongia vesparia*, Figure 5)— 16,352 shrimps.

Sponges are rarely eaten because the flesh contains noxious chemicals which render it unattractive to other animals. Thus, certain crabs live commensally with them, using them for protection as well as camouflage. Species of the crab genus *Dromia* place small pieces of sponge on their backs, holding them in place with the last pair of legs. Gradually the sponge grows over the back, covering it and disguising the crab. Some hermit crabs grow the monaxonid *Suberites* on the mollusk shells they inhabit. After the shell has been covered by a thick growth of sponge, it eventually disappears altogether (absorbed by the sponge?) and thereafter the hermit occupies a spacious cavity within the sponge.

Symbiotic relationships—those from which both host and guest derive some benefit—are common between sponges and algae. Blue-green algae live in *Hircinia* and filamentous green algae in *Halichondria*. Certain red algae are found entirely enclosed in sponge tissue. Unicellular biflagellated organisms with golden-brown chromatophores (zooxanthellae) are frequent occupants of marine species, and similar but bright green cells (zoochlorellae) are regularly found in the amoebocytes of fresh-water forms. Symbiotic plants play an important role in the excretory processes of the host because they utilize its nitrogenous and other wastes in their own metabolism. They also remove carbon dioxide, using it in photosynthesis, and release oxygen which the sponge can use. Undoubtedly the host may digest the plant cells, but whether this is frequent or unusual is unknown. This type of relationship has been studied in greater detail in coelenterates (see page 122).

Phylogeny

Discussions of phylogeny are mostly nothing more than educated speculation. In order to comprehend and participate in the speculation, the student must be equipped with a comprehensive knowledge of the anatomy, embryology, and biochemical characteristics of the groups involved, as well as of the geological record. For these reasons, our comments on phylogeny will be presented in only the most general terms.

Sponges are generally considered an evolutionary dead-end— that is, a group evolved eons ago from which no other groups have arisen. Some of their characteristics are unique, such as the system of canals and flagellated chambers, the presence of an

exhalant "oral" opening, the osculum, and the previously unknown sterols found in certain species; other characteristics are
unusual—for example, the fact that the blastopore is aboral rather
than oral as in other lower Metazoa. However, resemblances to
other Metazoa exist as well, among them the occurrence of three
body layers—dermal, mesenchymal and gastral—and similarities in
types of cells and in the processes of oogenesis and spermatogenesis. In gross structure, the parenchymella larva (Figure 40)
and many planula larvae (Figure 151) are basically the same,
both being ovoid free-swimming stereogastrulae, or two-layered
embryos, consisting of a solid mass of cells surrounded, or nearly
so, by a layer of flagellated cells. Indeed, many students of phylogeny believe that a common metazoan ancestor, a gastrula, gave
rise to those ancestral organisms which evolved into sponges as
well as those which evolved into other Metazoa. Some theorize
that the gastrula was solid at first and that later a space within
the central mass appeared which eventually developed into the
spongocoel of Porifera in one line of evolution and the gut of
higher Metazoa in another. Others propose that the ancestral
gastrula was hollow, its two-layered condition having come about
as a result of invagination, with the consequent formation of a
primitive gut or archenteron (Figure 150).

The other major theory on the derivation of sponges rests on
similarities to the Protozoa. It has been proposed that sponges
arose directly from colonial Choanoflagellata. The fact that choanocytes and choanoflagellates are very much alike structurally
was pointed out earlier in this chapter. The occurrence of similar
collared, flagellated cells in animals other than sponges has also
been mentioned. Some other students believe that the inversion of
the stomoblastula (Figures 33 to 35) in the development of
some Calcarea is strong evidence that sponges evolved from the
green colonial Volvocinae—for example *Volvox*, the daughter
colonies of which also invert (Figure 44). This resemblance can
also be considered a case of convergent evolution, without any
phylogenetic significance.

2

Phylum Coelenterata

Introduction

Coelenterates were known to the ancients, as the writings of Aristotle 2,300 years ago show us. Because of the plant-like form of many, they were thought to be marine plants by the scholars of the Renaissance period, and their seeming combination of plant and animal characteristics bedeviled scientists as their awareness of the living world grew along with the development of increasingly sophisticated means of observing it. Not until the work of a Frenchman, Peysonnel, early in the eighteenth century was the animal nature of coral recognized, and even then much controversy swirled about the notion—so much so, in fact, that the French Academy of Sciences suppressed Peysonnel's work, which was first published by the Royal Society in England. At about the same time, John Ellis in England and Abraham Trembley in Holland independently reached the conclusion that coelenterates are indeed animals, not plants. Trembley's work on *Hydra*, published in 1744, is a classic in experimental biology. He was the first to make permanent grafts of animal tissue and to demonstrate the artificial multiplication of animals by experimental means. He was also the first to observe cell division and to prove that animals may reproduce by budding. Although later workers may have contributed a greater mass of knowledge to science, Trembley's experiments remain a landmark and his scientific method a model for us all.

[25]

**Phylum
Coelenterata**

The coelenterates go back in geological time as far as the sponges do. Even though the soft, gelatinous bodies of jellyfishes do not seem capable of fossilization, many kinds are found in the fossil record, and the calcareous skeletons of the corals are very well represented. The record is reasonably rich and quite clear as far back as the Ordovician period, 350 million years ago, and can be traced even farther back, into Cambrian time. Recent discoveries in Australia show that coelenterates were well along the evolutionary path more than 600 million years ago. Fossils found in Pre-Cambrian rocks in the Ediacara Hills of South Australia represent several kinds of medusae, as well as sea pens, the most highly specialized of the flexible corals still living.

Although the coelenterates are of relatively little direct economic value, they are important to man in many other ways. Corals of the remote geological past formed reef structures that were highly favorable sites for the accumulation of petroleum deposits, so these animals are of great interest to petroleum geologists and the oil industry. A knowledge of the biology of modern reefs provides an insight into the circumstances that led to the production of oil in ages past. Coral limestone of ancient reefs is, in addition, quarried in the Florida Keys as a building stone and for decorative applications in architecture.

The coelenterates that are of the greatest direct importance to the most people undoubtedly are those whose nematocysts, or thread-capsules, are capable of stinging man. Although all coelenterates have nematocysts, in only a few groups are they strong enough to penetrate human skin. The classes Hydrozoa and Scyphozoa in particular contain species that are potent stingers. Notable among these are the attached hydroids, whose colonies form delicate, feathery growths on rocks, dock pilings, and even on marine grasses, and the stinging coral, which is common on coral reefs in tropical regions. Both stinging hydroids and stinging corals belong to the class Hydrozoa and are sessile, although their free-swimming medusae and planula larvae may also be capable of stinging. Another hydrozoan group containing violent stingers is the Siphonophora, which includes the beautiful but dangerous Portuguese man-of-war, well known to swimmers in all tropical waters. Members of the other major groups of stinging coelenterates, the Scyphozoa, are collectively known as sea nettles, a common name that goes back to the ancient Greeks. Because of these properties, Aristotle called medusae "acalephae," from the Greek word for nettles, and this term was used extensively in the scientific literature almost to the beginning of the Twentieth Century. If not scientific, it still is an appropriate word, as anyone who has felt the tingle of sea nettles while swimming along Atlantic and Gulf Coast beaches will agree. Also included here is the gigantic jellyfish of northern waters, known as the "lion's mane" (made famous by Arthur Conan Doyle in a Sherlock Holmes story), and the sea wasps, or Cubomedusae, which are prevalent in tropical Australia and are the most virulent stingers of all, now recognized as man-killers.

GENERAL FEATURES

The coelenterates are the lowest of the eumetazoan phyla—that is, those animals constructed of well-defined tissues, having distinct form and symmetry, and with a digestive tube called *coelenteron* lined with epithelium derived from entoderm. In this phylum, the digestive tract opens to the exterior by a mouth but lacks an anus. Unlike sponges, the body of coelenterates has a continuous surface that is not perforated by numerous pores. Although in their high degree of individuality the coelenterates show a marked advance over the sponges, they lack cephalization and show no trace of a centralized nervous system. They have simple digestive, muscular, nervous, and sensory systems, constructed out of the basic epithelial, muscular, and connective tissues. Definite respiratory, circulatory, and excretory systems are not present, and the genital system consists only of sex cells usually localized into gonads.

The Coelenterata have two morphological types of individuals, or *persons*, fundamentally similar but different in details, called the *polyp* and the *medusa* (Figure 45). The polyp is a tubular structure covered with epidermis and lined with gastrodermis, the two layers being separated by jelly-like mesogloea of varying thickness. It consists of (1) a *base*, usually attached to the substrate by a *pedal disc*, projecting rootlike *stolons*, or calcareous skeletal structures; (2) the cylindrical body; and (3) the oral end, either tall and conical as in the Hydrozoa, where it is called the *manubrium* or *hypostome*, or broadly expanded to form an *oral disc* as in the Anthozoa. In the latter, the mouth is elongated and extends into the coelenteron as a compressed tube, the *pharynx*, which has one or more ciliated grooves, the *siphonoglyphs*. In the hydrozoans the mouth is circular and lacks a pharynx. The *tentacles* which surround the mouth may contain hollow extensions of the coelenteron, lined with gastrodermis, or solid cores of gastrodermal cells in one or more columns. The tentacles are food-capturing structures and thus are densely charged with nematocysts, often clustered into *batteries*. Polyps structurally modified for predation and defense, ingesting food, and reproduction occur

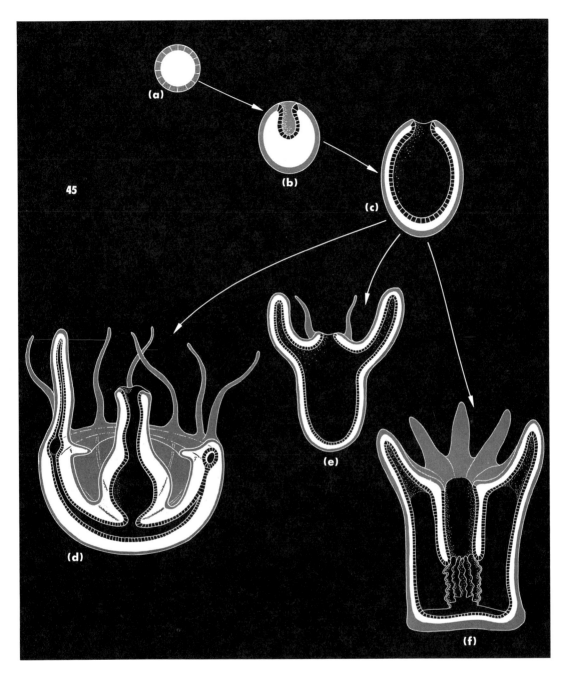

Figure 45. Body plan of coelenterates. The polypoid and medusoid forms are similar in basic structure. A ball of cells, for instance, a blastula (a), becomes two-layered by some developmental process, shown as invagination (b), and develops a hollow interior, the gastrovascular cavity (c). Appearance of tentacles around the oral end and further modifications of shape result in the medusoid form (d), shown inverted from its normal swimming position; also shown is the hydroid polyp (e), without radial partitions; and the anthozoan polyp (f), with radial septa and inturned pharynx.

in polymorphic species. In hydrozoans, the coelenteron is a simple, uncompartmented tube, but in scyphozoan polyps, called *scyphistomae*, it is partially subdivided by four longitudinal ridge-like *septa*, and in anthozoans, such septa fully compartmentalize it. Sometimes inaccurately termed "mesenteries," these septa extend from the body wall toward the pharynx, some or all of them fusing with it to become *complete*, the rest remaining *incomplete* (Figure 112).

The medusa is a free-living form. Typically, it consists of a bowl-shaped *bell* or *umbrella* of stiff mesogloeal jelly (Figure 45), from which the name "jellyfish" is derived. The *exumbrella* is the convex outer surface, and the *subumbrella* is the concave lower or oral surface, from the center of which hangs the *manubrium*, a tubular projection terminating in the *mouth*. The *gastric cavity*, often called *stomach*, occupies the central part of the umbrella, extending via *radial canals* to a marginal *ring canal* within the rim of the bell and opening to the exterior by way of manubrium and mouth. The stomach may be a simple sac or divided by septa into four gastric pouches. These, as well as the radial canals and other structures, display a four-part or *tetramerous symmetry* (Figure 46). The presence of a thin, circular flap or *velum* within the margin of the bell distinguishes the *craspedote* medusae of the Hydrozoa from the *acraspedote* medusae of the Scyphozoa, which never have such a structure. As in polyps, the entire external surface is clothed with epidermis and the internal surfaces are lined with gastrodermis. The bulky gelatinous intermediate layer is either an acellular *mesogloea* or a *collenchyme* containing amoeboid cells. The medusa is an organism adapted for swimming and has undergone numerous modifications just as has the polypoid form. It may become a purely locomotory swimming bell by elimination of all other structures. The medusa is also the sexually reproducing form in all coelenterates possessing it, but it may be so modified that it no longer resembles the familiar medusoid form.

The definite symmetry which appears for the first time in the coelenterates is of a radial nature and is arranged around the main oral–aboral axis of the body (Figure 45); as there is no head, there is no anterior and posterior. The number of units comprising this symmetry is usually four or six, or a multiple of these, but sometimes this is obscured by replication of parts and in some cases the number is indefinite. In hydrozoans and scyphozoans, any two diameters that are at right angles are identical and divide the animal into like halves (Figures 46, 47). The radial symmetry of anthozoans, however, is modified toward bilaterality in that the

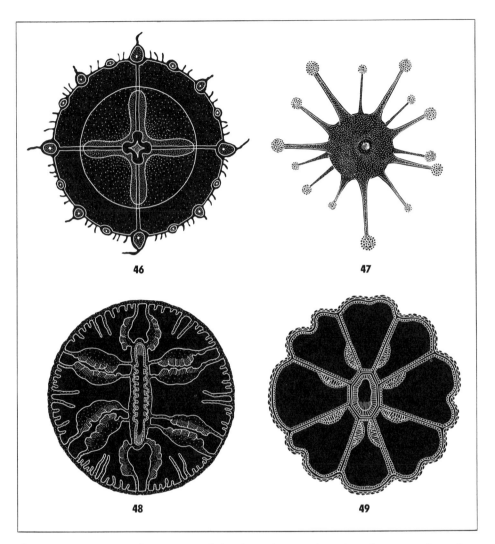

46

47

48

49

Figures 46 to 49. Types of coelenterate symmetry.
46. Hydrozoan medusa, oral view. [After Mayer, 1901.]
47. Hydroid polyp, oral view. [After Agassiz, 1860.]
48. Actinian polyp, cross-section at level of pharynx. [After Corrêa, 1964.]
49. Octocoral polyp, cross-section at level of pharynx. [After Moseley, 1876.]

mouth is often elongated so that there may be only two diameters that yield like halves, one through the long axis of the mouth (the *sagittal axis*). If the ends of these two axes are alike, the symmetry of the animal is *biradial* (Figure 48). In some cases, however, the ends of the sagittal axis are not alike due to the development of localized structures in the pharynx, hence the halves defined by the transverse axis differ. As there is thus only one axis that divides the animal into identical halves, the sagittal axis, the resulting modified radial symmetry is called *radiobilateral* (Figure 49).

Coelenterate construction is of the tissue level of complexity. Between the two fundamental germ layers, ectoderm and entoderm, a variously thick layer of mesogloeal jelly often contains inwandered cells and is an incipient mesoderm. Structural special-

[30]

izations, such as tentacles, pharynx, mesenterial filaments, and the like certainly foreshadow true organs.

The basic structural plan of the individual coelenterate body must be understood before its morphological variations can be fully appreciated. In simplest terms, a coelenterate resembles a gastrula: a hollow ball of cells pushed in on one side to form a two-layered tube open at one end. The opening, representing the blastopore of the gastrula, is the animal's mouth. The inner layer of cells, the entoderm, forms the gastrodermis which lines the gastrovascular cavity. The outer layer is ectodermal and is the epidermis of the adult animal (Figure 45).

HISTOLOGY

The tissues of coelenterates are arranged in three layers, two of which represent the primary germ layers, ectoderm and entoderm, while the third is either a noncellular mesogloea or a collenchyme consisting of jelly and cellular elements from the epithelia (Figure 50). The covering layer, or *epidermis*, is not a simple epithelium but contains three more or less distinct strata, seen most clearly in the anthozoans but discernible in all coelenterates. The superficial stratum consists of so-called *supporting cells*, or *cover cells*, which actually are cuboidal or columnar epithelium, sometimes very tall, together with *sensory* and *gland cells*. On a level with the bases of these cells there is a stratum of *nerve cells*, and below these, *muscle fibers* lie adjacent to or embedded in the underlying mesogloea.

The epidermis may be ciliated or flagellated, and it may secrete a cuticle. Not infrequently, cellular boundaries are ill-defined and the epidermis is syncytial. The epidermal cells are attached to the underlying mesogloea by pseudopodial strands which may be irregular and noncontractile, or regularly oriented and contractile due to the presence of *myonemes*. In the latter case, the special term *epitheliomuscular cells* is applied. Especially in the vicinity of the mouth and on the tentacles, the epidermis contains numerous *cnidoblasts* and their remarkable products, the nematocysts.

Two kinds of gland cells are found among the supporting cells of the epidermis, *mucous* and *granular*. The former are more abundant and produce secretions which serve adhesive or protective functions and which may also entrap food or debris; the latter are found only sparingly in the epidermis but are concentrated in the pharyngeal lining of anthozoans, where they produce secretions functioning in the ingestion of food.

Certain groups of coelenterates have independent muscle fibers instead of the epitheliomuscular type already mentioned. The independent fibers, often cross-striated, form layers or bundles adjacent to the mesogloea and are either attached to mesogloeal folds or embedded completely in it.

The sensory cell bodies, located rather deep in the epithelium, send out a sensory process topped with bristles, motile processes, or other terminal structures, to the surface of the epidermis, as well as nerve fibrils which connect with the nerve plexus below. They evidently serve as undifferentiated receptors. The presence of free sensory nerve endings has been alleged but not adequately demonstrated. The nerve cells are bipolar or multipolar. Those of the epidermal plexus lie deep in the epithelium near the mesogloea so that the inner terminations of the supporting cells pass between their fibers.

Situated here and there among the other epidermal cells are the so-called *interstitial cells*, which may be undifferentiated embryonic cells rather like the archaeocytes of sponges. They are capable of development into various cell types, such as cnidoblasts and germ cells, and thus are important in regenerative activities.

In both structure and cell types, the gastrodermis is very similar to the epidermis. Here, the predominant epithelial cells are the *nutritive cells*, cuboidal or columnar in form and often furnished with contractile basal processes just as are the epidermal supporting cells. When nutritive cells have such contractile processes, they are termed *nutritive muscular cells*. The mucous gland cells are common in the oral gastrodermis and their secretions aid in the ingestion of food; the granular cells are more abundant in the digestive areas in the coelenteron and presumably are responsible for the secretion of digestive enzymes. A nerve plexus is usually present at the level of the bases of the nutritive cells although it is not so well developed as in the epidermis. As in the epidermis, interstitial cells are present in the innermost stratum of the gastrodermis. Except in certain special regions, nematocysts do not occur in the gastrodermis. In many shallow-water coelenterates, the gastrodermis is densely packed with symbiotic algal cells. These are green in the fresh-water hydra and are called zoochlorellae, but are typically yellowish or brownish in most marine forms, where they are called zooxanthellae (Figure 51).

Figures 50 and 51. Histology of coelenterates. **50.** Diagrammatic cross-section of hydrozoan polyp wall, showing cell types (flagella of gastrodermal cells not shown). [Adapted from Hyman, 1940; Bouillon, 1957; and various other sources.] **51.** Cross-section of octocoral showing distribution of zooxanthellae in gastrodermis.

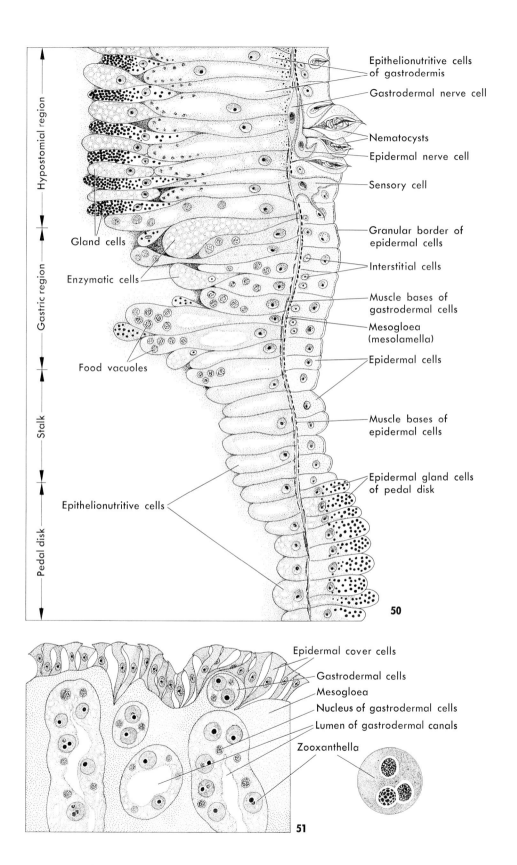

Hypostomial region

Gastric region

Stalk

Pedal disk

Epithelionutritive cells
of gastrodermis

Gastrodermal nerve cell

Nematocysts

Epidermal nerve cell

Sensory cell

Granular border of
epidermal cells

Interstitial cells

Muscle bases of
gastrodermal cells

Mesogloea
(mesolamella)

Epidermal cells

Muscle bases of
epidermal cells

Epidermal gland cells
of pedal disk

Gland cells

Enzymatic cells

Food vacuoles

Epithelionutritive cells

50

Epidermal cover cells

Gastrodermal cells

Mesogloea

Nucleus of gastrodermal cells

Lumen of gastrodermal canals

Zooxanthella

51

[33]

The former, when cultured outside of their coelenterate hosts, prove to be algae of the genus *Chlorella*, and the latter, long resistant to identification, have now been fairly well established as belonging to the class Dinoflagellata of the algal phylum Pyrrhophyta.

The mesogloea is the third of the major layers of the coelenterate body; although it is not a germ layer established in the embryo it arises early in the animal's development and may be acellular or a highly differentiated tissue containing many amoeboid cells often interspersed with abundant fibers embedded in a proteinaceous matrix. The cellular mesogloea justifiably can be regarded as a fibrous connective tissue corresponding closely with that of higher animals. It is characteristic of anthozoans and quite different from the noncellular gelatinous membrane seen in hydroid polyps, best termed a *mesolamella*. The hydromedusae have a mesogloea filled with fibrous elements of unkown nature but generally lacking cells, whereas in scyphomedusae there are also many amoeboid cells so that the term *collenchyme* is more appropriate.

The *nematocysts* (Figure 52) are the most characteristic structure to be found in the coelenterates. Aside from one known instance in the phylum Ctenophora, they are not to be found outside the Coelenterata. Though they are frequently called "stinging cells," they actually are structures produced by special cells, the *cnidoblasts* or nematocytes. These are modified interstitial cells which produce a large vacuole within which the capsule is secreted, but details of nematocyst formation are still incompletely known. The cnidoblasts, distributed abundantly in the epidermis of the oral regions and the tentacles where they may be clustered as wartlike "nematocyst batteries," anchor in the underlying mesogloea by means of a simple or branched stalk or rootlike projection. The exposed end of the cells bears a bristlelike *cnidocil*, often thought to function as a trigger. Groups of supporting rods surround the cnidocil as well as the periphery of the cell body, and a complicated system of fibrils, known to be contractile in some coelenterates and probably so in all, surrounds the body of the cell and extends down into its base. The nematocysts are minute (mostly 5 to 50 μ in length) capsules of thin, chitinous or keratin-like material which contain a narrow coiled tube as an extension of the capsular wall. Stated simply, they resemble a flask with an extremely long, narrow neck—the tube —open at the tip, which lies inverted and coiled within the body of the flask. It is usually said that the open base of the inverted tube is covered by a delicate lid, or *operculum*, but this structure

Figure 52. (a) Diagram of cnidoblast with nematocyst. [Adapted from Lentz, 1966.] (b) Exploded nematocyst. [After Schulze, 1922.] Code: *A*, supporting rods of cnidocil; *B*, cnidocil (oblique section); *C*, operculum of nematocyst; *D*, supporting rods of cnidoblast; *E*, stylets on invaginated base of tube; *F*, spines on proximal part of tube; *G*, mitochondria; *H*, coils of tube within capsule; *I*, myofibrils; *J*, nucleus of cnidoblast; *K*, capsule.

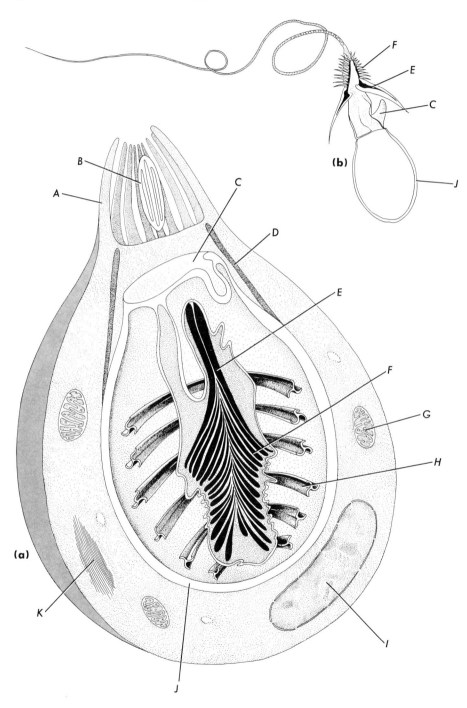

52

has been seen clearly in only one type of nematocyst and has not been definitely observed in the others.

There are two main structural types: (1) the true nematocysts with double walls and a tube usually armed with spines and often with a thicker basal and a thinner terminal part, and (2) the *spirocysts* with single walls and an unarmed tube of uniform diameter. The former are found in all coelenterate groups, but the latter are confined to the Zoantharia.

The capsules of the nematocysts contain a mixture of proteins and phenols, whereas those of spirocysts contain mucoprotein or glycoprotein. Under proper conditions and with proper stimulation the contents of the capsule can be discharged to the exterior by violent eversion of the coiled tube, which may serve to inject the material into the object touched. Although the chemistry of the nematocysts is still not completely known, its toxicity can be appreciated by those who have been stung by sea nettles or a Portuguese man-of-war. It is sufficiently powerful to subdue active animals such as fishes, and in some species of Cubomedusae it is virulent enough to be fatal to man. Several obvious functions— notably defense, holding and overcoming prey—are served by the nematocysts. To some extent, they also may aid the animal in locomotion and holding fast to the substrate. The mechanism of discharge has been much studied in recent years but still is not satisfactorily explained. There is no control by the nervous system of the animal, since the discharge response is wholly local and never transmitted. Sensory, excitor, and effector elements apparently exist within each cnidoblast and form a nervous circuit that can bring about discharge independently. Mechanical stimuli will not evoke discharge unless food substances in the water indicate proximity to prey, but these substances alone will not cause discharge. Such an arrangement prevents ineffectual expenditure of nematocysts upon contact with inert objects or before the prey is near enough to be struck by the everting threads. The mechanics of the discharge has not been clearly demonstrated as yet. It was long thought that uptake of water caused an increase in the volume of the capsule contents resulting in explosive eversion of the tube, and recent work on the nematocysts of the sea anemone *Corynactis* tends to support this view. However, investigations of other animals suggest the action of different mechanisms. In hydra, it appears that contraction of the cnidoblast causes tension of the capsule wall to exert enough pressure to evert the tube. Thus it appears that different nematocysts may operate in different ways in various animals.

In spite of their small size, the nematocysts have very distinctive features showing modifications in various taxonomic groups. Systematists have accordingly made much use of them in classification, especially of the sea anemones, and have evolved an elaborate terminology for the various sorts. Two main types are recognized, those with open tubes and those with closed tubes. The latter are adhesive devices and are of limited occurrence among the siphonophores and certain hydroids. Those with open tubes are distributed throughout the phylum and show extensive differentiation.

Morphology and Classification

Because of their simple construction and great adaptability, the fundamental medusoid and polypoid body plans of the coelenterates, by relatively minor modifications, have given rise to the various distinctive orders of the three great classes Hydrozoa, Scyphozoa, and Anthozoa. The diversity of these animals is astounding, and it is difficult to believe that such different-looking organisms as hydra, a jellyfish, a Portuguese man-of-war, a reef coral, and a sea pen are really nothing more than variations on a very simple body plan.

CLASS HYDROZOA

All members of the class Hydrozoa share certain distinctive characters that set them apart from all other coelenterates. For the most part they have both polypoid and medusoid stages in their life history, although some exist only as polyps and others only as medusae. Their symmetry is radial and either tetramerous or polymerous, the mouth is situated on an elongated manubrium and lacks a stomodaeum (pharynx), and there are neither septa nor nematocyst-bearing structures in the coelenteron. The medusae always have the thin marginal veil or *velum* that gives them the name *craspedote medusae;* they never have rhopalia (special marginal sense organs), and their sex cells ripen in the ectodermal layer.

The hydroid form is the familiar one in this class, as the medusae are mostly small, transparent, and rarely seen by the casual observer. It is usually, but not always, colonial (that is, composed of several physically united individuals), and consists of the simplest of the polypoid type of individual (Figure 53). This is divided into *base, stem,* and *hydranth.* The base is an area of attachment and ordinarily consists of a glandular zone that secretes adhesive substances. In solitary forms, for example, the familiar hydra, the proximal end terminates in a pedal disc. In colonial hydroids (Figures 54 and 55), tubular processes called *stolons* grow out from the base and produce a complicated meshwork, the *hydrorhiza,* which extends along the substrate anchoring the colony firmly. The hydrorhiza gives forth either simple stalks with

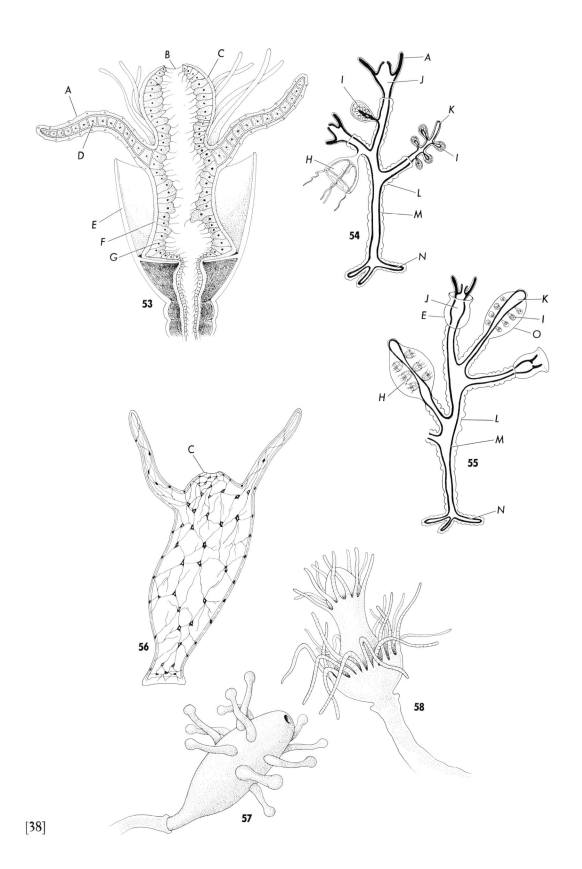

[38]

terminal hydranths, or the main stem of a colony with numerous side branches bearing hydranths. The upright colonial stalk, or *hydrocaulus*, is a tube continuous with the stolons of the hydrorhiza below and with the hydranths proper above. Its wall consists of outer epidermis, a thin lamellar mesogloea without cellular components, and an inner gastrodermis, together termed *coenosarc*. The epidermis produces around itself a thin, protective chitinous tube or *perisarc*, in some forms reduced to an inconspicuous and rather indefinite film, or completely missing as in the freshwater hydras.

The hydranths, the conspicuous terminal tentaculate portion of the polyps, are of diverse aspect. The body is flask- or vase-shaped, with an apical mouth. A distinct, projecting proboscis, often called *manubrium*, is frequently present. In the hydras and similar forms, the conical oral projection is termed *hypostome* (Figure 56). Tentacles surround the body of the hydranth in various arrangements. In primitive genera, such as *Clava*, they are scattered over the hydranth without any regular arrangement (Figure 57). More advanced genera have the tentacles arranged in definite whorls around the body, sometimes a proximal whorl with the distal tentacles remaining scattered, sometimes with the distal ones arranged in a second whorl (Figure 58). In the most advanced hydroid genera, the tentacles are reduced to a single whorl around the base of the hydranth. A very few kinds have the tentacles reduced to one or two, as in the peculiar little commensals called *Lar* (Figure 59) which live on the rim of polychaete tubes, and *Monobrachium* (Figure 60) which inhabit clam shells. Some parasitic and aberrant forms have lost the tentacles altogether.

The tentacles may be hollow and continuous with the coelenteron, as in the hydras, or partitioned off from it as in most other kinds; or they may contain a solid core of gastrodermal cells in one or more rows. They either terminate in a conspicuous knob of nematocysts and are then called *capitate tentacles* (Figure 57), or taper to a point and are called *filiform* (Figure 58).

Figures 53 to 58. Anatomy of Hydrozoa. **53.** Longitudinal section through hydranth of thecate hydroid, diagrammatic. [Redrawn from Parker and Haswell, 1940.] **54.** Composite diagram of athecate hydroid colony showing various types of reproductive structures. [Redrawn from Iwasa, 1953, adapted from Allman, 1872.] **55.** Composite diagram of thecate hydroid colony showing blastostyles producing sporosacs and medusae. [Redrawn from Iwasa, 1953, adapted from Allman, 1872.] **56.** Nerve net of hydra. [Redrawn from Parker and Haswell, 1940.] **57.** Hydranth with capitate tentacles. [Modified from Naumov, 1960.) **58.** Hydranth with two whorls of filiform tentacles. [Modified from Naumov, 1960.] Code: A, tentacle; B, mouth; C, hypostome; D, cellular core tentacle; E, hydrotheca; F, ectoderm of hydranth; G, gastrodermis of hydranth; H, medusa; I, sporosac; J, hydranth; K, blastostyle; L, perisarc; M, hydrocaulus; N, hydrorhiza; O, gonotheca.

The coelenteron, continuous throughout the hydroid colony, forms a stomach or gastric region by enlargement in the basal part of the hydranth. The gastrodermis is a completely flagellated epithelium composed of tall columnar cells in the digestive regions, where gland cells are numerous. In the stems and stolons, the gastrodermis is lower but likewise flagellated. The epidermis is usually not flagellated or ciliated and contains many sensory cells. The hydranths contain a nerve plexus that concentrates as a ring around the manubrium, and in the hydras there seems to be an incipient nerve ring also in the pedal disc. It is not known whether the epidermal and gastrodermal ganglion cells of the coenosarc are connected to form a nerve plexus extending throughout colonial forms, but observations of the way in which colonies respond to stimulation suggest that such is the case.

Extension and contraction of the hydranths are accomplished by the myoepithelial cells, whose bases are transversely arranged in the gastrodermis and longitudinally in the epidermis. The stems and stolons, immobile because of attachment to the substrate or protected by perisarc, apparently lack muscle fibers.

The hydroids are grossly divided into two main types according to the extent of development of the perisarc. Those in which the perisarc is entirely wanting or at most developed only around

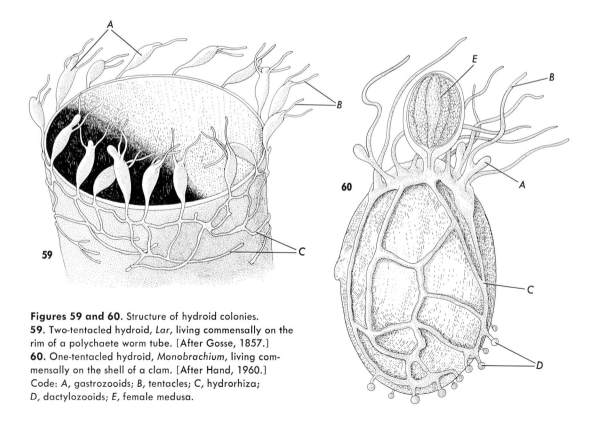

Figures 59 and 60. Structure of hydroid colonies.
59. Two-tentacled hydroid, *Lar*, living commensally on the rim of a polychaete worm tube. [After Gosse, 1857.]
60. One-tentacled hydroid, *Monobrachium*, living commensally on the shell of a clam. [After Hand, 1960.]
Code: *A*, gastrozooids; *B*, tentacles; *C*, hydrorhiza; *D*, dactylozooids; *E*, female medusa.

stolons and stems are called *athecate hydroids* (Figures 54, 56). Others have bell- or goblet-shaped expansions of perisarc called *hydrothecae* and *gonothecae* surrounding the hydranths and gonophores and are termed *thecate hydroids* (Figures 53, 55).

Hydroid colonies are composed of more than one type of polyp, also referred to as *zooids* or *persons* (Figure 61). The vegetative individuals that produce the colony by their asexual budding and function chiefly in feeding are commonly called *gastrozooids*. All colonial hydroids have a second type of person that produces the sexual medusoid stages which may be set free as medusae or retained as *gonophores*. Gonophores may be produced upon well-developed polyps with mouth and tentacles, called gonozooids, or upon polyps that have lost tentacles, mouth, and associated parts, known by the special name *blastostyle*. Sometimes individual gonophores spring from the body wall of the gastrozooids, either from the manubrium or from the stalk below the hydranths. In thecate hydroids the gonophores are commonly borne on blastostyles encased in special *gonothecae*, the complete structures being term *gonangia* (singular, *gonangium*).

In addition to the nutritive and reproductive polyps, several other kinds may be found among the many species of hydroids. Protective polyps, loaded with nematocysts and serving only for defense and capture of prey, have lost their feeding and digestive structures and simply resemble long, extensile tentacles; these are called *tentaculozooids*. If they retain vestiges of capitate tentacles, they are called *dactylozooids*. Certain thecate hydroids have characteristic small dactylozooids called *nematophores*, encased in nematothecae which are placed in very definite relationship to the ordinary hydrothecae (Figure 62). Some of these special dactyl-

Figures 61 and 62. Structure of hydroid colonies
61. *Hydractinia*, showing types of polyps. [Adapted from Agassiz, 1860.]
62. Branch of thecate hydroid with nematophores. [After Iwasa, 1953.] Code: A, gastrozooids; B, gonozooids; C, dactylozooids (spiral zooids); D, spines; E, nematophore with nematocysts; F, nematotheca; G, hydranth; H, hydrotheca.

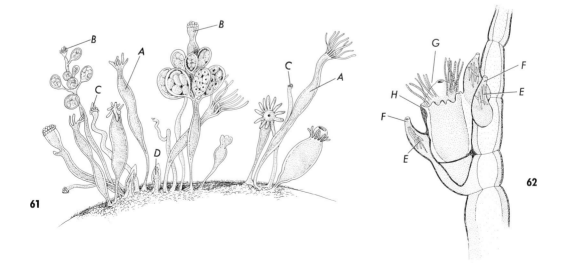

ozooids are abundantly supplied with gland cells that produce sticky mucus employed in entangling minute organisms.

Some hydroid colonies are simply encrusting mats of stolons or hydrorhizae directly giving rise to the polyps (Figure 63). Rarely, such hydrorhizal colonies send up a bundle of parallel stolons, thus forming a false stem. However, most branched colonies have one main stem formed by the erect tubular *hydrocaulus*, which produces side branches bearing hydranths. The arrangement of branches and placement of the hydranths is characteristic of each hydroid species. Colonies with one primary axial polyp that buds off lateral polyps forming the secondary branches are said to be *monopodial* (Figure 64), whereas those with a primary axis composed of a succession of polyps are said to be *sympodial* (Figure 65). In the former, the major axes have terminal hydranths and

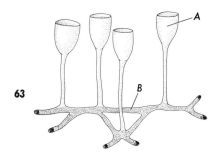

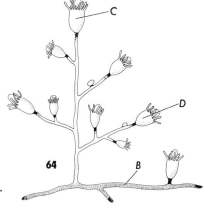

Figures 63 to 66. Structure of hydroid colonies. **63.** Growth form of a hydrorhizal colony, diagrammatic. **64.** Growth form of a monopodial colony. **65.** Growth form of a sympodial colony. **66.** Terminal branch of *Dynamene*, thecate hydroid with terminal growing point. [All after Naumov, 1960.] Code: A, hydrotheca; B, hydrorhiza; C, axial polyp; D, lateral polyp; E, terminal hydrotheca; F, terminal growing point; G, lateral hydranth covered by protective hydrotheca, H.

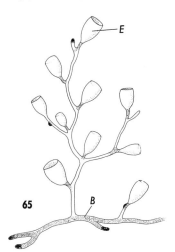

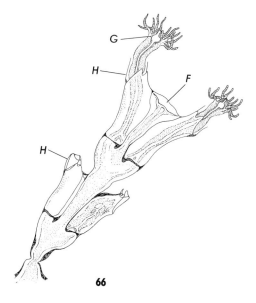

continue to elongate from a growth zone just below the hydranth. As growth proceeds, a succession of lateral buds is produced, some of which elongate to form side branches while others grow no longer. In the resulting colony, the terminal hydranth of the main stem is the original and oldest hydranth of the colony, and the bud immediately below it is the youngest. Some families of thecate hydroids produce monopodial colonies in which the hydrocaulus continues to elongate at terminal growing points (Figure 66), budding off hydranths and lateral branches also with terminal growing points. In such colonies, the lowest hydranths on the stem and branches are the oldest. This is true also in sympodial colonies, whose hydranths lack a growth zone and consequently do not elongate after they have attained full size. Instead, the stalk of the terminal hydranth has a budding zone which produces a new hydranth that exceeds the height of its parent and then becomes the new terminal hydranth. Ordinarily, these buds arise alternately on the two sides of the branches so the colonies consist of an alternating sequence of polyps.

Some species of hydroids remain solitary throughout life, either producing no buds or shedding them soon after formation. Most familiar of the solitary hydroids is the fresh-water hydra, which reproduces asexually by budding at the proximal part of the gastric region. When the buds have developed their tentacles and assumed the form of a complete diminutive hydra, they separate from the parent and take up independent existence. Less well known are the solitary marine hydroids such as *Corymorpha* and *Branchiocerianthus*. The flexible stalk of the polyp has rootlike holdfasts at the bottom which serve to anchor the animal in mud, and the terminal hydranth has two circles of tentacles, one around the base and another around the distal part of the manubrium. From the walls of the manubrium arise dense clusters of gonophores which, according to species, may or may not produce free medusae. These hydroids are among the largest known; individual polyps of *Corymorpha* reach a height of two or three inches, and the fantastic *Branchiocerianthus* may be nine feet tall. Both of these solitary types lack perisarc and thus are classed among the athecate hydroids. Other athecate forms are *Pennaria tiarella*, a common shallow-water species forming pinnate colonies with hydranths having capitate tentacles on the manubrium and filiform tentacles in a circle around their bases, and the only colonial fresh-water hydroid, *Cordylophora lacustris*. Familiar on the New England coast is the encrusting *Hydractinia*, which lives on shells inhabited by hermit crabs, and over which it forms a prickly brown hydrorhizal mat. From this mat arise the zooids.

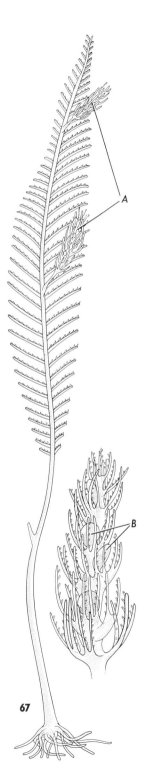

The thecate hydroids vary in growth form from low hydro-rhizal colonies sending up simple hydranths encased in thecae (Figure 63), as seen in *Clytia*, to the large, feathery or plumose colonies of *Plumularia*, *Aglaophenia*, and *Callicarpa* (Figure 67). Some thecate hydroids produce their gonophores on special branches or on special parts of branches, while others have developed a variety of protective structures, called *phylactocarps*, to enclose them.

Whereas many of the athecate hydroids produce free medusae, called *anthomedusae* (Figure 68), the majority of the thecate species do not, as the extensive development of protective corbulae would suggest. When medusae are formed by thecate hydroids, however, they are termed *leptomedusae* (Figure 69) and differ from the anthomedusae in the shape of the bell, position of sex organs, presence of statocysts, and number and arrangement of tentacles around the margin of the bell.

In general, the hydromedusae are free-swimming animals of small size with a bell of various shapes and proportions, ranging from a broadly open saucer-shape to a tall, thimble-, dome-, or bell-like structure (Figure 70). From the center of the subumbrellar surface depends the tubular manubrium with its terminal mouth often surrounded by lobes, tentacles, or frills. The lumen of the manubrium leads into the centrally located gastric region from which tubular extensions radiate outward to the margin of the bell as the *radial canals*. They usually have a definite tetramerous arrangement and usually are simple, although they may branch as they do in *Proboscidactyla* (Figure 70a), the medusa of the curious little two-tentacled hydroid *Lar*. Their outer ends join with a *circular canal* in the margin of the bell, and the flat gastrodermis with which they are lined extends between the canals as a one-layered *gastrodermal lamella*.

Projecting inward from the margin of the bell and partially cutting off the subumbrellar cavity is the thin flap known as the *velum*. This structure, with its strong circular muscle, helps control the expulsion of water from the bell and thus is important in swimming. The velum is characteristic of hydromedusae, although it is poorly developed or rudimentary in a few species.

The margin of the bell bears sense organs and tentacles. The latter are ordinarily simple but in some forms are branched or have stalked nematocyst-bearing structures known as *cnidophores* (Figure 72). The epidermis is liberally supplied with sensory cells

Figure 67. Structure of hydroid colonies. Colony of *Callicarpa gracilis*, with special branches (phylactocarps) modified for protection of gonangia. [Redrawn from Fewkes, 1881.] Code: A, phylactocarps; B, gonangia.

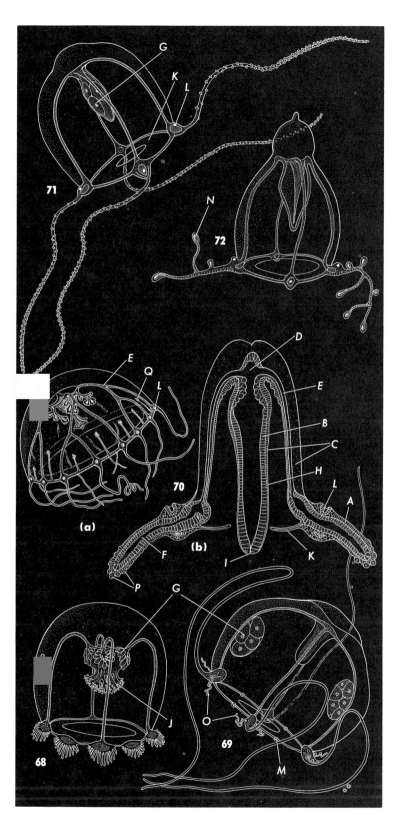

Figures 68 to 72. Medusoid
forms: hydromedusae.
68. Anthomedusa, *Rathkea
fasciculata*. 69. Leptomedusa,
Eucheilota duodecimalis var.
parvum. 70. (a) anthomedusa
Proboscidactyla, medusa of
Lar (see Fig. 59); (b) young
anthomedusa, *Sarsia*, in longitudinal section. 71. Four-
tentacled anthomedusa,
Sarsia eximia. [All redrawn
from Mayer, 1910.] 72. Two-
tentacled anthomedusa, *Gemmaria dichotoma*. [Redrawn
from Mayer, 1900.] Code: *A*,
epidermis; *B*, gastrodermis;
C, mesogloea; *D*, stomach;
E, radial canal; *F*, tentacular
extension of radial canal;
G, gonads; *H*, manubrium; *I*,
mouth; *J*, oral tentacles; *K*,
velum; *L*, ocellus; *M*, lithocyst;
N, cnidophore; *O*, cirri; *P*, nematocysts; *Q*, cluster of
nematocysts.

and with nematocysts arranged in annular, spiral, ridgelike or wartlike batteries. Commonly there are four tentacles, extending from the ends of the four radial canals, but some kinds of medusae have fewer (1 or 2) or more (8, 12, 16). As in hydroid polyps, the tentacles are often filled with a solid core of entodermal cells, but occasionally they contain an extension of the circular canal.

The members of two hydrozoan orders produce a massive, calcareous exoskeleton much resembling that of stony corals. The first of these orders, the Milleporina, or "millepores," contains the well known stinging coral, *Millepora* (from *mille*, a thousand; and *pora*, pore).

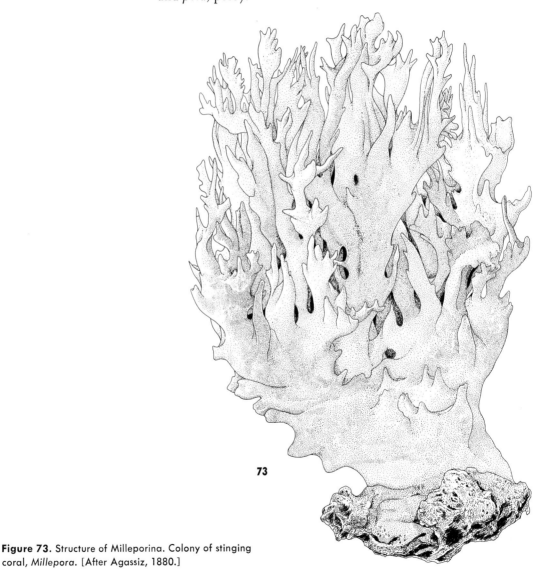

73

Figure 73. Structure of Milleporina. Colony of stinging coral, *Millepora*. [After Agassiz, 1880.]

The millepore skeleton is composed of hard but porous calcareous material or *coenosteum* which assumes many forms (Figure 73). Colonies may be irregular, lumpy masses, but often they form groups of upright, undulated plates which may be simply frondose or divided into finger-like or antler-like branches. Sometimes the colonies form a thin, sheetlike crust over the rocky sea bottom or over the solid parts of corals or gorgonians, whose shape they then assume. Innumerable variations have troubled the systematists who have attempted to classify them. The coenosteum is perforated by pores of two sizes which accommodate the two different kinds of polyps (Figure 74), the *gastrozooids* and the *dactylozooids*. The larger pores, which contain the gastrozooids, are the *gastropores*, and are usually surrounded by a circle of smaller *dactylopores*, containing the dactylozooids. A gastropore and its accompanying dactylopores together form a *cyclosystem*. The pores lead downward into the coenosteum and are closed off below by transverse stony partitions or *tabulae*, which are formed successively as growth proceeds.

The gastrozooids are short, columnar structures with an apical mouth surrounded by four to six knoblike tentacles. The dactylozooids, slender and much taller, have several capitate tentacles along the body but no mouth. Special chambers in the coenosteum, called *ampullae*, contain the gonophores, which are freed as tiny medusae. These have no velum, and the tentacles are reduced to low knobs of nematocysts. Radial canals are lacking, and the sexual products are borne on the manubrium.

Figure 74. Structure of Milleporina. (a) Cyclosystem of *Millepora* polyps. [Modified from Moseley, 1880.] (b) Section through ampulla of *Millepora* containing developing medusa, with liberated medusa above. [After Hickson, 1891.] Code: A, gastrozooid; B, dactylozooid; C, nematocyst batteries; D, umbrella; E, manubrium; F, eggs; G, epidermis; H, skeleton; I, canal.

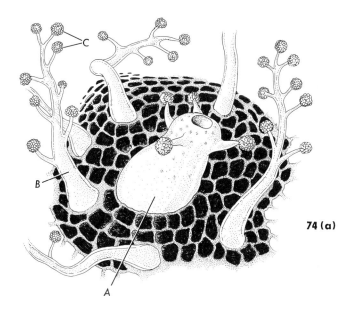

74 (a)

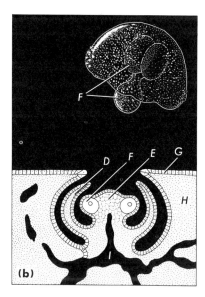

(b)

A complex system of tubes of coenosarc ramifying through the coenosteum interconnects the gastric cavities of the zooids, and a thin layer of coenosarc invests the entire surface of the coenosteum. The coenosarc tubes, which correspond to the hydrorhiza of hydroids, produce the coenosteum which thus corresponds to the perisarc of hydroids. Only the outermost layer of skeleton contains living tissue.

In life the colonies are greenish or yellowish brown or mustard colored, with a delicate furry white covering when the translucent polyps are expanded out of their pores. The nematocysts are very powerful and of two or three kinds. They are capable of producing a severe stinging sensation even on the tougher parts of the human body.

The second hydrozoan order in which a calcareous skeleton is found is the Stylasterina. These hydrocorals are similar to the millepores but are more delicately branched (Figure 75) and usually colored some shade of purple, pink, red, or yellow, although some are white. In these corals the large gastropores usu-

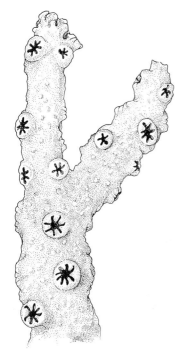
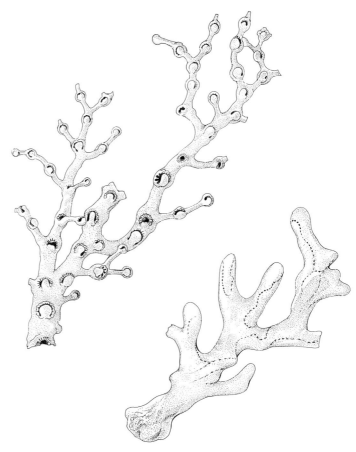

75

Figure 75. Colonial form in Stylasterina. Branches of *Allopora* (left), *Crypthelia* (center), and *Distichopora* (right). [After Moseley, 1880, and Naumov, 1960.]

ally have a notched margin, each of the notches representing a dactylopore (Figure 76). Commonly, a spine, the *style*, rises from the bottom of the gastropores, giving the order its name. The resulting *cyclosystems* are superficially similar to the calyces of stony corals, as the ridges between the dactylopores look like the septa of madrepores. The development and arrangement of the cyclosystems are quite diverse and achieve bizarre form in some genera, such as *Crypthelia*, in which an arching flap of coenosteum forms a sort of roof over each cyclosystem (Figure 75). In *Spinipora*, the dactylopores have projecting, gutterlike spouts, and in *Distichopora*, one of the commonest genera, the gastrozooids are arranged in a row along the narrow edge of the branches and are flanked on each side by a row of dactylopores.

The gastrozooids of stylasterine corals have a number of stubby tentacles, but the dactylozooids are simple projections without mouth or tentacles. The gonophores are very degenerate and do

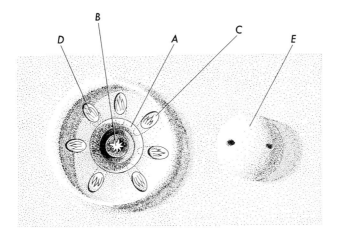

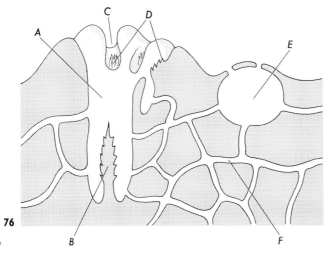

76

Fiure 76. Structure of Stylasterina. Diagram of cyclosystem of *Allopora*: plan view above, section below. [After Naumov, 1960.] Code: A, gastropore; B, gastrostyle; C, dactylopore; D, dactylostyle; E, ampulla; F, canal.

not produce free medusae. They occupy blister-like chambers in the coenosteum, called ampullae as in the millepores. The young are freed as planulae. The coenosteum is constructed very much as in the Milleporina, but as the colonies are less massive the entire skeleton is permeated by living tissue rather than just a superficial layer.

Although the stylasterine corals are well represented in tropical waters, they seem to achieve their peak of development in cooler areas such as the west coast of North America where a number of handsome species are found, and representatives are also present in both the Arctic and Antarctic Seas as well as in deep water.

Whereas the hydrozoan orders Milleporina and Stylasterina are predominantly polypoid, the order Trachylina is almost completely medusoid. It contains two groups of jellyfishes, the Trachymedusae and the Narcomedusae. These medusae are similar in appearance to those of the hydroids, mostly of small or moderate size, with a velum, and similar in general aspects of histology. However, in the Trachylina, the polypoid generation is very greatly reduced or eliminated altogether.

The trachyline medusae are separated from the hydroid medusae chiefly because of the gastrodermal nature of their sensory lithocytes. Both Trachymedusae and Narcomedusae have only a single type of nematocyst, but these are different in the two groups, suggesting that they are not especially close. Moreover, the two kinds of medusae differ in anatomical particulars. The trachymedusae (Figure 77) have a conventional gastrovascular

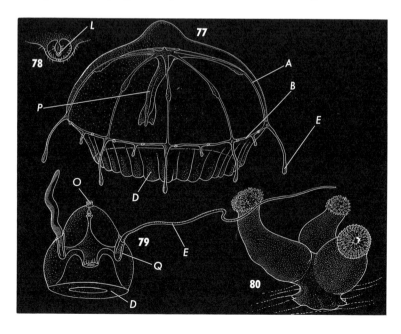

Figures 77 to 80. Form and structure of Trachylina. **77.** Trachymedusa, *Rhopalonema velatum*. [After Mayer, 1910.] **78.** Statocyst of *Rhopalonema*. [After Mayer, 1910.] **79.** *Hydroctena*. [After Mayer, 1910.] **80.** *Microhydra*, the polypoid of *Craspedacusta*. [From Naumov after Dejdar, 1934.] Code: A, radial canal; B, ring canal; D, velum; E, tentacle; L, statolith; O, apical sense organ; P, pseudomanubrium; Q, tentacle sheath.

system, with the mouth at the end of a manubrium which itself may be situated on a long, tubular projection of the subumbrella called the *pseudomanubrium*. The stomach leads into a ring canal by way of tetramerously arranged radial canals. The narcomedusae (Figure 81) lack a manubrium, however, and the mouth leads directly into the stomach. Large, tetramerously arranged gastric pouches extend out toward the margin of the bell, the radial canals are reduced or absent, and the ring canal may be reduced to a solid strand of cells or completely missing. The tentacles often are not marginal as in the hydroid medusae, but instead project from the exumbrella at some distance from the edge of the bell. In the Narcomedusae, the rim of the bell is divided into scallops or marginal *lappets* by epidermal extensions from the base of the tentacles (Figure 81). Two kinds of static organs occur around the bell between the tentacle bases, the *lithostyles* and the *statocysts*. Many narcomedusae have lithostyles on the margin of the bell (Figure 82), club-shaped projections with a low sensory epidermis and a core of gastrodermal lithocytes containing statoliths (Figure 83), set on a basal cushion of sensory cells. Statocysts, commonly found in trachymedusae, are lithostyles that have become more or less enclosed in a pocket formed by the basal sensory cells (Figure 78).

The trachymedusae include some very small jellyfishes, notably the bottom-dwelling forms like *Gonionemus*, which clings to algae and other objects by adhesive suckers, and the fresh-water jellyfishes *Limnocnida* and *Craspedacusta* (Figure 84).

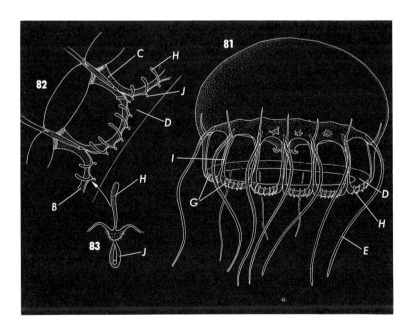

Figures 81 to 83. Form and structure of Trachylina.
81. Narcomedusa, *Cunina prolifera*. [After Mayer, 1910.]
82. Part of the bell margin of *Cunina*. [After Mayer, 1910.]
83. Lithostyle of *Cunina*. [After Mayer, 1910.] Code: B, ring canal; C, peronial canal; D, velum; E, tentacle; G, marginal lappet; H, otoporpa; I, peronium; J, lithostyle.

Phylum
Coelenterata

The latter, now familiar in man-made bodies of water in many parts of the United States, was first discovered in a botanical garden in London, living in a pond containing water lilies from South America, presumably brought from Brazil along with specimens of the plant. The hydroid stage is a very small form without tentacles known under the name *Microhydra ryderi* (Figure 80). The gonads of *Craspedacusta* occur on the radial canals as in most other trachymedusae, but those of *Limnocnida*, an African fresh-water jellyfish, are in the stomach region, and those of certain marine forms are on the pseudomanubrium. The curious jellyfish called *Olindioides formosa* (Figure 85) is a trachymedusa with adhesive tentacles sprouting from the exumbrella and long, nematocyst-bearing tentacles from the bell margin.

The narcomedusae are mostly marine jellyfishes, distinctive by their scalloped margins (Figure 81) but not ordinarily encountered except in the open ocean. Several curious coelenterates of obscure affinities have been placed in this group of medusae be-

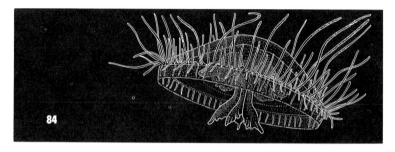

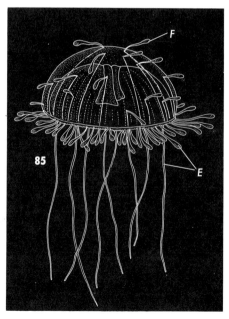

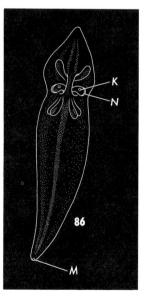

Figures 84 to 86. Form and structure of Trachylina.
84. Fresh-water jellyfish, *Craspedocusta*. [From Naumov after Dejdar, 1937.]
85. Trachymedusa, *Olindioides formosa*. [From Mayer 1910, after Goto, 1903.]
86. *Tetraplatia.* [After Komai, 1939.] Code: *E*, tentacle; *F*, exumbrellar tentacle; *K*, statocyst; *M*, mouth; *N*, swimming flap.

cause of their distinctive and uniform nematocysts. Among these are the strange solitary polyps known as *Polypodium*, which creep about on their tentacles. These animals parasitize sturgeon in the region of the Black and Caspian Seas. How they infect the sturgeon is unknown, but by some means parasitic stolons invade the ovarian eggs of the fish and produce buds that develop into the polyps after the eggs are laid. Another enigmatical medusa is *Tetraplatia*, a bipyramidal creature with four swimming flaps projecting from pockets around its middle (Figure 86). The flaps contain statocysts and presumably represent the medusoid velum. *Hydroctena*, so named because of similarities to ctenophores, is the only medusa with a distinct apical sense organ in the adult stage (Figure 79). It also has only two tentacles, contained in sheaths as in ctenophores, but it has a definite velum and is placed near the narcomedusa *Solmundella*, which has an apical organ in its young stages.

Among the most remarkable of all coelenterates are the Siphonophora. In this class, known best for *Physalia*, the Portuguese man-of-war, polymorphism is more highly developed than in any other group of coelenterates. Although *Physalia* (Figure 87) is the most familiar siphonophore because it is commonly washed ashore on ocean beaches, it is not a good example of the order as

Figure 87. Portuguese man-of-war, *Physalia*, stranded on a Florida beach.

a whole as its structure is not representative of the majority of species. Siphonophores are colonial coelenterates, exclusively marine and planktonic or pelagic, composed of several kinds of polypoid and medusoid persons more or less strongly modified and specialized for the various vital functions. The polypoid individuals consist of zooids modified for feeding, capture of prey, and production of reproductive persons, named, as in the Hydroida, *gastrozooids*, *dactylozooids*, and *gonozooids*. A number of special terms have been given to the persons and structures of siphonophore colonies, but as they are of interest only in the detailed description of the animals, only the principal ones with homologies elsewhere in the Hydrozoa will be mentioned here.

The gastrozooids (Figure 88), specialized for feeding, are polyps with a mouth but only one long, hollow tentacle with branches called *tentilla*, richly supplied with nematocysts in special knoblike or spiral thickenings. The dactylozooids (Figure 89) sometimes called *palpons*, lack a mouth but also have a single tentacle, in this case unbranched. Some dactylozooids are simple, atentaculate structures located near the gonophores and designated as

Figures 88 to 90. Structure of siphonophores: types of zooids. **88.** Gastrozooid. **89.** Dactylozooid. **90.** Gonodendron. [After Haeckel, 1888.] Code: A, mouth; B, tentacle; C, tentillum; D, basal mass of nematocyst batteries (basigaster); E, nematocyst batteries; F, cluster of nematocyst batteries; G, female gonophores; H, male gonophores.

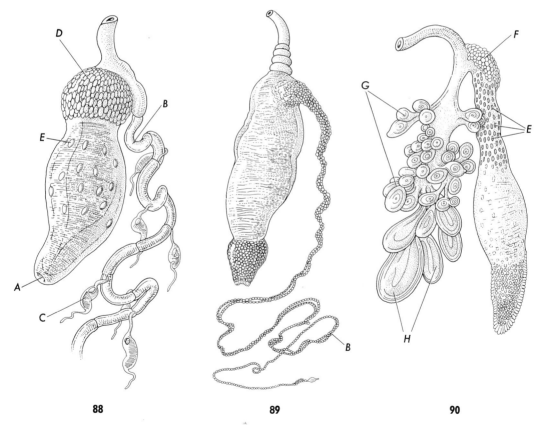

88   89   90

gonopalpons. The gonozooids are usually branched structures called *gonodendra* (Figure 90), often accompanied by gonopalpons. The gonophores produced by the gonodendra are medusoid persons but usually are not set free.

The medusoid forms are concerned with locomotion, flotation, and reproduction. The swimming bells are obviously medusoid forms with a bell furnished with velum and distinct radial and ring canals. As they have no nutritive functions, they have lost mouth, manubrium, and tentacles; sense organs are also lacking. These swimming bells, also called *nectophores,* are typically medusoid in shape in some species (Figure 91), fantastically modified in others (Figure 92), strongly muscular and responsible for propulsion of the colony. The gonophores are usually obvious medusoids (Figure 93), with the usual medusoid structures including a manubrium bearing the gonads. Although more or less strongly modified forms are present, the medusoid nature of most siphonophoran gonophores is usually evident.

The curious gelatinous structures called *bracts* (Figure 96), of diverse and complicated shapes, were commonly thought to be modified medusae as apparently intermediate forms exist, but a recent viewpoint maintains that bracts are modified tentacles instead. Regardless of their derivation, these structures, of various prismatic and foliate forms, are a conspicuous component of certain siphonophores. They contain simple or branched extensions of the gastrovascular canal and supposedly are protective.

Another siphonophoran structure, once thought to be a modified medusoid but now recognized as derived from an aboral invagination of the larva, is the *float* or *pneumatophore* (Figure 96). This is a double-walled chamber lined with a chitinous epidermal secretion and furnished at the bottom with a *gas gland,* consisting of a glandular epithelium lining a pit or chamber called the funnel. The wall of the float is strongly muscular, allowing control of contents or of shape, according to species. The gas gland may be simple or very complex, and it secretes a gas usually similar to air in composition. In *Physalia,* however, there is a surprisingly large proportion of carbon monoxide. As a structure, the float reaches its greatest development in *Physalia,* where it has the form of an ovate bladder nearly a foot long, with an erectile crest whereby the animal maneuvers in the wind (Figure 87). Many other kinds of siphonophores are furnished with a float which is smaller, acting as a hydrostatic organ to keep the animal at a particular bathymetric level rather than as a raft to maintain it at the surface. Other kinds lack a float entirely.

Siphonophores in general are capable of stinging violently due to their numerous large and powerful nematocysts.

The different kinds of zooids are grouped into complex colonies. Three suborders are recognized on the basis of the colonial structure: the Calycophorae include colonies with swimming bells but no float; the Physonectae have a small float and a long train of swimming bells; and the Cystonectae have a large float and no bells.

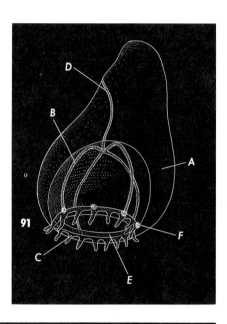

Figures 91 to 93. Structure of siphonophores. 91. Bell-shaped nectophore of *Desmophyes*. [After Haeckel, 1888.] 92. Three modified nectophores: Helmet-shaped *Hippopodius*. [After Fewkes, 1880.] Spirally twisted *Eudoxoides*. [After Cervigón, 1958.] *Vogtia* with gelatinous projections. [After Haeckel, 1888.] 93. (a) Female gonophores of *Diphyopsis* and *Praya* with umbrella more or less modified. [After Haeckel, 1888.] (b) Cluster of male gonophores of *Desmophyes*. [After Haeckel, 1888.] Code: A, umbrella; B, radial canals; C, ring canal; D, peduncular canal; E, velum; F, ocellus; G, ova; H, gonad.

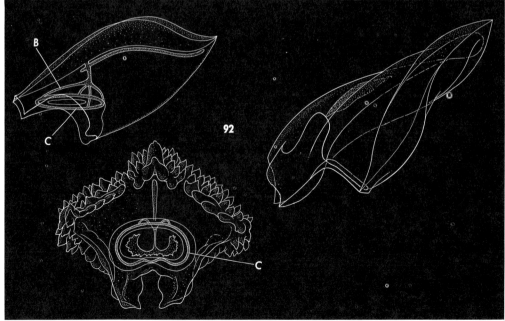

A calycophoran colony (Figures 94, 95) is topped by one or more bells, set singly, two side by side or one higher than the other, in an alternating series or in a circle. Extending from the bell is a tubular *stem* from which various types of zooids are budded in groups called *cormidia*. Each cormidium is ordinarily composed of a bract, a gastrozooid, and one or more gonophores which may function also as swimming bells. The stem has a growing point near the top and continues to produce cormidia in a long chain. The cormidia commonly break loose from the parent colony and live an independent existence. In this condition they are termed *eudoxids* and, being sexually functional, they vastly

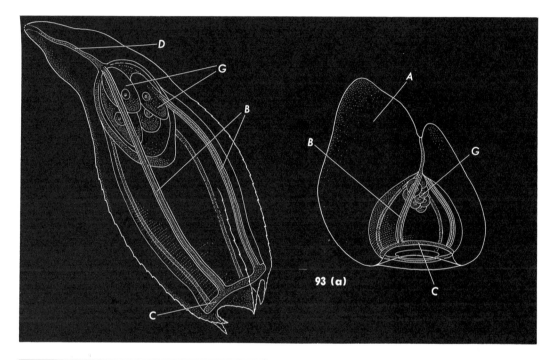

93 (a)

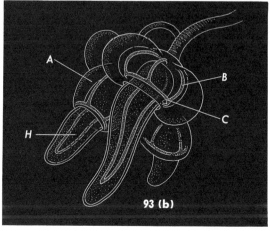

93 (b)

(a)

(b)

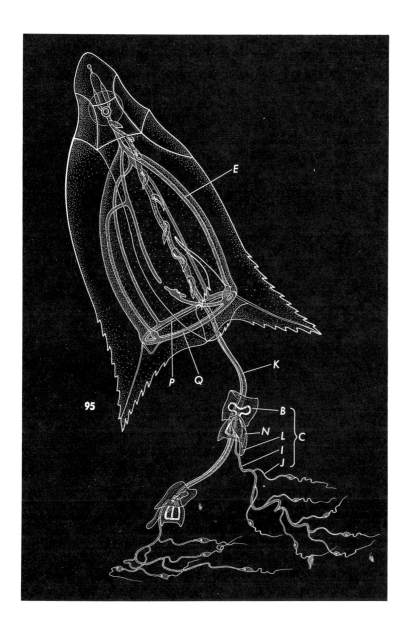

Figures 94 and 95. Structure of siphonophores. **94.** (a) Single cormidium of
the calycophoran *Praya*. [After Haeckel, 1888.] (b) Complete colony of *Praya*.
[After Fewkes, 1888.] **95.** Colony of *Abylopsis*, a calycophoran. [After Fewkes,
1879.] Code: *A*, nectophore; *B*, bract; *C*, cormidia; *D*, dorsal canal; *E*, radial
canal; *F*, left canal; *G*, right canal; *H*, ventral canal; *I*, tentacle; *J*, tentilla;
K, stem; *L*, gastrozooid; *M*, mouth; *N*, gonophore; *O*, bell; *P*, velum; *Q*, ring
canal.

increase the possibilities for cross fertilization. Great diversity of shape is found in calycophoran bells, which form a striking component of the oceanic plankton. They may resemble ordinary jellyfishes as in *Praya*, or elegantly sculptured and faceted helmets as in *Muggiaea*.

The Physonectae have an apical float from which depends a long stem bearing first a series of nectophores and then a long train of cormidia (for example, *Agalma*, Figure 96).

The well-known Portuguese man-of-war (Figure 87) is an example of the Cystonectae. In this genus the stem consists only of the large budding zone on the bottom of the float. This produces the various persons of the colony, most conspicuous of which are the large dactylozooids with their enormously long and dangerous tentacles. Also present are smaller dactylozooids, gastrozooids, and gonodendra with their gonopalpons and gonophores. The float is an intense blue with pink or violet along the edge of the crest, the gonodendra are lavender, and the long tentacles are blue.

Long treated as a subgroup of physophorid siphonophores, the Chondrophorae are now considered to be a separate group with phyletic ranking equivalent to siphonophores. These animals lack an elongated stem, having the form of a round or oval disc consisting of a chitinous, many-chambered float from which hangs one central gastrozooid surrounded by gonozooids that give rise to free-swimming medusae and marginally fringed with dactylozooids. *Porpita* and *Porpema* (Figure 97) have a flat, circular disc; *Velella* (Figure 98), the by-the-wind sailor, familiar along Florida beaches, has an oval float with a thin, triangular sail. Both are colored intense blue, with the sail of *Velella* edged with purple.

CLASS SCYPHOZOA

The class Scyphozoa includes the most familiar of all coelenterates, the common jellyfishes and sea nettles, as well as the largest, the gigantic *Cyanea*, a medusa that may be as much as seven feet across the umbrella. Among the coelenterates, the latter is exceeded in size only by the largest of the massive reef corals, and these are colonies, not individual animals. In the Scyphozoa, the medusoid phase (Figure 99) dominates and the polypoid stage is reduced to an inconspicuous organism called the *scyphistoma* (Figure 110), and even this is lacking in some species.

Scyphozoan medusae are much larger than the hydromedusae discussed previously, commonly six inches to one foot or more in diameter, and they never have a velum. Their tetramerous symmetry is a conspicuous feature, seen also in the scyphistoma. The umbrella varies in form from cuboidal or tall dome-shaped to a

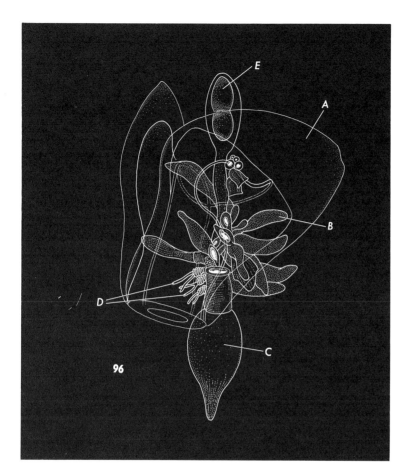

96

Figure 96. Structure of
siphonophores. Young colony
of *Agalma*, a physonectid.
[After Cervigón, 1961.] Code:
A, nectophore; *B*, palpon;
C, gastrozooid; *D*, tentilla;
E, pneumatophore.

97

Figure 97. Discoidal chondrophoran, *Porpema* (top
view). [After Haeckel, 1888.]

shallow saucer, almost discoidal. It is ordinarily of a firm, even cartilaginous, consistency because of the thick mesogloea containing many fibers and wandering amoeboid cells. The edge of the bell is notched, producing marginal lappets, and fringed with tentacles. Sense organs occur in the notches and alternate with the tentacles in a definite sequence arranged in some multiple of four. The tentacles may be filiform or capitate, solid or hollow. Nematocysts of two or three kinds may occur on both surfaces of the umbrella and on the tentacles, either in definite aggregations or generally scattered.

In some scyphozoans, the gastrovascular system (Figure 100) bears a resemblance to that of the hydromedusae, but in many it diverges rather widely from that type. The quadrangular mouth is situated on a prominent manubrium located at the center of the subumbrella. Its four corners are produced as lobes that in some families form complicated *oral arms* or *mouth arms*. In many of the jellyfishes with elaborate mouth arms, the original mouth is closed over by fusion of the edges of the arms and is replaced by a large number of porelike *suctorial mouths* scattered over the arm lobes. The mouth opens via the endoderm-lined manubrium into the *stomach*, a cavity partially divided by four *septa* projecting inward from the periphery. This results in a stomach with four *gastric pouches*. A hole through the outer end of each septum forms the *ring sinus*, which provides communication between the gastric pouches.

Toward their inner ends, the four septa are more or less thickened where they receive the *subumbrellar funnels*, deep pits in the subumbrella which dip down into them. The thickened ends of the septa partially close off the gastric pouches from the central undivided stomach. Digitate projections, the *gastric filaments*, project into the stomach from the ends of the septa; these have no counterpart in the hydromedusae. In some forms, the septa degenerate early in the development of the medusae, so that the stomach is essentially undivided. Radial canals, often elaborately branched and anastomosed, run from the periphery of the stomach out toward the edge of the bell where there may be a ring canal. In some species, excretory pores lead from the radial canals to the subumbrellar surface, forming the first hint of an excretory system. Due to the loss of the septa, the gastric filaments are located on the floor of the stomach, and the funnels are replaced by *subgenital pits*. The gonads occupy a position in the floor of the stomach and may bulge down into the subumbrellar cavity.

The musculature, involved chiefly in swimming activities, is concentrated in the margin and lower surface of the bell. All

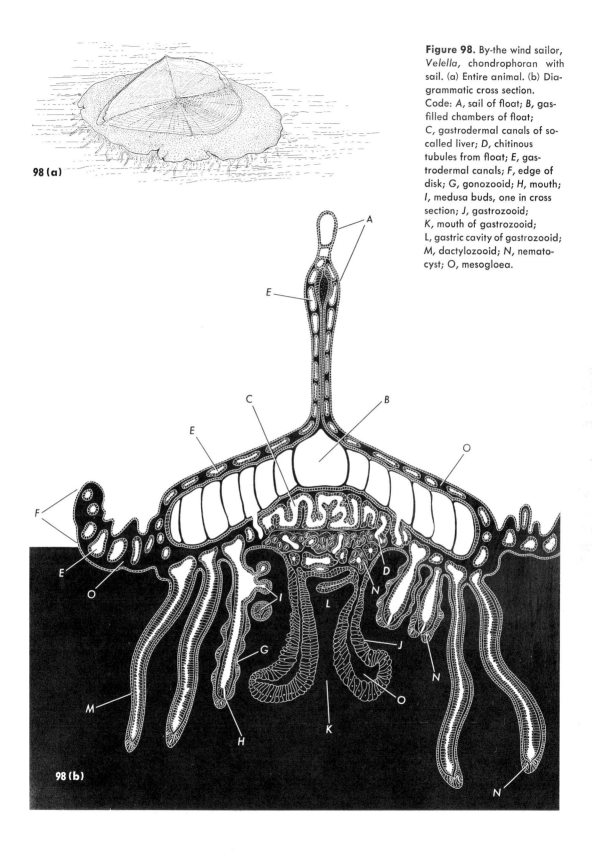

Figure 98. By-the wind sailor, *Velella*, chondrophoran with sail. (a) Entire animal. (b) Diagrammatic cross section. Code: *A*, sail of float; *B*, gas-filled chambers of float; *C*, gastrodermal canals of so-called liver; *D*, chitinous tubules from float; *E*, gastrodermal canals; *F*, edge of disk; *G*, gonozooid; *H*, mouth; *I*, medusa buds, one in cross section; *J*, gastrozooid; *K*, mouth of gastrozooid; *L*, gastric cavity of gastrozooid; *M*, dactylozooid; *N*, nematocyst; *O*, mesogloea.

98 (a)

98 (b)

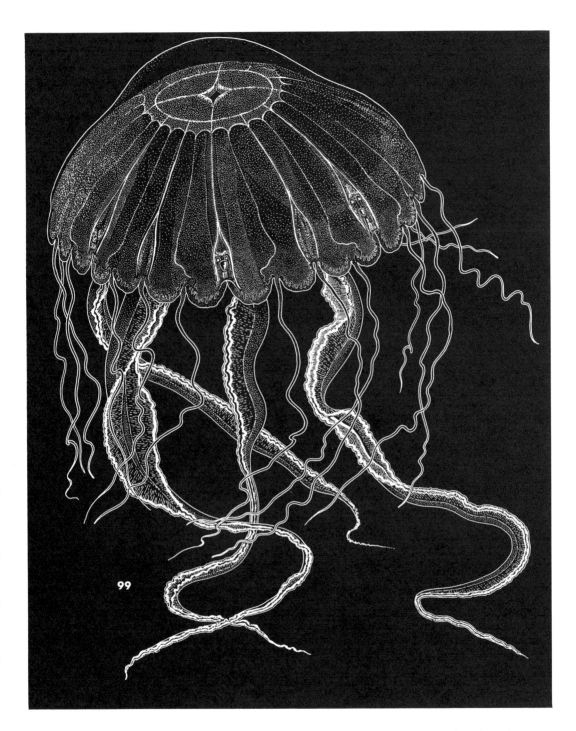

99

Figure 99. Adult scypho-
medusa, *Chrysaora.*
[After Naumov, 1961.]

Figure 100. Anatomy of Scyphozoa. General anatomy of scyphomedusa,
diagrammatic. [After Naumov, 1961.] Code: *A,* epidermis of exumbrella;
B, epidermis of subumbrella; *C,* exumbrella; *D,* gastric pouch; *E,* gastric fila-
ments; *F,* mouth; *G,* gonad; *H,* subgenital pits; *I,* ring canal; *J,* gastrodermis;
K, radial canal; *L,* subumbrella; *M,* mesogloea; *N,* oral arms; *O,* rhopalium;
P, pigment-cup ocellus; *Q,* statocyst; *R,* pigment-spot ocellus; *S,* hood;
T, stomach.

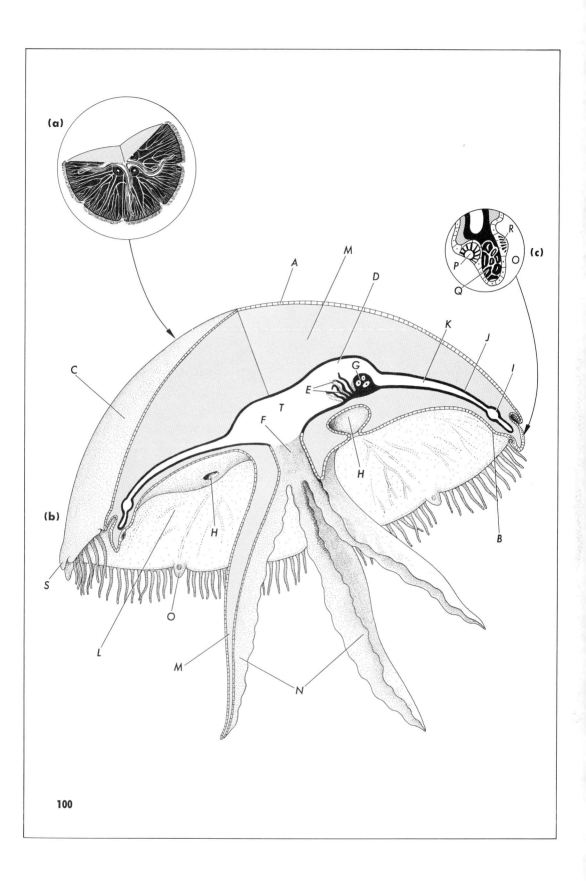

(a)

(c)

(b)

medusae, except for the attached forms that do not swim, have a strong, circular coronal muscle around the edge of the subumbrella. In scyphistomae and the medusae with strong septa, such as the Stauromedusae, longitudinal septal muscles are well developed and function as contractors.

Sensory structures occur in various positions along the edge of the bell or on the enlarged tentacle bases known as *pedalia*. These sensory organs, called *rhopalia* (Figure 101), are hollow, club-shaped structures situated in a *sensory niche* partially closed over by a protective *hood*. They have a sensory epithelium whose cells have hairlike projections, and a gastrodermal lining whose cells at the distal end contain concretions of calcium sulphate, the *stato-*

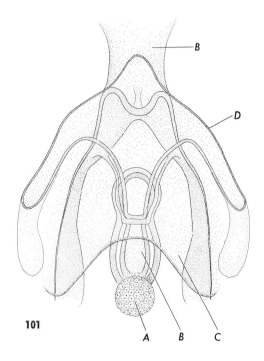

Figures 101 and 102. Anatomy of Scyphozoa. **101.** Rhopalium of *Aurelia* ephyra. [After Agassiz, 1860.] **102.** Rhopalium of *Carybdea*, longitudinal section showing ocelli. [After Mayer, 1910.] Code: A, statocyst; B, gastrovascular canal; C, hood; D, wall of canal; E, statolith; F, mesogloea; G, ocelli.

101

A   B   C

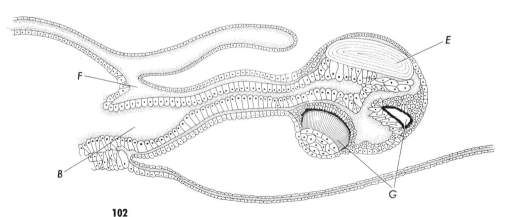

102

liths. Sensory pits also may occur in the roof of the sensory niche and in its floor. Some kinds of medusae have still another kind of sense organ, the *ocelli* (Figures 102, 103), which are photoreceptors located on the rhopalia. They are of several kinds, of various degrees of complexity, and with or without a lens.

The nervous system is in the form of a plexus in the subumbrella, extending onto the manubrium and tentacles. Concentrations into radial strands and clusters of ganglion cells in the vicinity of the rhopalia are the chief specializations.

On the basis of shape, structure of the manubrium, arrangement of sense organs, distribution of tentacles, presence of septa, and other anatomical features, the 200 or so species of Scyphozoa are allocated to five orders. One of these, the Stauromedusae, contains the peculiar, permanently polypoid, sessile scyphozoans of the genera *Lucernaria* and *Haliclystus* (Figure 104). Attached to the substrate by a narrow stalk, they are completely unable to swim and some cannot even change locations, being immovably cemented down by a pedal secretion. The Stauromedusae are animals of small or moderate size, one or a few centimeters in diameter at the expanded oral end. The flared margin of the funnel-shaped body (Figure 105) has eight projections terminating in a cluster of capitate tentacles. The concave oral end of the animal, actually the subumbrella, has a mouth with four small

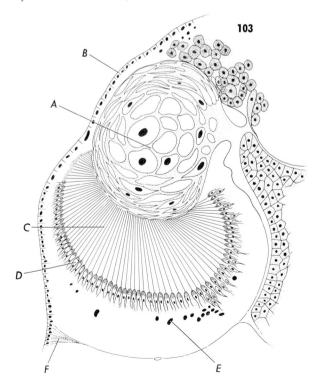

Figure 103. Anatomy of Scyphozoa. Ocellus of *Carybdea*, diagrammatic section. [Redrawn from Berger, 1900.] Code: A, lens; B, cornea; C, sensory fibers; D, retinal cells; E, ganglion cells; F, fibers in mesogloea.

oral lobes and four deep subumbrellar funnels. The four septa which partition the stomach and also bear the gonads are strong and furnished with longitudinal retractor muscles. The circular muscle has no function in this sedentary animal and is reduced to a thin marginal band. As would be expected from the polypoid nature of these animals, the sides—actually the exumbrella— contain a rich exumbrellar nerve plexus, contrary to the usual scyphozoan condition. Stauromedusae are inhabitants of cool inshore waters; *Haliclystus* is especially common along the northwestern coast of the United States, and *Lucernaria* occurs along New England shores. They often cling to marine plants where they are very inconspicuous because of their green or brownish coloration. Their development is direct and they never produce a free-swimming stage.

The Carybdeida (or Cubomedusae) is the order containing the most dangerous of all coelenterates, the sea wasps, sometimes

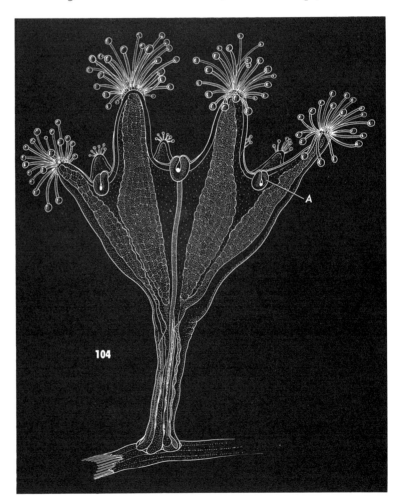

Figure 104. Anatomy of Scyphozoa. Stauromedusa, *Haliclystus*. [After Clark, 1878.] Code: A, anchor, a modified tentacle superficially resembling a rhopalium but not sensory.

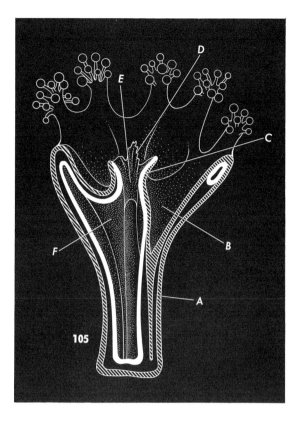

105

Figure 105. Diagram of stauromedusan anatomy. [After Naumov, 1961.] Code: A, stalk; B, subumbrellar funnel; C, manubrium; D, oral lobes; E, mouth; F, septum.

called box jellies because of the cuboidal shape of the bell. They are transparent, colorless medusae with one or several tentacles springing from the four corners of the quadrangular bell margin (Figures 106, 107). The edge of the bell is bent inward to form a marginal flap, the *velarium*, that in swimming functions like the velum of the hydromedusae although it differs structurally. The subumbrellar space contains the manubrium, usually small and quadrangular. The mouth leads into the stomach, which occupies the top of the bell, with the four gastric pockets extending down the four sides. The pockets are connected by a ring sinus. The gonads are long, thin flaps attached by their edges to the septa, one on each side. The rhopalia are hollow, their cavities communicating with the gastric pockets by way of a canal; they bear ocelli, which may be elaborate structures with lens, retinal cup, and vitreous body (Figure 103).

The sea wasps are found mainly in tropical and subtropical regions where they are a danger to bathers in shallow waters. Many documented cases of fatal jellyfish stings have occurred in tropical parts of Australia, the Solomon Islands, Borneo, Malaya, and the Philippines where species of the genera *Chiropsalmus* and *Chironex* are common (Figure 107). Sea wasps are present also in the Caribbean area but appear not to be sufficiently common there to create any serious hazard to swimmers. Even where abundant, they are rarely noticed because of their highly transparent substance.

Jellyfishes of the third scyphozoan order, the Coronatae, differ from the others by the circular *coronal groove* around the exumbrella, in some cases placed near the summit of the bell, in others closer to its margin (Figure 108). The margin of the bell is conspicuously scalloped and bears broad radial ribs that marginally give rise alternately to tentacles and sense organs, which lie in the notches between the lappets. These peripheral structures are, as usual, symmetrically arranged in multiples of four. The central part of the stomach is cut off from the peripheral part by

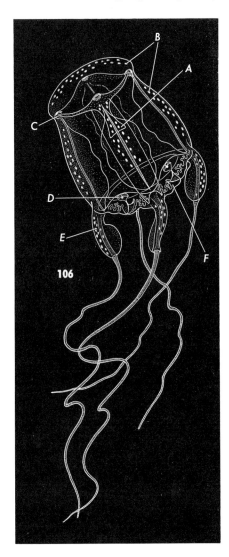

Figures 106 and 107. Forms of Scyphozoa. **106.** Cubomedusa, *Carybdea*. [After Mayer, 1910.] **107.** Cubomedusa, *Chironex*, the deadly sea-wasp of Australia. [After Southcott, 1956, 1959.] Code: A, manubrium; B, nematocyst batteries; C, gastric filaments; D, rhopalium; E, pedalia; F, velarium; G, gonad.

a thin membrane running between the peripheral ends of the septa. Due to the fact that the outer ends of the septa do not extend from floor to roof of the stomach, the ring sinus is so wide that the gastric pouches are combined into one broad circular chamber. Canals extend from this into the lappets and rhopalia.

Most coronate medusae are typical bathypelagic forms of the open ocean, but a few are known from shallow coastal waters. *Linuche*, the brown thimble jelly, sometimes swarms in countless thousands around Florida and in the West Indies. *Nausithoe* is common both in the Atlantic and Pacific and is remarkable because its scyphistomae (Figure 109), called by the separate generic name *Stephanoscyphus*, are covered by an annulated, horny perisarc, and in Japan and elsewhere in the western Pacific form extensive colonies with notable stinging powers. The deep-sea Coronatae are often large and deep red, purple, or maroon in color.

The orders Semaeostomae and Rhizostomae, once united under the name Discomedusae, are the large medusae best known col-

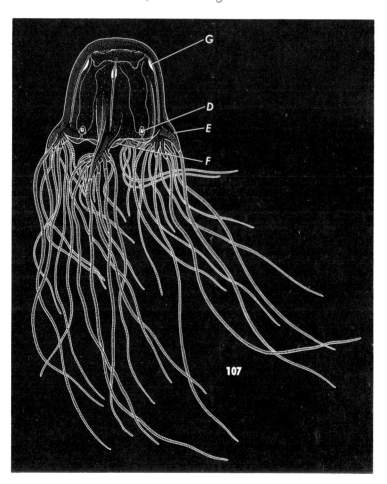

lectively as "jellyfishes." The two orders differ in the construction of the oral arms. In the semaeostomes (Figure 99) these are broad, open lobes with flounced edges, whereas in the rhizostomes the frilled edges fuse over and close the mouth, forming instead a complicated system of canals opening by way of many small *suctorial mouths*. In both orders the septa have disappeared entirely, and with them the subumbrellar funnels. Four subgenital pits often occur in the location of the funnels, their cavities expanding and uniting in the interior to form a quadrangular chamber lying below the stomach. The semaeostomes have gastric filaments, which are located on the floor of the stomach, but the rhizostomes have lost these structures. The stomach sends out radial canals, which may branch or form a complicated network, and a ring canal is present in some groups, absent in others. Both orders have

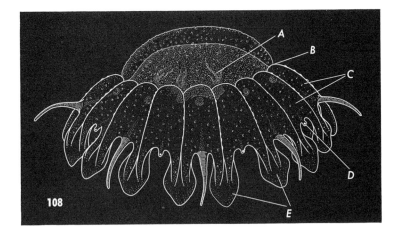

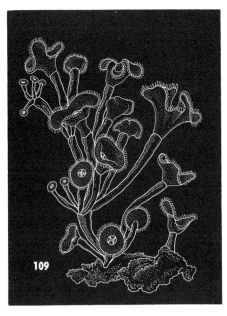

Figures 108 and 109. Forms of Scyphozoa. 108. Coronate, *Nausithoe*. [After Mayer, 1910.] 109. *Stephanoscyphus*, the scyphistoma stage of *Nausithoe*. [After Komai, 1935.] Code: A, gastric filaments; B, coronal groove; C, pedalia; D, rhopalium; E, marginal lappet.

rhopalia. The polypoid stage is typically a scyphistoma (Figure 110) which buds off numerous ephyra larvae at intervals over several seasons, each thus producing a large number of medusae during its lifetime. The scyphistoma stage has been eliminated from the life cycle of species inhabiting the open and deep sea where there is neither suitable substrate nor sufficient food for its survival. In *Pelagia*, young medusae develop directly from the planulae, and in *Stygiomedusa* the young jellyfishes, produced in an unknown way, are brooded to substantial size in cysts in four subumbrellar brood-chambers, escaping as well-formed young adults. The most familiar semaeostomes are the troublesome sea nettle, *Dactylometra quinquecirrha*, of our eastern coast, the huge

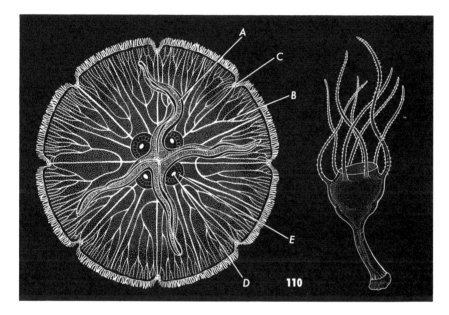

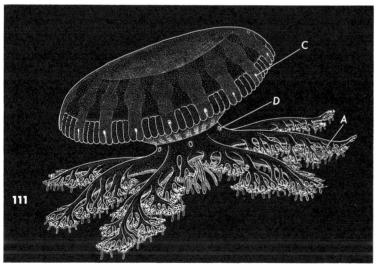

Figures 110 and 111. Forms of Scyphozoa. 110. Semaeostome medusa, *Aurelia*, and its scyphistoma. [After Mayer, 1910.] 111. Rhizostome medusa, *Cassiopea*. [After Mayer, 1910.] Code: A, oral arms; B, gastrovascular canals; C, rhopalium; D, subgenital pit; E, gonad.

Cyanea of northern waters, and the common moon-jelly, *Aurelia aurita* (Figure 110), generally described in textbooks as the typical scyphozoan. Rhizostomes are less frequently encountered, although two species of *Cassiopea* (Figure 111) are abundant in the Caribbean area from Florida south to Curaçao, where the animals lie on the bottom, umbrella downward, almost inert except for marginal pulsations. Less common is the large, stiff, spheroidal *Stomolophus*, handsomely splotched with rich brown, which swims in conventional fashion.

CLASS ANTHOZOA

The Anthozoa, third of the great coelenterate classes, is characterized by the complete suppression of the medusoid stage. Included here are the well-known sea anemones, stony corals, soft and horny corals, and sea pens. The polyps (Figure 112) differ in many ways from the hydrozoan polyps. Most noticeably, they are larger, short and squat instead of tall and slender, with a flattened oral end, the *oral disc*, which is usually surrounded by hollow tentacles in one or several circles. The cylindrical body of the polyp is commonly called the *column*, especially in the sea anemones and similar forms. The mouth opens into a tubular *pharynx* which extends down into the gastrovascular cavity. The latter is divided into compartments by thin longitudinal partitions, the *septa* (called "mesenteries" in many texts but having nothing to do with the mesenteries of coelomate animals), some or all of which extend from body wall to pharynx in their upper parts, joining with the oral disc above, and hanging free in the gastric cavity below the lower end of the pharynx. The free edges of the septa are thickened into convoluted, cordlike structures, the *septal filaments* (Figures 113, 114). The interior of the pharynx, which is a flattened tube, has a groove lined with flagellated cells along one, sometimes both, of its narrow edges. This flagellated groove, which serves to propel water into the polyp, is termed the *siphonoglyph* or *sulcus* (Figure 115).

Figures 112 to 115. Anatomy of Anthozoa. **112.** Diagrammatic longitudinal section of actinian polyp. Code: A, mouth; B, siphonoglyph; C, pharynx; D, column wall; E, fosse; F, collar; G, incomplete septum; H, complete septum; I, longitudinal retractor muscle; J, transverse septal muscles; K, basilar muscle; L, septal filament; M, gonads; N, acontia; O, oral disk; P, pedal disk; Q, internal stoma; R, external stoma. **113.** Cross section of septal filament from upper part of septum near pharynx. [After Duerden, 1901.] Code: A, cnidoglandular band with nematocysts B; C, flagellated band; D, mesogloea containing wandering cells. **114.** Cross section of septal filament from lower part of septum. [After Duerden, 1901.] Code: A, cnidoglandular band with nematocysts B and gland cells C; D, mesogloea. **115.** Cross section of siphonoglyph. Code: A, pharynx; B, C, gland cells and flagellated cells; D, mesogloea of pharynx; E, gastrodermis of gastrovascular cavity F; G, mesogloea of septum.

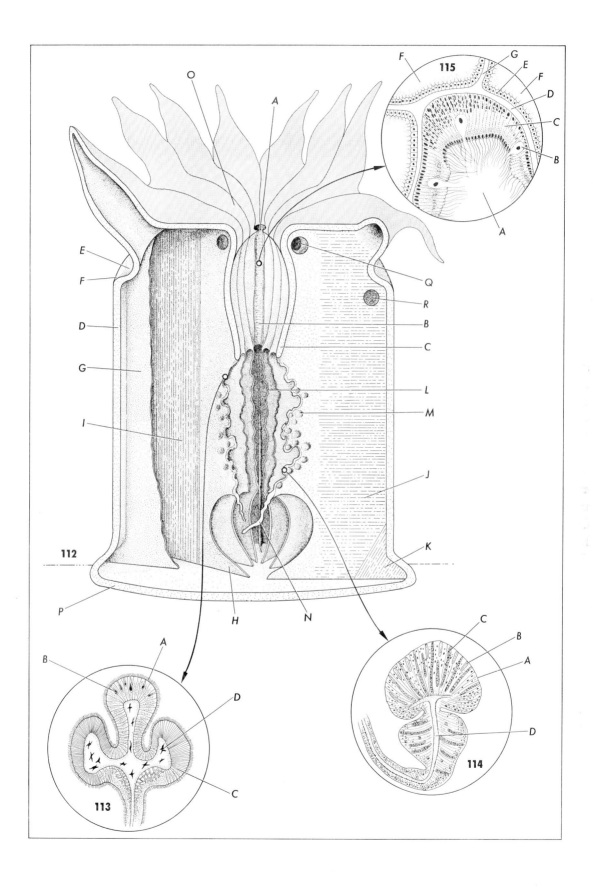

The histological structure of the anthozoan polyp consists of epidermis and gastrodermis with an intervening layer of mesogloea (Figure 116). The septa, which originate as projections from the gastrodermis, are lined with gastrodermis on both faces. Unlike the situation in the hydrozoan polyp, the mesogloea is usually quite thick and richly cellular (Figure 117). In some anthozoans, the cells of the mesogloea secrete calcareous spicules and there may also be a horny ectodermal secretion that forms a supporting structure for the colonial aggregation of polyps. In others, the ectoderm secretes a calcareous substance known as *coral* around the base of the polyps. Certain forms produce no skeleton at all or incorporate foreign material, such as sand grains and sponge spicules, into the column wall as a means of support. The epidermis is syncytial or composed of columnar or inverted pyramidal cells, sometimes flagellated. The flagellated cells may have microvilli forming a collar-like structure around the base of the flagellum as in the choanocytes of sponges. Mucous and sensory cells as well as nematocysts are abundant among the epidermal cells. Muscle fibers lie under the epidermis of oral disc and tentacles, and sometimes also in the column wall where they may take a longitudinal direction. Strong retractor muscles lie longitudinally in the gastrodermis along one side of the septa, where the mesogloea is thrown into prominent folds supporting the fibers. Circular muscles occur in the gastrodermis of the tentacles, disk and column wall, and transverse strands in the septa.

On the basis of their symmetry and many other characters, the Anthozoa are divided into two subclasses, one homogeneous as to

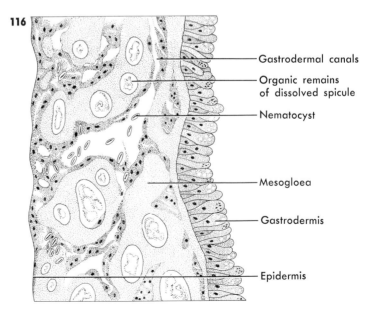

116

Gastrodermal canals

Organic remains
of dissolved spicule

Nematocyst

Mesogloea

Gastrodermis

Epidermis

Figure 116. Anthozoan structure. Cross section of body wall of gorgonian polyp.

all essentials but showing diversified specializations, the other quite heterogeneous but showing much less diversity of modification. The former, the subclass Octocorallia, also known under the equivalent name Alcyonaria, is comprised of colonial forms whose polyps are basically of a very uniform construction. Their symmetry is invariably octomerous (Figure 118), with eight septa and eight pinnate tentacles, one siphonoglyph, and muscle bands always on the sulcal side of the septa. The colonies almost always produce a calcareous skeleton in the form of spicules in the mesogloea, and very commonly a woodlike epidermal secretion, the *horny axis*, as well (Figure 117). The nematocysts are uniformly of a single type. Diversity in the alcyonarians is expressed in various modifications of the calcareous spicules and in variations in the structure of the axis and organization of the colony.

The second subclass, the Hexacorallia or Zoantharia, is a heterogeneous assemblage of forms whose symmetry, as the name implies, is based on multiples of six (Figures 119, 120, 121), although it is not always so. The tentacles are never pinnate and septa may be very numerous, the muscles do not always face in the same direction on the septa, and there may be more than one siphonoglyph. Polyps may be either solitary or colonial, with or without a skeleton of epidermal origin. In the Antipatharia, the skeleton is horny, like the axis of some alcyonarians, and calcareous in the Madreporaria (Scleractinia), the stony corals. The Actiniaria, Ceriantharia, and Zoantharia produce no intrinsic skeleton, but the latter may incorporate foreign matter as a supporting agent.

Although the size may vary, the basic plan of the alcyonarian polyp (Figure 122) is universal in the subclass. The body is cylin-

117

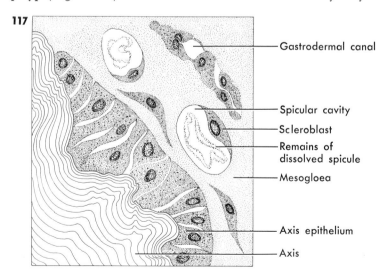

Gastrodermal canal

Spicular cavity

Scleroblast

Remains of
dissolved spicule

Mesogloea

Axis epithelium

Axis

Figure 117. Anthozoan structure. Cross section of part of gorgonian branch showing axis-secreting epithelium.

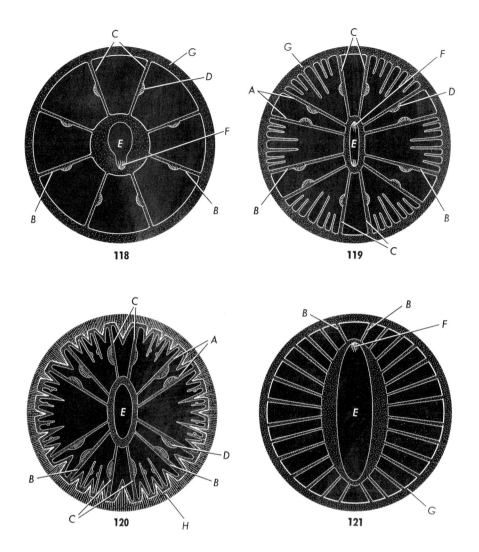

Figures 118 to 121. Anthozoan symmetry. Diagrammatic cross sections of polyps. **118.** Octocorallia. **119.** Actiniaria. **120.** Scleractinia (with skeleton). **121.** Ceriantharia (septa coupled but not paired). Code: In all diagrams, the septa marked *A* are pairs, those marked *B* are couples, and those marked *C* are directives; *D*, retractor muscle; *E*, pharynx; *F*, siphonoglyph; *G*, body wall; *H*, skeleton.

drical, its upper part encircled by a ring of eight tentacles which surround the flattened oral disc. The tentacles bear a series of finger-like processes, the *pinnules*, in a feather-like arrangement along both sides. The mouth leads from the center of the oral disc into a flattened tubular pharynx with a flagellated groove, or siphonoglyph, down only one of the narrow edges. Alternating with the tentacles are eight radial septa all of which extend completely from body wall to pharynx. The edges of the septa that hang free below the pharynx have a thickened, convoluted margin, the *septal filament*. Those of the two septa opposite the siphonoglyph (that is, the *asulcal septa*) are formed by flagellated ectodermal cells that have grown down from the pharyngeal lining and continue to the base of the polyp. They are part of the water transport mechanism and serve to create an out-flowing current. The remaining six filaments do not extend so deeply into the gastric cavity. They are not so strongly flagellated and are formed of richly glandular gastrodermis which functions in digestion. The gonads are borne in the edges of the six septa nearest the siphonoglyph; those of the asulcal pair never have gonads. As alcyonarian colonies are for the most part immovably fixed, their chief movements consist of the food-capturing actions of the polyps and the withdrawal of the upper portion of the polyps into the colonial coenenchyme in times of danger. These activities are accomplished by a rather weak epidermal muscular system in the tentacles and pinnules, extending onto the oral disc, and by a gastrodermal system consisting of circular fibers in the body wall, transverse fibers on the asulcal faces of the septa, and bands of strong longitudinal retractor muscles on the sulcal faces of the septa. The longitudinal muscles are set on projecting plates of mesogloea. Due to the distinctive nature of the two asulcal filaments, the presence of only one siphonoglyph, and the position of the retractor muscles, only one plane divides the polyp into identical halves. Thus the alcyonarian polyp displays a strongly bilateral trend in its symmetry, termed radiobilateral (Figure 118).

The lower part of the body wall of the alcyonarian polyp is greatly thickened by development of the mesogloea containing calcareous spicules and tubular gastroderm-lined extensions from the gastrovascular cavity known as *solenia*. New polyps originate from these solenial tubes, thus producing a colonial aggregation of polyps interconnected by way of a complex canal system. The epithelium next to the substrate may produce a horny cuticular

Figure 122. Anthozoan form. Fully expanded polyps of the young octocoral colony *Erythropodium.*

**Phylum
Coelenterata**

lamella which in arborescent forms is raised into upright, branching woodlike or horny projections over which the colony is spread. In other branching forms, the stems are the elongated polyp bodies stiffened by profuse development of mesogloea, and the daughter polyps which form the branches are budded off from solenia in the thickened wall of the parent polyp.

Liberally strewn through the colonial mesogloea, best called *coenenchyme*, are calcareous spicules (Figure 123) of diverse form and size, produced by mesogloeal cells called *scleroblasts* (Figure 117), derived from interstitial cells that have migrated inward from the epidermis. The various modifications of the spicules are characteristic of the different systematic categories and constitute a taxonomic character of major importance. The basic form of the alcyonarian spicule is the slender, pointed, monaxial *spindle*. This may develop tubercular, spinous, or foliate sculpturing arranged in distinctive ways and may undergo curvature or flattening to form platelike structures often with ornamented edges.

The subclass Octocorallia is divided into six orders, two very distinct and four intergrading almost completely. Colonies be-

Figure 123. Skeletal structures in octocorals. Various types of spicules. [Adapted from Bayer, 1958.]

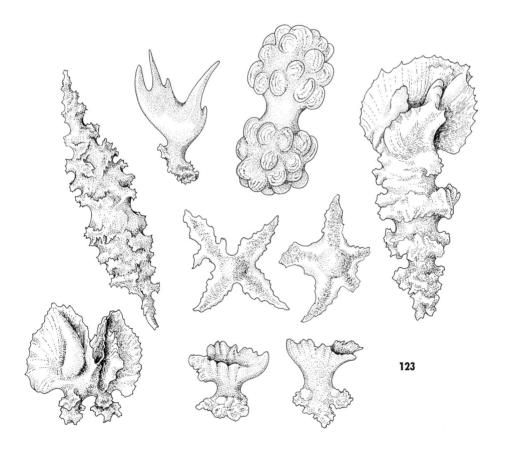

123

longing to the order Stolonifera (Figure 125) consist of simple, cylindrical polyps connected at the base by narrow ribbons of coenenchyme, the *stolons*, growing on rocks and shells. Species of the order Telestacea are similar, but the polyps grow tall and bud off lateral daughter polyps (Figure 126) so the colonies are branched and sometimes quite bushy. Colonies of the order Alcyonacea are usually massive because the long polyps are embedded in a thick mass of mesogloea filled with spicules (Figure 127). The order Gorgonacea contains the most familiar octocorals, the sea fans and related forms (Figure 128). These all have a firm supporting skeleton, often branched, over which the polyps are spread in a layer of coenenchyme containing spicules (Figure 129). In some, the axis is horny or woodlike, in others made of separate calcareous spicules, and in certain families it is solidly calcareous. In the last, the axis may be bright red or pink, as in the familiar precious coral, and either interrupted by flexible, horny joints or quite unjointed. These four orders show a regular progression of complexity and perhaps represent an evolutionary sequence. Two other orders stand apart without definite intergrades. These are the massive blue coral, order Coenothecalia, the bright blue colonies of which resemble millepores or stony corals and the sea pens, order Pennatulacea. The Pennatulacea are the most complex of the octocorals, being composed of several modified types of polyps. The highly organized colonies (Figure 130)

124

Figure 124. Anthozoan form. Expanded polyp of the sea anemone *Bunodeopsis*.

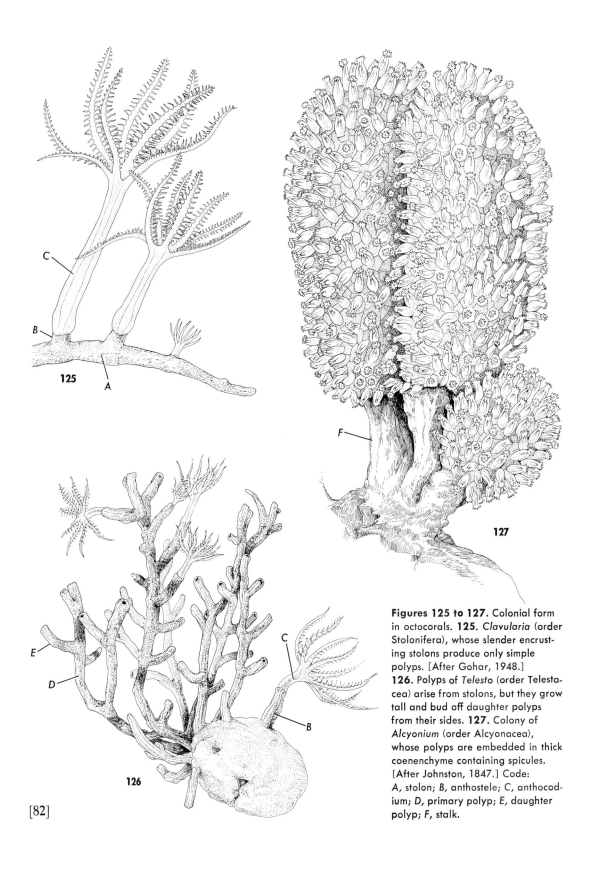

Figures 125 to 127. Colonial form in octocorals. **125.** *Clavularia* (order Stolonifera), whose slender encrusting stolons produce only simple polyps. [After Gohar, 1948.] **126.** Polyps of *Telesto* (order Telestacea) arise from stolons, but they grow tall and bud off daughter polyps from their sides. **127.** Colony of *Alcyonium* (order Alcyonacea), whose polyps are embedded in thick coenenchyme containing spicules. [After Johnston, 1847.] Code: *A*, stolon; *B*, anthostele; *C*, anthocodium; *D*, primary polyp; *E*, daughter polyp; *F*, stalk.

are built around one primary polyp which buds off lateral polyps in a very regular way, eventually losing its own individuality by becoming the main stem of the colony. It is anchored in the soft sea bottom by its muscular lower end and from its side produces many polyps, arranged in distinct whorls or rows and sometimes united into crestlike projecting "leaves."

The members of the subclass Zoantharia are as diverse as the alcyonarians are homogeneous, and it is virtually impossible to define the group in terms compatible with all of its orders. Included are the Actiniaria or sea anemones, the Madreporaria or stony corals, the Antipatharia or black corals, and the Ceriantharia or burrowing sea anemones.

One of the principal differences between the Alcyonaria and the Zoantharia is the tendency toward hexamerous symmetry of the septa (Figures 119, 120, 121) in the latter, as suggested by its alternate name Hexacorallia. The Zoantharia never have only eight perfect septa all with retractor muscles on the sulcal side; their tentacles are simple or at most bifurcated, and if there is a skeleton it is either massive and calcareous or arborescent and horny, but never made up of spicules. The nematocysts show a great diversity which is a further indication of the heterogeneous nature of this anthozoan group.

The body plan (Figure 112) in the various orders follows the general organization of the alcyonarian polyp, differing in details. The zoantharian polyp is either solitary or colonial, with a columnar body divided by radial septa symmetrically disposed in regard to position of the longitudinal muscle. The oral end is expanded as a flattened *oral disc* surrounded by one or several circlets of hollow tentacles which in some forms occupy most of the disc. The aboral end may be a flattened, adhesive *pedal disc*, or it may be rounded for insertion into a soft substrate. In colonial species the polyps may encrust rocks or other solid objects, or the common basal epidermis secretes a skeletal substance, either horny and arborescent, or calcareous and massive or branched, over which the polyps, united in colonial coenenchyme, are distributed.

As in the Alcyonaria, the mouth opens into a flattened tubular pharynx which usually has a flagellated groove or siphonoglyph along one or both narrow edges. If there are two siphonoglyphs, the major one is the *sulcus* and the secondary one is the *sulculus*. Complete or perfect septa extend from column wall to the pharynx, which opens into the gastrovascular cavity. The edges of the septa hanging free below the pharynx are thickened into filaments. The thickened edge actually consists of three cords or ridges (Figure 113). The central one is composed of gland cells

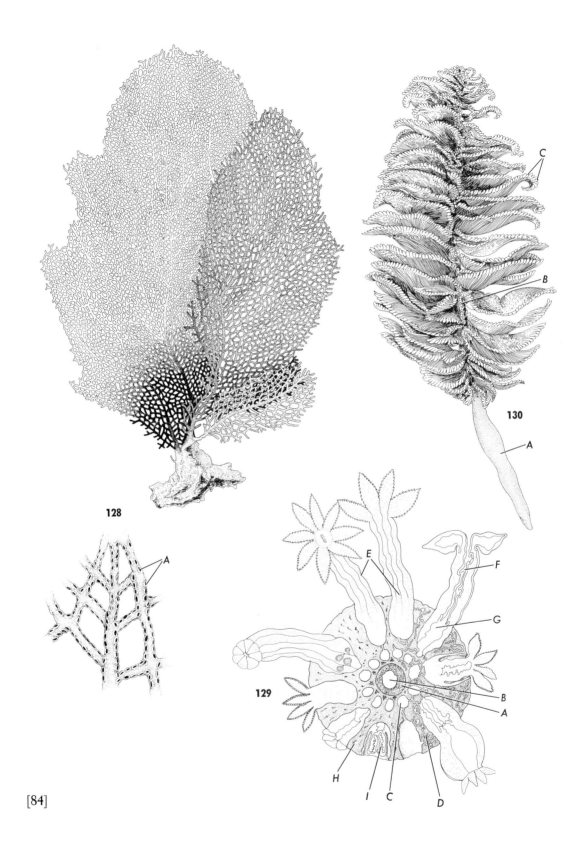

[84]

and numerous nematocysts and is called the *cnidoglandular band*; it participates in digestion and corresponds to the filaments of the six asulcal septa in Alcyonaria. The two lateral cords are strongly flagellated and are termed the *flagellated bands*; they correspond to the filaments of the two asulcal septa in the Alcyonaria.

The order Actiniaria comprises the sea anemones (Figure 124), familiar animals in tide pools along rocky coasts, as well as on reefs and in many other habitats. They are always solitary and completely lack a skeleton. The tentacles are hollow and may correspond in number with the interseptal spaces, although some kinds have more than one tentacle per chamber. They are usually slender and tapered, but may vary in shape and size, and in a few cases may branch. The oral end of the anemone may be set off from the column by a groove or *fosse* (Figure 112) bounded below by a ridgelike *collar*, and further regional differentiation may occur in some species. The column may have various structures of special function, such as glandular *warts, tenaculi, nemathybomes,* and *acrorhagi* filled with nematocysts, *fronds, pseudotentacles* (Figure 131), and *vesicles*. The column may also have pores (*cinclides*—Figure 132) leading to the interior, through which water is expelled during sudden contraction. As the chambers bounded by the complete septa may be deep, blind pockets, water flow between them is facilitated by perforations through the septa near their union with the oral disc. There is usually one hole, the *internal stoma*, near the pharynx, and another, the *external stoma*, near the column wall (Figure 112).

Below the pharynx the septa curve back to the body wall more or less abruptly, thus forming a spacious gastrovascular cavity, and then widen again, extending out onto the pedal disc to which they are attached. The free margins of the septa have filaments, as mentioned before, consisting of three bands. In some families, the lower ends of the cnidoglandular bands may project as free threads called *acontia* which protrude from the cinclides when the animal contracts and presumably have a defensive function.

Figures 128 to 130. Structure and colonial form in octocorals. **128.** Net-like colony of the common sea fan, *Gorgonia* (order Gorgonacea) and detail of branching. [After Agassiz, 1880.] Code: A, apertures of retracted polyps. **129.** Cross section of gorgonian branch, *Pseudoplexaura*. [After Chester, 1913.] Code: A, axis; B, chambered core of axis; C, longitudinal canals; D, fine gastrodermal canals connecting polyps with each other and with the major canals; E, polyps; F, pharynx; G, gastrovascular cavity of polyp; H, mesogloea containing spicules; I, section of retracted polyp. **130.** Colony of *Pennatula* (order Pennatulacea), the sea pen. [After Kölliker, 1870.] Code: A, stalk; B, rhachis bearing leaf-like clusters of polyps; C, calyces of retracted polyps.

The epidermal muscle system is represented by fibers longitudinally arranged in the tentacles, radially in the oral disc, and rarely present on the column. The gastrodermal musculature is strong, circular in the column, where it may be thickened as a sphincter at the upper end, oral disc, and base. The septa have transverse gastrodermal muscle fibers and a longitudinal *parietal muscle* on one side, and the powerful *retractor muscle* on the opposite side.

The orderly arrangement of the septa is very conspicuous in a cross section of a sea anemone (Figure 119). Here, the longitudinal retractor muscles are not always on the same side of the septa, as they are in alcyonarian polyps, but on adjacent septa also may face either toward or away from each other. As the two halves of an anemone divided along the siphonoglyph are identical, each septum on one side of the animal has its exact counterpart on the other side. Such corresponding septa are called *couples*, whereas on either side of the animal the septa facing each other in two's are called *pairs*. Although the arrangement of septa with regard to the position of the retractor muscle, the relationship of complete and incomplete types, and occurrence of septal filaments and gonads, are extremely regular within certain taxonomic groups, the major kinds of arrangements throughout the Zoantharia is so diverse that no one organization can be considered typical of the order.

The gonads (Figure 133) are located along the edges of the septa just behind the filaments. Hermaphroditism occurs, but the sexes also may be separate.

The tissues of actinians are composed of much the same type of cells as described for hydrozoans. The nervous system is an

Figures 131 and 132. Form of Actiniaria. **131.** Stinging sea anemone, *Lebrunia*. **132.** Sea anemone, *Calliactis*. [Both after Corrêa, 1964.] Code: *A*, pseudotentacles with acrorhagi *B*; *C*, tentacles; *D*, oral disk; *E*, mouth; *F*, column; *G*, cinclides; *H*, edge of pedal disk.

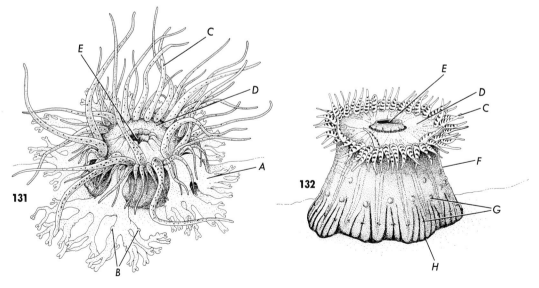

131

132

epidermal plexus connected through the mesogloea to a gastrodermal plexus. The mesogloea contains numerous amoeboid cells of ectodermal origin and may be gelatinous, more or less firm, or fibrous, in which case many fibers occur in addition to the amoebocytes, resulting in considerable thickness.

The Madreporaria are hexamerously symmetrical anthozoan polyps much like the Actiniaria but with two very conspicuous differences. First, they secrete an epidermal skeleton of calcium carbonate; and second, they are predominantly colonial animals because of their rapid asexual reproduction.

The skeleton is produced by the aboral epidermis, and the polyp sits in it as in a cup or *calice*; the skeleton of a single polyp is called a *corallite* (Figure 134). The bottom of the calice has several radially arranged stony partitions or *sclerosepta*, which grow up in folds of the aboral wall between the soft septa of the polyp. They are composed of fused, rodlike skeletal elements called *trabeculae* arranged in one or more fanlike groups. The outer wall or *theca* of the calice is either a cuplike structure surrounding the sclerosepta, the thickened ends of the sclerosepta themselves fused to form a wall, or barlike *synapticulae* joining the outer ends of the sclerosepta like a latticework.

Some stony corals are solitary, resembling a sea anemone with a calcareous skeleton. The corallite is a simple cup, more or less widely open, with numerous radial sclerosepta (Figure 134). Most species are colonial, however, because of profuse budding (Figure 135). Those whose polyps have a wide, collar-like expansion of the column wall surrounding the tentacles commonly produce new polyps from this edge. Thus each calice is a simple, rounded cup, in groups forming a colonial skeleton called the *corallum*. Others produce additional polyps by forming secondary mouths in the oral disc, inside the circle of tentacles. This kind of budding, called *intratentacular*, results in long, sinuous, physically

Figure 133. Form of Actiniaria. Cross section of actinian septum. Code: A, gastrodermis; B, gonads; C, filament; D, mesogloea; E, plates of mesogloea bearing the retractor muscles F; G, transverse septal muscles; H, parietal muscle. [Diagram combined and modified from Duerden, 1901; Hyman, 1940.]

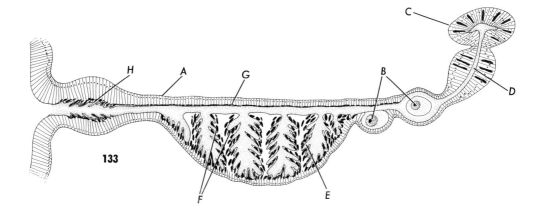

133

Phylum
Coelenterata

Figure 134. Form of scleractinian coral. Solitary coral *Oulangia*. Expanded living polyp on left, cleaned skeleton on right.

Figure 135. Form of scleractinian coral. Colonial coral *Montastrea*. One of the most important reef builders in the tropical Atlantic. Cleaned skeleton.

joined polyps which form the large masses called *brain corals* because of their convoluted surfaces. In these, the cycles of septa and sclerosepta become confused and the hexamerous arrangement is largely obliterated.

The polyps occupy only the upper surface of the corallum, which enlarges marginally (terminally in branched kinds) and increases in thickness as new polyps are budded off and consecutive layers of skeleton are secreted. Increase in skeletal thickness results as the polyps grow upward in their calices. The rim of the wall and the septa increase in height, and the bottom of the calices are sealed off by transverse, blister-like calcareous partitions or dissepiments. The skeleton between the calices, produced by the expanded margin of the polyps, grows upward by a similar process.

In addition to these features, coral polyps differ from sea anemones in that they lack a siphonoglyph in the pharynx and their septal filaments consist only of a cnidoglandular band. Their nematocysts are of three kinds and show little diversification, indicating the homogeneous nature of the stony corals.

Five small but distinct groups of anthozoans must also be mentioned briefly. Two of these have recently been separated off from the Actiniaria. In one order, the Corallimorpharia, a strong tendency to intratentacular budding results in a polystomodaeal condition as in the Madreporaria, differing chiefly in the lack of a calcareous skeleton. Another divergent group of sea anemones lacks muscle fibers in the base of the polyps and has no flagellated tracts on the septal filaments. For these and other histological reasons, such forms are now considered as a separate order named Ptychodactiaria.

The Zoanthidea (Figure 136) is a small order of anthozoans, mostly colonial in nature, in which the polyps arise from a basal stolon or mat containing gastrodermal canals or are embedded in a thickened mesogloea, much as in certain alcyonarian orders. However, zoanthids have many tentacles, never pinnate, and do not form calcareous spicules. The septa are numerous and arranged in a distinctive fashion quite different from other anthozoan orders. Their filaments have exceptionally wide, thin, lateral flagellated bands projecting back from edge of the septa. Although the oral disc and tentacles can be infolded and closed by a marginal sphincter, the animals are sluggish and not strongly retractile and the septal musculature is weakly developed. The highly developed capacity for asexual reproduction is shown in the colonial nature of most zoanthids. As in Alcyonaria, new polyps are budded from the gastrodermal solenia in the stolons rather than from the old polyps.

Similar to sea anemones, but without a basal disc, are the burrowing anemones, order Ceriantharia. They have a tall, columnar body aborally rounded and buried in sand or mud (Figure 137). There is a terminal pore in the aboral end; the tentacles are arranged on the oral disc in two circles, one around the mouth, one at the margin, and the circles may be from one to four tentacles wide. The septa are set in couples, one on each side of the siphonoglyph, and are added indefinitely in the interseptal space at the end of the pharynx opposite the siphonoglyph. All septa are perfect, but some are long and others short, arranged in a very definite pattern. Most of the septa are too short to reach from oral disc to aboral end of the body. The gonads occur only on alternate septa, and the animals are protandrous hermaphrodites. The complete life cycle is not known, but the larval forms have been frequently collected and various stages reported.

The cerianthids often line their burrows with a protective tube of mucus and agglutinated bottom material. They have no sphincter muscle and very weak longitudinal muscles which do not form distinct retractors on the septa, so they do not contract the oral disc and tentacles as they withdraw into this tube for protection.

The cerianthids differ from the actinians in the presence of a complete layer of longitudinal epidermal muscles in the column, permitting great contractility in connection with a tubicolous way of life.

Although the black corals, order Antipatharia, are different in appearance from the Ceriantharia, the two groups are sometimes combined in a single order on the basis of the way new septa are formed, the fact that the septa of each couple are never also paired, and the similarity of cerianthid larvae to adult antipatharian polyps. However, the Antipatharia are so different in general features that they are best treated separately. The polyps are colonial and produce a horny, arborescent skeleton resembling the axis of gorgonians except that they are covered with thorns. The colonies may be fanlike, plumose, or covered with short branchlets all around like a bottle brush. Some are simple and whiplike and may exceed 20 feet in length; the arborescent kinds may be several feet tall. Most antipatharian polyps (Figure 138) have six simple tentacles, and three, five, or six couples of septa. The polyps may be so elongated along the skeletal axis that the tentacles are in widely spaced pairs along the branch. The epidermis is ciliated. Only the transverse couple of septa have filaments and produce gonads. The muscular system is very weakly

Figure 136. Anthozoan. Colony of zoanthids, with polyps expanded.

136

developed as would be expected from the general sluggishness of the polyps, which are only slightly contractile. As the coenenchyme is very thin, the polyps are unable to retract into it, and the retractor muscles are very weakly developed. The development is unknown.

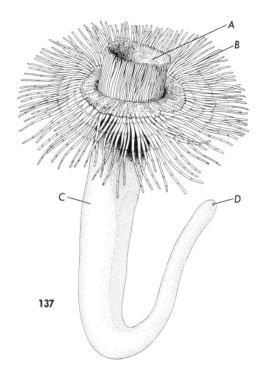

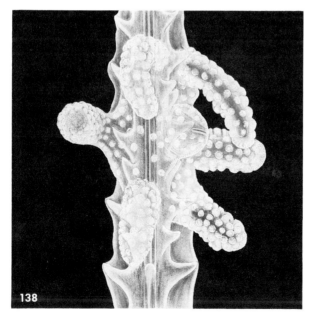

Figures 137 and 138. Anthozoans. **137.** Ceriantharian polyp. [Redrawn from Verrill, 1922.] Code: A, oral tentacles; B, marginal tentacles; C, column; D, terminal pore. **138.** Single polyp from an antipatharian colony.

I. Class Hydrozoa. Coelenterates usually with both polypoid and hydroid stages (although one or the other may be reduced or suppressed); gastric cavity of polyps is undivided tube, its mouth without pharynx; medusae with velum; gonads epidermal.

    A. Order Hydroida (the hydroids). Polypoid stage usually predominant, producing free medusae or their attached equivalents.

        1. Suborder Gymnoblastea, or Anthomedusae (the athecate hydroids). Hydranths of the hydroid stage without protective hydrothecae; medusae with gonads on manubrium.

        2. Suborder Calyptoblastea, or Leptomedusae (the thecate hydroids). Hydranths protected by hydrothecae; medusae with gonads on radial canals.

    B. Order Milleporina (the stinging corals). Polypoid stage producing a massive coral-like skeleton perforated by pores containing polyps of two types; medusae produced in special chambers, becoming free swimming, but without mouth, canals, or tentacles.

    C. Order Stylasterina (the hydrocorals). Polypoid stage producing massive or branched calcareous skeleton, with polyps of two kinds arranged in circular cyclosystems; medusoid stage very reduced and retained in special chambers.

    D. Order Trachylina. Medusoid stage dominant, polypoid minute or absent altogether. Tentacles of medusae often springing from exumbrellar surface well above margin.

        1. Suborder Trachymedusae. Bell margin not scalloped; gonads on the radial canals.

        2. Suborder Narcomedusae. Bell margin divided into lobes by bases of tentacles; gonads on stomach floor.

    E. Order Siphonophora. Free-living colonies composed of both hydroid and medusoid stages, the latter not freed.

        1. Suborder Calycophora. Colonies with one or several swimming bells at upper end.

        2. Suborder Physophorida. Colonies with gas-filled float.

    F. Order Chondrophorae. Free-living colonies consisting of central gastrozooid surrounded by many gonozooids producing free medusae, and marginal circle of dactylozooids, all hanging from circular or oval chitinous float.

II. Class Scyphozoa (jellyfishes). Coelenterates with predominant medusoid stage; medusae mostly of moderate or large

size, usually free swimming, without velum, gonads entodermal; polypoid stage produces young medusae by transverse
fission, or develops directly to adult condition, or absent
entirely.

   A. Order Stauromedusae. Medusoid stage develops directly
      from scyphistoma and remains permanently attached by
      stalk.

   B. Order Cubomedusae (box jellies and sea wasps). Free,
      cuboidal medusae with inturned margin; tentacles one or
      several at four corners of margin.

   C. Order Coronatae. Free discoidal medusae with scalloped
      margin bounded by furrow around bell.

   D. Order Semaeostomeae. Free discoidal medusae with scal-
      loped margin but no circular furrow. Mouth with four
      long, frilled lobes at corners.

   E. Order Rhizostomeae. Free discoidal or globular medusae
      with scalloped margin but no furrow. Mouth lobes very
      complicated and fused over, leaving many tiny mouth
      openings.

III. Class Anthozoa. Coelenterates with polypoid stage only; gastric cavity divided by radial partitions, the mouth with an
inturned pharynx, gonads formed in the entoderm of the
septa.

IIIa. Subclass Octocorallia, or Alcyonaria. Colonial polyps with
eight pinnate tentacles, eight septa and one siphonoglyph.

   A. Order Stolonifera. Simple polyps growing up from creep-
      ing stolon; skeleton of calcareous spicules in mesogloea.

   B. Order Telestacea. Polyps tall, growing from stolons, but
      producing arborescent colonies by lateral budding.

   C. Order Alcyonacea (soft corals). Bases of polyps fused
      into fleshy mass of mesogloea filled with calcareous
      spicules.

   D. Order Gorgonacea (flexible and horny corals). Attached
      colonies of small polyps supported by treelike horny or
      calcareous axial skeleton covered by thin layer of meso-
      gloea filled with spicules (two suborders).

   E. Order Pennatulacea (sea pens). Colonies composed of
      stalklike axial polyp loosely anchored in mud or sand,
      bearing many lateral polyps in regular arrangement, often
      feather-like; usually central axial rod as well as calcareous
      spicules.

IIIb. Subclass Zoantharia. Colonial or solitary polyps with tentacles usually unbranched and more than eight in number.
Skeleton present in some forms.

A. Order Actiniaria (sea anemones). Contains solitary polyps with no skeleton at all, and septa paired and often in multiples of six.

B. Order Scleractinia, or Madreporaria (the stony corals). Contains solitary or colonial polyps with massive, cup-like or branched calcareous exoskeleton.

C. Order Zoanthidea (the colonial anemones). Contains polyps without intrinsic skeleton but often with extraneous inclusions, having two cycles of marginal simple tentacles; usually pairs of septa consist of one complete and one incomplete septum; septa form only in spaces on either side of ventral directives.

D. Order Corallimorpharia (the coral-like anemones). Solitary or colonial polyps lacking skeleton, lacking basilar muscles, siphonoglyphs, and flagellated bands on septal filaments.

E. Order Ceriantharia. Long, solitary anemones without pedal disc but instead a rounded or pointed base for burrowing in sand or mud; tentacles are in two whorls, one around mouth, other at edge of disc.

F. Order Antipatharia (the black corals). Colonial polyps with 6, 10, or 12 complete septa, 6 or 8 tentacles, and 2 siphonoglyphs; they form gorgonian-like branching skeleton of black, horny substance covered with thorns, but soft tissues never contain spicules.

Reproduction and Embryology

ASEXUAL REPRODUCTION

The habitual manner of asexual reproduction among coelenterates is *budding*, in which a new individual or a new part of a colony is produced. In the polypoid form, budding of new polyps results in *monopodial* (Figure 64) or *sympodial growth* (Figure 65); or, as in madrepores, budding from the edge zone of the polyp or from the oral disc results in arborescent or massive colonies. Hydrozoan polyps may arise from stolons, stems, and, in a few species, from another polyp (for example, *Hydra*); medusae are usually budded from the stolons, stems, and hydranths of the polyps (Figure 54). However, medusae may also arise from the radial canals, manubrium, and tentacular bulbs of medusae (Figures 139, 140, 141).

Scyphozoa reproduce asexually only during the reduced polypoid stage (scyphistoma, Figure 142) by a number of types of budding, some of which produce new polyps and others, young medusae (*ephyrae*, Figure 143).

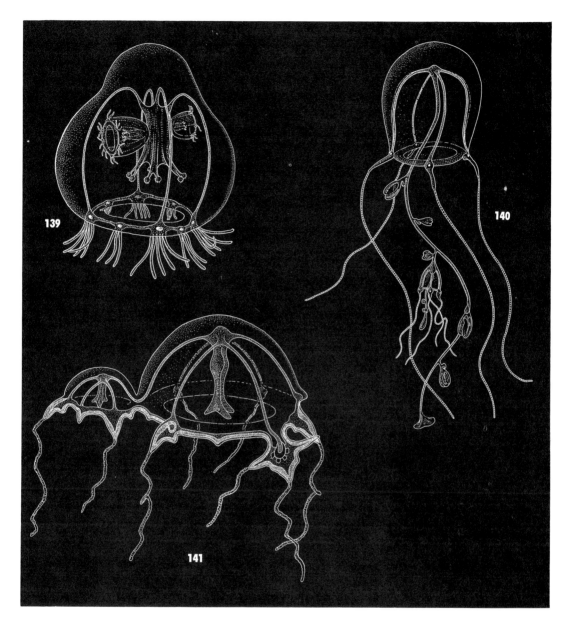

Figures 139 to 141. Asexual reproduction in medusae. **139.** *Rathkea* budding from manubrium. [Redrawn from Naumov, 1960.] **140.** *Sarsia* budding from manubrium with daughter medusae budding in the same manner. [Redrawn from Mayer, 1910, after Chun, 1895.] **141.** *Niobia* budding from the tentacular bulbs. [Redrawn from Mayer, 1900.]

Budding is uncommon in sea anemones. It may take place from the column, the pedal disc, or, in the curious anemone *Boloceroides*, from the tentacles. *Pedal laceration*, in which projections of the pedal disc are constricted off and left behind as the animal moves, each piece growing into a complete anemone, is of frequent occurrence. The new anemones may, however, be quite atypical in septal arrangement and other organizational aspects.

Some anemones and a few hydrozoans also may reproduce by longitudinal or, rarely, transverse *fission*, in which the body separates into two pieces and each then develops into a whole individual.

SEXUAL REPRODUCTION

The life cycle of coelenterates may or may not include an alternation of a sexually reproducing generation with one which reproduces asexually (*metagenesis*). If this alternation occurs, it is the polyp which reproduces asexually and the medusa is the sexual individual. Among the Hydrozoa, most Hydroida and the Milleporina have a life cycle which includes metagenesis, but some Hydrozoa are exclusively polypoid (for example, the hydras) and others are entirely medusoid (some Trachylina) (Figures 144, 154). In the Scyphozoa, the medusoid generation is always dominant and the polypoid generation is either relatively very small or else absent altogether (Figures 161, 162). The Anthozoa have no medusoid generation at all; the polyp reproduces sexually as well as by budding, fission, and so on.

Although the type of life history varies from group to group, the fertilized egg of all coelenterates eventually develops into an ovoid, ciliated, two-layered structure, the *planula larva*. In most species, the planula is a free-swimming planktonic larva, but in others it may remain attached to the parent, developing until it is ready to commence independent life.

CLASS HYDROZOA. Coelenterate reproduction is frequently exemplified by hydra in introductory texts and thus is relatively

Figures 142 and 143. Asexual reproduction in Scyphozoa. **142.** Scyphistoma stage of *Aurelia*. [After Agassiz, 1860.] **143.** Ephyra larva of *Nausithoe*. [After Komai, 1935.]

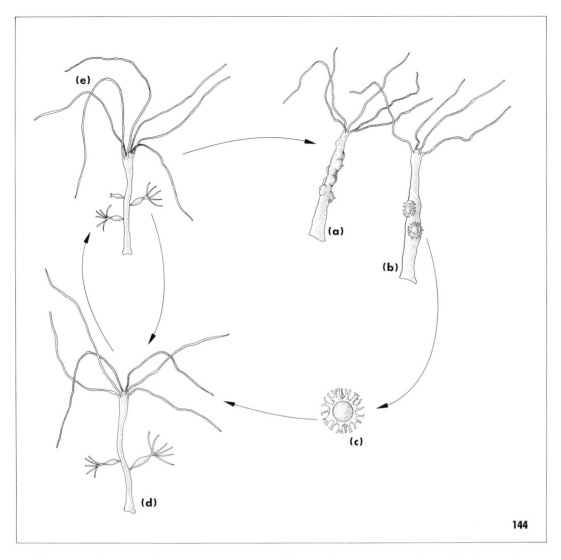

144

well known. However, the hydras are quite different from most hydrozoans in that the medusoid stage is completely lacking and the embryo does not develop into the typical planula larva (Figure 144). We will therefore first consider the general features of sexual reproduction in the hydras and then go on to examine embryology and development as they occur in the other Hydrozoa.

Sexual reproduction in hydra typically occurs after a change in temperature, hence often in spring or fall, according to species, although this is is by no means universal. Hydras in culture may reproduce sexually without any known previous change in conditions. The sexual cells are derived from interstitial cells of the epidermis which accumulate to form protruding bulges in the

Figure 144. Reproduction in coelenterates. Life cycle of *Hydra*. [Redrawn from Naumov, 1960.] Male polyp (a) fertilizes eggs of female (b); during cleavage the eggs secrete around themselves a chitinous embryonic theca which may be spiny (c) or smooth. After hatching, the embryos grow into polyps that reproduce asexually by budding (d and e) until environmental conditions trigger sexual reproduction.

[97]

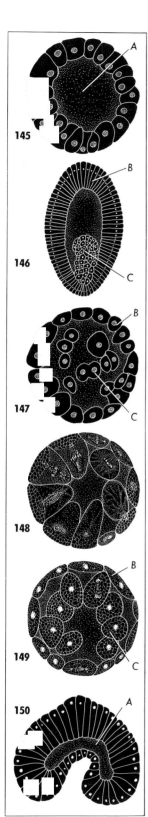

body wall of the gastric region. Some forms are dioecious, others hermaphroditic. In the latter case, the testes are situated toward the oral end and the ovaries below; in dioecious species the testes occur throughout the gastric region but the ovaries are usually in its lower part, though never on the stalk.

The testes are more or less conical in shape, opening to the exterior by way of a pore sometimes set on an apical, nipple-like protuberance. The ovaries are larger, rounded swellings, each containing a single egg. When an egg is ripe, the epidermis over it ruptures and withdraws to form a cuplike receptacle containing the exposed egg. After fertilization, the egg undergoes cleavage *in situ*, and in a late stage secretes a chitinous shell or *theca* around itself, variously shaped and sculptured. The thecate embryos fall off the parent and can then endure the adverse conditions of winter or periods of drought. After a dormant period of several weeks or more, the embryo will hatch under favorable conditions into a partially differentiated polyp which already has coelenteron and tentacle buds. The life history (Figure 144) thus has the scheme: polyp → egg → polyp.

The medusae of most hydrozoans are dioecious, the males forming numerous spermatozoa and the females, only a few ova and rarely just one ovum. An exception is the hermaphroditic *Eleutheria* in which both kinds of gamete develop in a chamber above the stomach. Some species shed both eggs and sperm into the water where fertilization occurs. Others—for example, those with sessile gonophores—retain their ova, sperm are carried to the eggs via water currents, and the embryo may develop to an advanced stage while still attached to the parent.

The zygote cleaves in a radial pattern which is equal and holoblastic. As the cells divide they become smaller and, of course, more numerous, and soon there appears in the center of this cleaving mass a space, the *blastocoel*. It is also called the segmentation cavity. The *blastula* of coelenterates typically has a commodious blastocoel, and this stage is therefore termed the *coeloblastula* (Figure 145). In species which shed their eggs, the coeloblastula is a ciliated free-swimming larva, and it undergoes *gastrulation* whereby the *entoderm* develops by a process called *unipolar ingression* (Figure 146). Cells in the vicinity of the vegetal pole

Figures 145 to 150. Embryology of coelenterates. **145.** Coeloblastula. [Redrawn from Metschnikoff, 1886.) **146.** Unipolar ingression. [Redrawn from Metschnikoff, 1886.) **147.** Multipolar ingression. [Redrawn from Wulfert, 1902.] **148 and 149.** Coeloblastula (148) forming entoderm by primary delamination (149). [Redrawn from Metschnikoff, 1881, 1886.] **150.** Invagination of coeloblastula. [Redrawn from Hyde, 1894.] Code: A, blastocoel; B, ectoderm; C, entoderm.

divide rapidly, forming cells which move into the blastocoel and eventually fill it. The embryo is now a solid gastrula or *stereo-gastrula*, the common free-swimming *planula* of the coelenterates (Figure 151). The body is elongated, with a broad anterior end and narrower posterior end, and it consists of a columnar, flagellated ectoderm enclosing a mass of entoderm. Nerve, sensory, gland, and muscle cells and even cnidoblasts containing nematocysts may be present. Soon a space, the beginning of the *gastric cavity*, appears in the entoderm, which eventually forms the lining epithelium of that cavity. The duration of the free-swimming, planktonic phase is governed by many factors, mostly poorly understood. In due course, the larva settles on a solid object, anterior, broad end down. The mouth with associated structures will form at the free end, which was posterior in the planula, and will become continuous with the gastric cavity. In athecate and many thecate hydroids, the settled planula grows directly into a hydranth, forming tentacles and mouth at the apex and stolons at the base. Budding produces the colonial form. In other thecate species the apex does not develop into a hydranth but forms a growing point, leaving below a stem, from the sides of which branches and polyps arise. Rarely the planula attaches on its side rather than on the anterior end, and forms a hydrorhiza from which the colony buds.

If the embryo is retained ("incubated") by the parent, the coeloblastula will usually gastrulate by *multipolar ingression* in which the entoderm cells arise from all parts of the embryo (Figure 147). Some species lack the blastocoel entirely and thus develop into a solid blastula. Gastrulation occurs by a process of *delamination*: the inner cells separate from the outer layer, or ectoderm (Figures 148, 149).

There are many variations on this scheme of development in the Class Hydrozoa. In the hydroid family Tubulariidae (*Tubularia*), which lacks the free medusoid stage, the planula is not

Figure 151. Embryology of coelenterates. Planula larva of the hydroid *Gonothyraea*, longitudinal section. [After Wulfert, 1902.] Code: A, ectoderm; B, entoderm; C, gastrovascular cavity; D, nematocyst; E, nerve cell; F, sensory cell; G, ectodermal gland cell; H, entodermal gland cell.

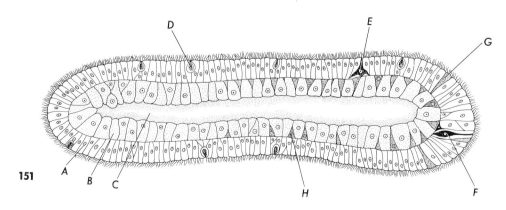

151

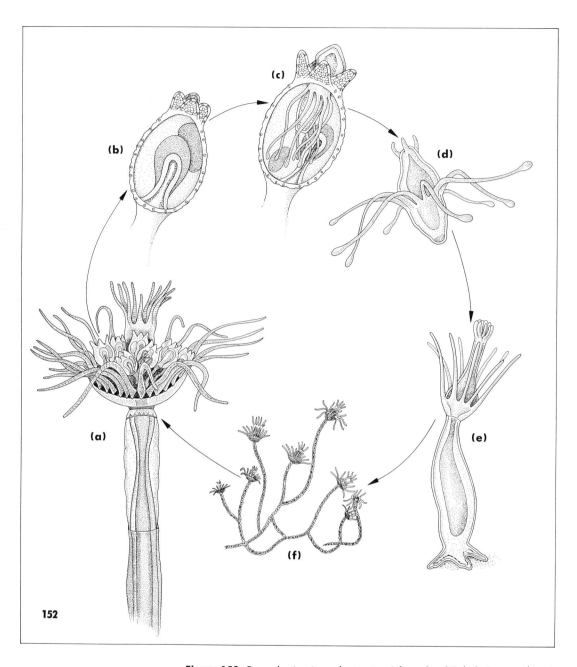

Figure 152. Reproduction in coelenterates. Life cycle of *Tubularia*, an athecate hydroid. The polyp (a) bears many gonophores whose eggs develop *in situ* into planulae (b), then into actinulae (c) before release. The liberated actinula (d) transforms directly into a polyp (e) that by asexual proliferation forms a tubularian colony (f). [Adopted from Allman, 1872.]

freed either but develops into a tentaculate larva, the *actinula* (Figure 152). The actinula does become free, settles on a substrate, and develops directly into a polyp. The life history thus has the scheme: polyp → egg → planula → actinula → polyp (Figure

152), in contrast to the familiar pattern of most hydroids: polyp → medusa → egg → planula → polyp (Figure 153).

In the Order Trachylina, the polypoid stage is either absent altogether or very small and simple in form. The commonest life cycle, as in *Aglaura* and *Liriope*, follows this pattern: medusa → egg → free-swimming planula → actinula → medusa (Figure 154). In others (*Gonionemus* and *Limnocnida*) the planula settles and develops into a tiny polyp (Figure 155). This reproduces asexually by budding nonciliated planula-like structures (*frustules*) which develop into polyps, and gonophores which form medusae. This life cycle thus is identical in pattern with that typical of most hydroids; however, instead of the hydroid being the larger, more conspicuous form, the medusa is "dominant" in the Trachylina.

Apparently the actinula is a labile form which may be primitive in the evolutionary sense. The actinula develops into a polyp in the hydroid *Tubularia*; but in the trachyline medusae, it grows into a medusa. This illustrates the basic unity of form in the hydrozoan polypoid and medusoid phases.

Development in the Order Siphonophora is modified in keeping with the totally pelagic habit of these creatures. The colonies are hermaphroditic but the gonophores are dioecious. These may remain attached to the parent colony or a cormidium budded from it (Figure 90), or they may be released as tiny medusae—

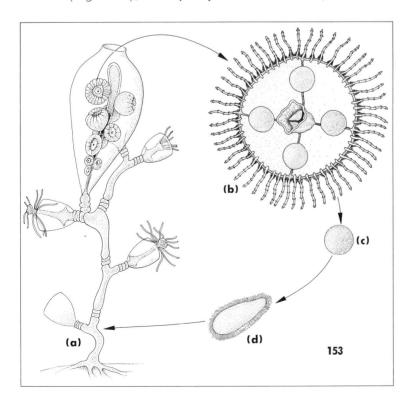

(b)

(c)

(d)

(a)

153

Figure 153. Reproduction in coelenterates. Life cycle of *Obelia*, a thecate hydroid with free medusae: hydroid with gonangium containing developing medusae (a); medusa (b); fertilized egg (c); planula larva (d). [Adapted from Naumov, 1960.]

Phylum
Coelenterata

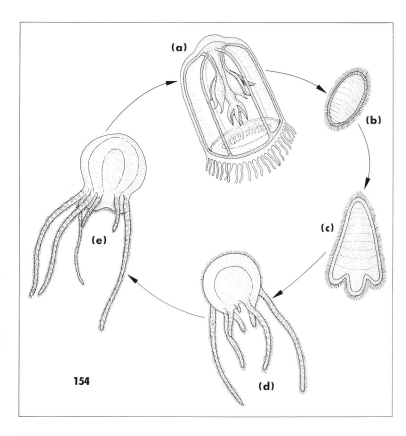

Figure 154. Reproduction in coelenterates. Life cycle of *Aglaura,* a trachyline medusa: medusa (a), whose fertilized eggs develop into planula larva (b), which forms mouth and tentacles (c) and becomes an actinula (d) that transforms into a young medusa (e). There is no attached stage in the life cycle. [Adapted from Metschnikoff, 1886; Uchida, 1953; Mayer et al, 1910.)

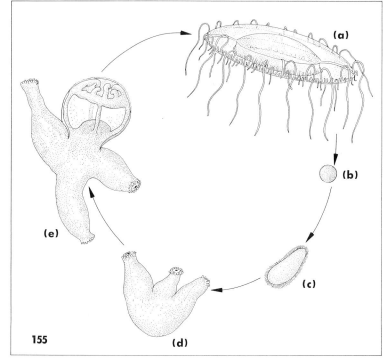

Figure 155. Reproduction in coelenterates. Life cycle of *Limnocnida,* a fresh-water trachyline with an attached hydroid stage: (a) medusa; (b) fertilized egg; (c) planula; (d) hydroid with three polyps; (e) hydroid colony with medusa bud, which eventually will be set free. [Adapted from Günther, 1893; and Bouillon, 1955.)

for example, those of the by-the-wind sailor, V*elella* (Figure 156).
Little is known about development in siphonophores, but it
appears that gastrulation occurs by delamination. As in Hydrozoa
generally, the posterior end of the planula becomes oral, developing into the primary gastrozooid. In the Calycophora (*Diphyes*)
the swimming bell is budded from one side of the advanced planula (Figure 157). The float of the Physophorida develops at the
anterior end of the larva and beneath it appears the pneumatophore (Figure 158). In V*elella*, special names are applied to the
larval forms into which the planula grows, the *conaria* (Figure
159) and *rataria* (Figure 160). The fundamental adult morphology can be seen in the rataria.

The Siphonophora are essentially polypoid forms, highly modified for planktonic existence. They reproduce by budding off
sexual units, whether sessile gonophores or free medusae, which
reproduce sexually, giving rise to a planula. The planula develops
into a modified polypoid colony, the adult siphonophore. Again
the life cycle is fundamentally the same as in hydroids: polyp →
medusa → egg → planula → polyp.

CLASS SCYPHOZOA. Life cycles resemble hydrozoan cycles
except those which lack the medusa—for example, the hydras
and *Tubularia*. Most Scyphozoa undergo metagenesis, in which a
conspicuous medusa reproduces sexually and the embryo develops
into a planula which settles and grows into a small polyp. In the
specialized terminology, the polyp is known as *scyphistoma* until
it commences producing young medusae (*ephyrae*) by transverse
fission (*strobilation*), when it is called a *strobila* (Figure 161).
Rarely, as in *Pelagia*, there is no scyphistoma stage at all. The

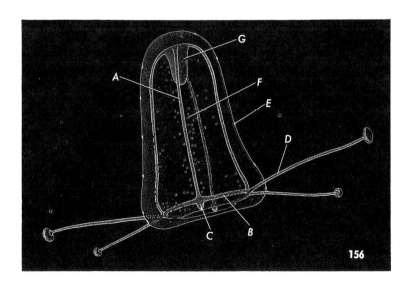

Figure 156. Reproduction in
coelenterates. *Chrysomitra*,
the medusa of the chondrophoran V*elella*. Code: A, radial canal; B, ring canal;
C, tentacular bulb without
tentacles; D, tentacle; E, nematocyst batteries on bell;
F, zooxanthellae; G, manubrium.

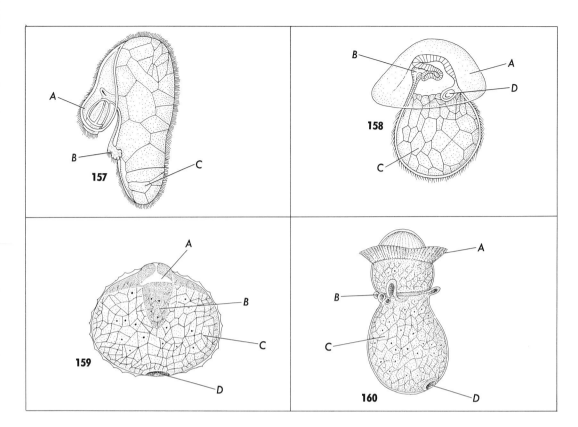

Figures 157 to 160. Reproduction in coelenterates. **157.** Bell budding in a calycophoran larva. [After Metschnikoff, 1874.] Code: A, bell with radial and ring canals; B, budding zone which will produce the stem; C, incipient gastrozooid. **158.** Juvenile *Agalma*, a physonectid. [After Metschnikoff, 1874.] Code: A, primary bract; B, first definitive bract; C, primary gastrozooid; D, pneumatophore. **159.** Conaria larva of the chondrophoran *Velella*. [After Leloup, 1929.] Code: A, pneumatophore; B, entoderm; C, primary gastrozooid with mouth D. **160.** Rataria larva of *Velella*. [After Leloup, 1929.] Code: A, disk; B, budding zone; C, primary gastrozooid with mouth D.

planula develops directly into an ephyra by flattening and pushing out eight bifurcated lobes (Figure 162). This is similar to the direct mode of development of some trachyline medusae in which the benthic, polypoid stage is altogether lacking.

Generally, Scyphozoa are dioecious. The gametes emerge into the gastric cavity and pass out of the mouth. Fertilization and subsequent development may take place in the folds of the oral arms or freely in the sea water. The blastula may gastrulate by an ingression of cells, or *invagination* may occur (Figure 150). In the latter case, the *blastopore* later closes and the two-layered embryo, with gastric cavity enclosed, becomes free-swimming as the planula larva. When it settles on its anterior end, the mouth then appears at the former posterior end—that is, the place where the blastopore was before it closed. The polypoid larva, the *scyphistoma*, develops an adhesive pedal disc, a basal stalk, an expanded oral end with manubrium, mouth and tentacles, four septa within, and four subumbrellar funnels. The scyphistomae of some species are known to live for years, budding new scyphistomae and periodically producing ephyrae by transverse fission. If only one ephyra is released at a time, the process is called *monodisc strobilation*; if several, *polydisc strobilation*. The ephyra (Figures 143, 161) is an incomplete medusa which develops directly into the adult.

CLASS ANTHOZOA. The anthozoans as a group are like the hydras in having a direct life history, but they ordinarily produce a ciliated free-swimming planula. Their life history is schematically represented: polyp → egg → planula → polyp (Figure 163). They are either dioecious or hermaphroditic. In the latter case, it is usual for the male stage to ripen in advance of the female, a condition known as protandry, but they may also mature almost or quite simultaneously. Fertilization may be external or internal. If it is internal, cleavage takes place within the gastrovascular cavity and results in a stereo- or coeloblastula that gastrulates by delamination, invagination, or ingression to form the ciliated planula. The blastopore either remains open, in the case of invaginate gastrulation, or an aperture appears sinking into the gastric cavity to form the inner opening of the stomodaeum, which accordingly is a tube lined by ectoderm. Septa then commence to grow inward in couples on opposite sides of the animal until several couples have formed. When there are four couples of septa, the symmetry of the organism is bilateral, subsequently becoming biradial upon development of the adult septal arrangement. The

Figure 161. Reproduction in coelenterates. Life cycle of *Aurelia*, a scyphomedusa with scyphistoma stage: (a) adult medusa; (b) fertilized egg; (c) planula; (d) scyphistoma, which either buds off more scyphistomae (e) or becomes a strobila (f); (g) ephyra larva budded from strobila. [Adapted from Agassiz, 1860; Friedemann, 1902; and Naumov, 1960.]

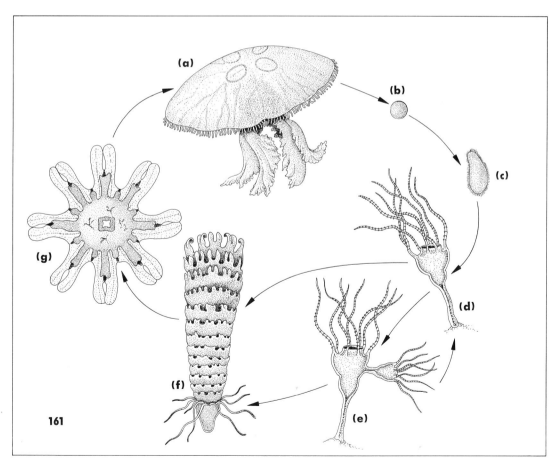

161

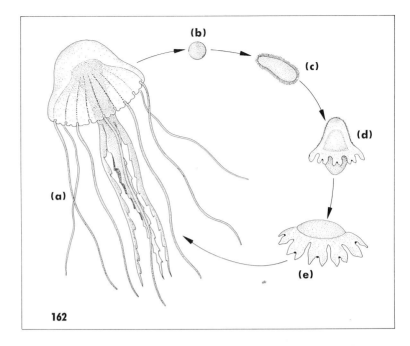

Figure 162. Reproduction in coelenterates. Life cycle of *Pelagia,* a scypho-medusa (a) with direct development. The fertilized egg (b) develops into the planula larva (c), which forms a bell with marginal lappets (d) and develops directly into an ephyra (e) without any intervening scyphistoma. [After Naumov, 1961.]

Figure 163. Reproduction in coelenterates. Life cycle of anthozoans: (a) adult polyp, either solitary, as shown, or colonial; (b) egg; (c) planula larva; (d) larva forms septa and mouth and transforms directly into the polyp form. [Adapted from Hedgpeth 1954, and other authors.]

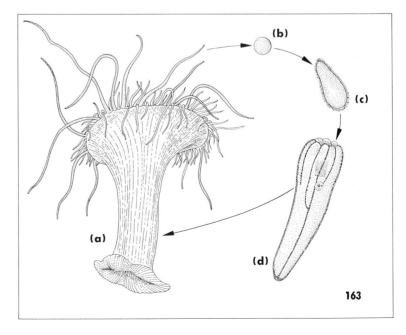

planula thus has developed into an ovate, ciliated larva with mouth, stomodaeum, and several septa but no tentacles or only buds. When conditions are favorable the larva settles out of the plankton, attaches by the aboral pole, and grows tentacles.

Physiology

RESPIRATION

Coelenterates are found chiefly in clean water with high oxygen content, and in all known cases their respiration is aerobic in nature, requiring oxygen and releasing carbon dioxide. In animals of such simple organization, no specialized respiratory system is developed and gas exchange takes place across the general body surface. Because of the direct contact of all epithelia with the aqueous medium, no transport mechanism is required, even by the relatively large forms such as the scyphomedusae and the larger anthozoans. The only respiratory requirement—that is, the circulation of oxygenated water across the respiratory surface (the whole surface, interior as well as exterior)—is accomplished either by the movement of the animal itself or by the action of flagellated epithelia which constantly renews the water in contact with the tissues. In most anthozoans, the strongly flagellated siphonoglyph propels a current of water into the gastrovascular cavity. The exaggeration of the siphonoglyph in the siphonozooids of dimorphic alcyonarians specializes those zooids for the transport of water and represents an incipient respiratory system. Respiratory functions have been attributed to the subumbrellar funnels of scyphozoans for no very compelling reasons.

Due to the small amount of solid organic material relative to volume, the respiratory rate of scyphomedusae is very low. That of anthozoans is somewhat higher but depends upon the state of expansion, being notably lower in contracted individuals. If the oxygen content of water is reduced, the respiratory rate of medusae declines, and if the salinity is altered in either direction the rate at first increases and then declines.

NERVOUS SYSTEM AND BEHAVIOR

The nervous system of coelenterates, the simplest in the animal kingdom, is usually described as a nerve "net" or plexus. It is divided into two main layers, one in the epidermis and one in the gastrodermis, connected by way of fibers through the mesogloea. The epidermal plexus is the better developed, although it is weak in the exumbrella of medusae and completely missing in the epidermis of the nectophores of siphonopores. Both epidermal and gastrodermal nets of certain scyphozoans and anthozoans and possibly of most coelenterates consist of two components, the main net and a secondary net, more diffuse and with smaller cell bodies in Scyphozoa, more complex in Anthozoa. The main net is a nonpolarized, through-conduction system controlling general responses such as bell pulsations in medusae and column contraction and retraction of the oral portion in anthozoans. The secondary net is in charge of local responses.

Efforts to generalize the nature of the coelenterate nervous system as either a continuous plexus or a synaptic system are shown to be pointless by the strong evidence that the system is synaptic in actinians and scyphozoans but continuous in hydras. As in either case conduction travels in a wave outward from the point of stimulation, behavior is that of a continuous network. Aside from the righting responses of medusae and anthozoans and feeding responses in the presence of food, reflexes are generally lacking.

Conduction pathways between receptors and effectors vary in complexity. Direct innervation of a contractile fiber by a sensory cell is the simplest mechanism, but one, two, or even more motor ganglion cells may lie between the sensory cells and the muscle fibers. Transmission is in any direction and is relatively slow, from about 7 cm/sec to 120 cm/sec, but does not attenuate or fatigue.

The photosensory activity of the ocelli has been demonstrated in certain medusae in which the normal reaction to light is abolished by excision of the eyespots. Moreover, forms such as *Cyanea*, which lack ocelli, are indifferent to light, although other eyeless medusae do respond. Therefore the general epithelium appears to be light sensitive. The function of the elaborate eyes of the Cubomedusae has not been demonstrated.

The behavior of coelenterates encompasses predatory, feeding, and defensive reactions often involving locomotion. This is achieved by swimming or passive floating in practically all medusae and siphonophores, whereas the polypoid forms, including hydroids, the scyphistoma stages of scyphozoans, and most anthozoans are benthic, mostly sessile animals with limited powers of locomotion or immovably fixed.

All medusae swim in essentially the same way, by a series of pulsations of the bell-shaped body which produces a form of "jet propulsion" in which water is expelled from the mouth of the bell and the animal is propelled forward. As motion is poorly directed, this activity serves chiefly to keep the animals near the surface of the water where currents carry them along in the prevailing direction. Not infrequently the medusa rises to the surface by a series of pulsations and then slowly sinks with tentacles outspread in a

fishing attitude, repeating the process over and over as long as
light is neither too bright nor too dim. Others fish by trailing the
long tentacles behind in continuous swimming movements.

Hydrozoan medusae swim by contracting the subumbrella and
velum, thus forcibly expelling water. from the bell. By asymmetrical contraction the medusa is able to direct the jet of water to
one side or another and so alter direction. The pulsation originates
in the bell margin and is initiated by the sense organs. Extirpation
of these diminishes the power of the contractions but does not
eliminate them. If the margin is cut, the various sectors pulsate
independently at different rates, and if the margin is removed,
the remainder of the bell ceases to pulsate.

The inturned marginal velarium of the box jellies serves the
same function as the velum in the hydromedusae and makes the
Cubomedusae the strongest swimmers of the Scyphozoa. Lacking
velum or velarium, the other jellyfishes of this class swim by
contraction of the radial and coronal muscle fibers of the subumbrella. In swimming, the radial muscles are the first to contract, shortening the bell, followed by the coronal muscle which
contracts the margin thus expelling a spurt of water. The function
of the rhopalia in initiating pulsations is as yet not clear. Depending on species, extirpation may have little effect or may abolish
spontaneous contractions. In the latter case, pulsations may or
may not resume after a time (up to two or three days). One
rhopalial center can maintain virtually normal pulsation. As there
is no marginal nerve ring, cuts in the margin do not affect pulsation unless they are very deep, in which case each sector contracts
at a different rate. The nervous stimulation of rhythmic bell contractions originates in the subumbrellar plexus but is in some way
controlled by the rhopalial centers.

The nectophores of siphonophores are characteristically strong
swimmers and act as the propulsive force of calycophoran colonies.
The eudoxids of certain kinds can dart about with astonishing
speed, whereas large colonies progress in a more sedate manner.
Those siphonophores that lack nectophores—the Chondrophorae
and Rhizophysaliae—are drifters wafted by winds and currents,
trailing their tentacles in passive fishing activity which succeeds
only by chance contact. Forms such as *Porpita* and *Velella* have
no control over their courses, but *Physalia* has an erectile crest on
its float which can be both raised and lowered, and it can bend
the float one way or the other so as to alter the shape, size, and
orientation of the sail surface and thus change its direction to
some extent.

A few polypoid forms have developed flotation devices and

taken to drifting in the plankton. Notable are the hydroid *Pelago-hydra* and the sea anemone *Minyas*.

Locomotor activities of polypoid forms are limited at best and totally absent in many species. Attached hydroids, alcyonarians, antipatharians, most stony corals, zoanthids, and many sea anemones are incapable of locomotion, all movement consisting merely of the expansion and contraction of the polyps and manipulation of the tentacles attendant upon feeding and defensive reactions, and normal diurnal patterns of expansion and contraction.

The colonial hydroids ordinarily remain in an expanded state, many showing little response to mechanical stimulation but responding to contact with food by appropriate motions of the tentacles and manubrium. The same is true of antipatharians, corals, and alcyonarians, although the latter two can withdraw the polyps into the protection of the general colonial mass, and at least the shallow-water forms—especially reef corals—show a definite tendency to expand at night and contract by day. A few stony corals, such as the solitary "mushroom corals" of the Pacific, have limited powers of movement and can right themselves if upset, in spite of their heavy skeleton. They accomplish this by asymmetrically inflating the gastric cavity with water until the discoidal skeleton is upended and finally topples over.

Some sea anemones are immovably attached but others are capable of limited movement. Some progress by a slow pedal gliding, advancing one edge of the pedal disc and withdrawing the opposite one. Others move in the fashion of hydras and other solitary hydroids, detaching the basal disc while holding on with the tentacles, then reattaching it in a different location. A few species of sea anemones and many cerianthids are sand-dwellers that burrow by peristaltic waves of the column. Among the burrowing anthozoans the pennatulids are remarkable for their ability to thrust the colony well out of the sand or mud, supported by its axial rod and to withdraw it almost or quite completely by peristaltic contractions of the stalk.

A few medusae are sedentary in habit and, in the case of *Cassiopea*, lie on the bottom sluggishly pulsating, thus bringing food-bearing currents of water to the oral arms and constantly renewing water for respiratory purposes. Other kinds, among them *Eleutheria* and the olindiids such as *Gonionemus*, have sucker-like tentacles or adhesive pads on the ordinary tentacles, by which they creep on marine vegetation. Such forms are capable of limited swimming activities, but the polypoid stauromedusae have abandoned the classic medusoid form and with it all powers of swimming. These species are either permanently fixed or else can move about in polypoid fashion by detaching the pedal disc while holding on with the tentacles and then relocating.

Feeding behavior has been observed carefully in hydra and has been known for more than 200 years. The manner in which the polyp snares passing organisms such as copepods with its tentacles and then reels them in to be grasped and engulfed by the manubrium is so familiar that it does not require detailed description. Feeding behavior is very similar in all polypoid forms. Sea anemones in general feed in this fashion, paralyzing larger prey, such as fishes, that come in contact with their tentacles. When subdued, the victim is taken into the gastric cavity whole by way of the mouth, which is capable of enormous distension. Many reef corals feed in the same manner but by their smaller size are limited to preying upon zooplankton such as copepods, pteropods, chaetognaths, and small fishes. Some, if not all, corals depend heavily upon the rain of organic particles that falls upon them. These are trapped in a mucous coating on the oral disc and drawn into the mouth by ciliary action.

Medusoid forms feed in both of the above-mentioned ways for polypoid individuals. Food organisms, large or small, may be snared and paralyzed by the trailing tentacles, which then contract and draw them up to the mouth. The large medusae and siphonophores such as *Physalia*, which have tentacles several meters long, are capable of capturing fishes of large size. Prey is ingested whole by most medusae, or cooperatively attacked by the numerous gastrozooids of siphonophores. *Porpita* captures planktonic crustaceans with its outspread tentaculozooids, which then bend inward and hold the prey against the central gastrozooid.

Medusae may also feed upon small organisms and organic particles that become trapped in mucus on the exumbrella. The mucus is carried by flagellar action to the margin, where it may be transferred to the mouth arms and thence to the mouth, or it may be transported to the manubrium by additional flagellar currents on the subumbrella. The multitude of small mouths of rhizostome jellyfishes can accept only small particles, hence the prey usually consists of minute organisms; animals too large to be ingested whole probably are partially digested and broken down by enzymes exuded upon them from the mouths. Mucus-trapped particles entering the mouths are moved by flagellar currents to the interior, where they can be reached by the gastric filaments and pulled into the stomach.

The nematocysts of most coelenterates serve the double purpose of defensive and predatory functions. They are so potent that most potential predators are satisfactorily discouraged without any other special defensive mechanisms and reactions. Nevertheless, coelenterates show more or less marked avoidance reactions, and polypoid types generally are able to contract both tentacles and body, sometimes pulling the contracted oral end down into the body cavity and covering it over with the distal edge of the body wall, sometimes merely folding the tentacles over the mouth in a protective attitude. Many sea anemones have a marginal sphincter muscle which draws tight, enclosing the tender oral parts of the body in a tough bag formed by the column wall. Very remarkable are the avoidance reactions performed by certain sea anemones in the presence of noxious echinoderms. The anemone first expands widely, then commences to thrash the oral end about in circular movement, followed by detachment of the pedal disc. Violent flexion of the column from side to side then serves to propel the creature into the water above, where currents can carry it out of range of the troublesome echinoderm. Although undirected, this activity is the closest approach to swimming to be found in the Anthozoa. Alcyonarians as a whole can retract the entire distal part of the polyps into the spicular colonial coenenchyme, and similar abilities are found in hydrocorals and some stony corals. Thecate hydroids retract the hydranths into the hydrothecae, but naked forms often show little or no reaction to irritation.

DIGESTION

As coelenterates are chiefly carnivorous, their digestive processes concentrate upon the utilization of protein. Both extracellular and intracellular digestion is employed in the assimilation of food materials. The first stage of the digestive process is extracellular and occurs within the gastrovascular cavity or, less commonly, outside the body as in the case of large prey first macerated by enzymes exuded upon it either from the many mouths of the rhizostome medusae, or from the gastrozooids as in the Portuguese man-of-war, and then ingested in fluid state. The gastrodermal gland cells, either generally scattered or concentrated in special digestive regions, produce the proteolytic enzymes necessary to accomplish the initial stages of digestion. The resulting liquid containing particulate food is then phagocytized by epidermal cells, in which digestion continues much the same as in the protozoans. In addition to other proteolytic enzymes of the nature of pepsin, trypsin, and rennin, coelenterates have been found to contain maltase, amylase, and lipase. Preliminary digestive processes take place rapidly, and the intracellular phase is completed in probably not longer than 12 hours. Food storage is mostly in the form of fat and glycogen.

Transport of food materials after digestion is accomplished largely by action of the amoebocytes, but in colonial forms in which only one or a few of the many polyps may feed at any one time, the fluid gastric contents probably are distributed by peristaltic and flagellar action through the gastrodermal canals to remote points where intracellular digestion takes place.

The larger indigestible materials are ejected via the mouth by contractions of the body. In many medusae the radial canals open on the subumbrellar surface by pores through which smaller undigested particles and, presumably, other wastes, are discharged.

Other aspects of coelenterate excretion are poorly known. The mouth and the subumbrellar pores of the radial canals of medusae are the major excretory routes. In some siphonophores, such as *Velella*, the cells of the gastrodermal canals concentrated under the float are presumed to be excretory from the presence of guanine crystals, and xanthine crystals in the septal filaments of anthozoans seem to suggest a similar function for those structures. The principal waste product of protein metabolism in coelenterates is ammonia, which is eliminated by simple diffusion, and there seems to be no production of urea or uric acid.

The role of zooxanthellae in the nutrition of coelenterates has been much debated, but it probably varies in different groups. Some alcyonarians have been found to depend completely on their zooxanthellae, but the method of utilization has not been determined. Many reef corals, sea anemones, and jellyfishes are able to survive without their zooxanthellae and thus are trophically independent of them.

Ecology and Distribution

A number of coelenterate species inhabit fresh or brackish waters, but by far the majority are exclusively marine and can tolerate little reduction in salinity. They are both benthic and planktonic in their way of life, and, ordinarily, it is the polypoid stages that are fixed and the medusoid stages that swim free.

Best known of the fresh-water coelenterates are the hydras, found attached to submerged plants and other objects in roadside ditches, ponds, and lakes in many parts of the world. They were among the first coelenterates admitted to be animals by scientists of the eighteenth century, as well as one of the first to be used experimentally. Several species are known but their classification is still not settled because of insufficient taxonomic research. *Cordylophora lacustris* is the only fresh-water hydroid forming extensive colonies, which attain a height of 100 mm. The largest colonies are found in brackish inlets and estuaries, smaller ones in completely fresh water. The species is widely distributed in northern Europe, North America, and elsewhere. A very few species of jellyfishes, notably *Craspedacusta sowerbyi* and *Limnocnida tanganyicae*, are known to live in fresh water. Their hydroid stages are minute inconspicuous forms and thus commonly overlooked. The former species is native to South America but has spread to many localities in Europe and North America by way of aquatic plants imported by man. The latter is an inhabitant of fresh waters in Africa.

The polypoid phases of coelenterates usually are benthic forms more or less firmly attached to the substrate. The marine colonial hydroids usually are permanently attached to solid objects such as shells, rocks, and pilings, and the smaller kinds not infrequently grow as epiphytes on submerged plants. Those infesting floating algae such as *Sargassum* may be limited to that community. A few kinds of hydroids anchor themselves in soft bottom by sending out hydrorhizal extensions which agglutinate a lump of sediment as a sort of anchor.

Sea anemones are benthic animals with very few exceptions. They inhabit a range of situations, mostly attached to solid objects, but a few species anchor in sandy or muddy bottom, and some drift around in the open sea attached to floating algae. Because of their habit of incorporating grains of sand in the column wall, zoanthids are so heavy that they are typically benthic, living attached to rocks and corals in reef situations. On soft bottoms in deeper waters they are usually found attached to other organisms, such as the anchor spicules of glass sponges, the axis of gorgonians, and shells inhabited by hermit crabs. Polypoid forms that secrete a calcareous skeleton obviously are confined to a bottom-dwelling existence. Hydrozoan corals are typical of reef habitats in shallow water in the tropics and on rocky bottoms in deeper water. The massive colonial madreporarian corals are the foundation of the reef structure, but the smaller forms, often solitary, are found also at very great depths where some lie unattached on soft oozes and others attach to any solid objects present. Alcyonarian colonies also are invariably sedentary, usually attached to rocks in the reef community but also living on soft bottom in deep water by means of various anchoring devices such as rootlike projections from the base of the axis, or by enclosing a lump of mud in a sacklike membranous expansion of the trunk. The lucernarid medusae have assumed a permanently or semipermanently attached condition and thus lead a benthic existence, and a few medusae of conventional form have unusual sedentary habits. Notable among these are the olindiid trachymedusae such as *Gonionemus* and the anthomedusa *Eleutheria*, which creep about on sucker-like appendages of the tentacles, and the sluggish rhizostome *Cassiopea*, which lies on the bottom, bell downward in shallow water, languidly pulsating.

The free-swimming and planktonic forms generally are the medusoid stages, although some polyps have assumed planktonic life. Among the latter are the sea anemone *Minyas*, which produces a gas-filled float in its pedal disc, and *Pelagohydra*, a hydroid with similar adaptations. Other than such oddities, and the polymorphic siphonophores whose complex colonies consist of both polypoid and medusoid persons, the planktonic forms are medusae. Hydrozoan and scyphozoan medusae occur as free swimmers both in coastal waters and on the high seas, at the surface as well as at great depth.

Coelenterates can stand little or no desiccation and therefore rarely are common much above the low-tide line. In tropical areas, reef corals, reef-dwelling alcyonarians, actinians, and hydrocorals may extend down to a depth of 80 meters or more, but below a depth of about 25 meters the corals do not actively form reefs due to reduction of illumination at those depths. Large numbers of sea anemones and hydroids are inhabitants of shallow waters in temperate climates, and the majority of the hydroid medusae, siphonophores, and scyphomedusae are surface or near-surface dwellers. However, members of these groups descend to the ocean deeps. Gorgonians have been taken at 5,850 meters, hydroids at 7,000 meters, and sea anemones from more than 10,000 meters —about six miles beneath the surface. The rhizostome, semaeostome, and carybdeid medusae are chiefly shallow-water or surface-dwelling forms, whereas the coronates are mostly deep bathypelagic animals. Trachyline medusae inhabit the open ocean where some species may live as deep as 3,000 meters.

The geographical distribution of coelenterates is extremely wide. As would be expected, the range of planktonic species often is very great because the animals are carried far and wide by ocean currents. Benthic species are similarly broadcast by planktonic larvae or by free-swimming medusoid stages in the life history. Coelenterates occur in all seas from the polar regions to the tropics, though certain kinds may be prevalent in tropical regions and others in temperate or arctic areas, due to various controlling factors. Notable for their distribution in warm, shallow waters are the reef corals, millepores, zoanthids, several families of gorgonians, semaeostomes, rhizostomes, and cubomedusae. Certain stony corals, hydrocorals, and gorgonians typically are inhabitants of

Arctic and Antarctic seas, some of them descending into deep water in the tropics, thus showing the phenomenon of equatorial submergence. In general, the Antarctic fauna is richer in number of species than that of the Arctic, where comparatively few are found although these few may be numerically abundant. A major factor controlling distribution is thus seen to be temperature, although light also is important, for reasons that will be shown subsequently.

REEFS

Perhaps the most interesting of all coelenterates to man are the stony corals because of their capacity to produce reefs of calcareous rock and hence, ultimately, dry land. In addition to being what amounts to a living geological phenomenon, reef corals in life form one of the most complex and fascinating of marine communities, and thus are of immense interest from ecological and biological standpoints.

Coral reefs are strictly tropical and do not grow where water temperatures drop below 70° F. The coral reef zone around the world thus lies within 30° north and south of the equator, and extends beyond these limits only in places where the 70° isotherm also extends beyond them. Very important in the distribution and development of reefs is the fact that reef corals do not thrive in water deeper than about 30 meters although they do live as deep as 80 meters and more, contrary to many general accounts. The reason for this limitation to comparatively shallow water is dependence upon the light necessary for photosynthesis of algae living symbiotically in the tissues of the coral.

Although the various types of reef organisms, including corals, have a circumtropical distribution, they form reefs only in certain broad geographical areas. The eastern shores of the continents are regions of active reef growth whereas the western coasts, such as those of Africa and Central America, have corals but no reefs.

T. Wayland Vaughan, one of the greatest students of corals and reefs, defined a coral reef as a ridge or mound of limestone the upper surface of which is near the surface of the sea and which is formed of calcium carbonate by the action of organisms, chiefly corals. The uppermost layer is a living stratum composed of growing corals, alcyonarians, and millepores, together with a virtually endless array of other organisms that live on or in this framework, some acting to break down the coral skeletons, others serving to cement the resulting debris together into a conglomerated mass that can act as a foundation for further coral growth. Boring sponges, mollusks, worms, and barnacles permeate the coral substance and open it to erosional forces that weaken it until it crumbles. Algae, sponges, hydroids, tunicates, and other organisms, as well as chemical processes, consolidate the fragments and provide a platform for new growth.

With its myriad of interstices, crevices, and other hiding places, and the sheltering branches of the corals themselves, the reef is a haven to a host of other animals. Sponges, sea anemones, annelids, mollusks, crustaceans, and echinoderms are among the conspicuous invertebrates, and the species of fishes may number several hundreds in the thriving reef communities of the tropical Pacific.

Reefs in the western Atlantic are in a flourishing state but differ from Pacific reefs in several ways. First, the coral fauna of Atlantic reefs consists of approximately 50 species and of these only about 20 are important reef builders, whereas the number of species on tropical Pacific reefs is nearer 250. In the Atlantic, gorgonians are a predominant part of the reef community, often being more conspicuous than the corals themselves, whereas they have only a minor place on Pacific reefs. There, the fleshy, spicule-filled soft corals assume an important role, in which they play a greater part in reef formation than do the West Indian gorgonians.

Although their forms are infinitely varied, reefs can be classified into four major categories: fringing reefs, barrier reefs, atolls, and banks. The origin of the curious ringlike form of atoll reefs prompted much speculation on the part of scientists in past years, and the resulting theories of reef formation and development are still discussed with interest today. The simplest and youngest reef type is the fringing reef, which lines coasts with a narrow, shelf-like ledge consisting of a zone of active coral growth called the reef front, separated from shore by a slightly lower reef flat of living and dead corals, covered by shallow water. The barrier reef differs from this by standing farther off shore, from which it is separated by a lagoon up to several miles wide and as much as 300 feet deep. Barrier reefs often encircle islands, which stand in the center of the lagoon. The atoll is a ringlike reef, more or less circular and often with islands along the reef flat, enclosing a deep basin-like lagoon without a central island.

To explain the genesis of these observed forms, Charles Darwin theorized that reefs begin growing as a fringe around slowly sinking shores, continuing to grow upward and outward as the land sinks. Thus, the fringing reef becomes a barrier reef as the coast subsides and the lagoon separating it from the reef grows wider and wider. Islands surrounded by barrier reefs ultimately sink beneath the lagoon, leaving only the encircling reef on which islands of wave-tossed rubble may accumulate, thus forming atolls.

An alternate theory, propounded by Reginald Daly, held that the lowered sea level resulting from the formation of the ice caps during glacial periods cut platforms along shorelines, on which corals began to grow as temperatures rose and water level returned to normal. Corals continued to grow upward as the water rose, resulting in reefs of the various types depending upon the nature of the wave-cut platform.

Other theories were postulated at various times, including one supported by Sir John Murray of the *Challenger* Expedition (1873–1876), who held that reefs grow on sea mounts that have been built up to a depth suitable for corals by accumulation of sediments. More active growth of corals around the periphery results in outward growth, and lagoons are solution features. Barrier reefs and atolls could have arisen in this way but almost certainly did not. In actual fact, since there are many possible kinds of foundations on which corals can grow and many geological processes whereby such foundations can be produced, it is likely that no single theory can account for all cases, but the idea of an antecedent platform is a necessary postulation for all reef growth.

Obviously, compelling evidence for the processes of reef formation could be had by sinking holes on reefs and examining the cores for the nature and age of the underlying strata. The first effort to obtain such evidence, a core sunk to a depth of 1,114 feet on Funafuti Atoll in 1904, showed that reef corals that lived in shallow water are present in the atoll at that depth, thus indicating more than a thousand feet of subsidence. That core penetrated nothing but reef material and did not reach its foundation. More recently, at Eniwetok Atoll in the Marshall Islands, two cores were sunk to a depth of more than 4,000 feet and these did reach volcanic bedrock. The atoll began growing on a volcanic mountain rising two miles above the bottom some 50 million years ago during Eocene time, and has reached a thickness now of over 4,000 feet. As Darwin postulated, the Pacific basin in general has been subsiding, although the fossils in the Eniwetok cores show that the atoll was periodically thrust high out of water and then resubmerged. Although the processes of subsidence have operated in many parts of the Pacific, giving much credence to Darwin's basic concept of reef formation, other principles surely operate elsewhere as in the Indian Ocean, where evidence shows that foundations are rising. Thus it is necessary to think of reef development in terms of many processes rather than just one.

The great concentration of diverse forms of life in the reef community provides an ideal situation for the development of biological relationships between various kinds of organisms. As might be expected from their abundance on the reefs, many coelenterates are involved in commensal, symbiotic, and other biological associations. Such relationships are by no means limited to reef-dwellers, however, and are found among coelenterates of all kinds of habitats.

Some of the relationships involving gorgonians and reef corals are nothing more than fortuitous spatial associations without biological implications. Fishes take refuge among coral branches, and echinoderms, notably unstalked crinoids and gorgonocephalid brittle-stars, cling to them for support and to gain a situation favorable for filter feeding.

The association between several species of small, brightly colored crabs (*Trapezia*) with branched reef corals is more intimate and seems to be obligatory for the crabs, as they never inhabit dead corals. Other crabs (*Hapalocarcinus*) actually induce the coral branches to form chamber-like galls in which they live, safe from predation, only to be entombed by the growth of the coral. Whether these associations are merely elaborate means of obtaining shelter from the sessile coelenterates or have a deeper physiological basis is not yet known. The case of the coralliophilid snails, which always inhabit living reef corals, is more clearly cut, however. This is an instance of parasitism, as the snails suck juices from the coral polyps and can exist in no other way. The soft corals and gorgonians are similarly infested with snails of the related family Magilidae, which often live embedded in the host tissues and presumably are parasitic, but in addition they harbor snails of the family Ovulidae which actually devour the polyps of the coelenterates. The ovulids are so restricted in their diet that they are unable to feed on other organisms, and so are obligate ectoparasites of the coelenterates.

Alcyonarian polyps also are parasitized by various kinds of arthropods, which enter the gastric cavity as larvae, often stretching it to an unrecognizable shape by their growth. Among these are pycnogonids, or sea spiders, of which some species spend their larval period encysted in deep-sea gorgonian polyps, ascothoracic barnacles which attain adult form within the polyps of deep-water gorgonians, and copepods of the family Lamippidae, which live in the polyps and solenial canals of species within all alcyonarian orders. Though nothing is known of the physiological relationship of these animals with their hosts, it must be presumed that they are parasites from the fact that they have no means of obtaining food from any source but their hosts. Gorgonians, soft corals, and sea pens harbor various species of creeping ctenophores, most of which are known only in such associations. As they are predators able to feed on microcrustaceans, it appears that they are specialized for feeding upon the small copepods that normally inhabit alcyonarians. The ophiuroids and crinoids that so often are found clinging to gorgonian colonies may depend on their hosts only for support, but the association is so constant that it seems likely to have some undetected physiological basis. Most curious is a small fish of the goby family which clings tightly to gorgonian colonies by means of its sucker-like pelvic fins and leaves them only when driven off.

One of the most familiar cases of commensalism in the sea is that between large sea anemones and the colorful clownfishes of the Indo-Pacific region. Although the sea anemones are capable of killing and eating fishes larger than the clownfishes, the latter are completely immune to the nematocysts of the coelenterates and actually hide among the tentacles when danger threatens. The nature of their immunity is unknown, but it may be conferred by eating bits of the tentacles. Clownfishes often have been seen to drag pieces of food material to the anemones, and it is possible that they lure other fishes within range of the tentacles. This relationship is of evident mutual benefit and is of a very specific nature, as the various species of clownfishes usually associate with a preferred host species in nature. However, the relationship is not inflexible and the fish are able to live quite happily in aquaria with sea anemones from a completely different part of the world, and they can exist perfectly well apart from the anemones as long as they are protected from predators. They depend upon the coelenterate only for protection.

Sea anemones are also associated with other invertebrates, mostly crustaceans. The best known examples are the species carried about on the shells of hermit crabs, on the carapace of crabs, and on snail shells. By the mobility that they afford, these relationships give the anemones a better chance to obtain food, and the crustaceans may benefit by sharing prey caught by the coelenterate. The nature of the relationship between tropical sea anemones and the small shrimps and porcelain crabs that often live among their tentacles is not understood. The anemone obviously affords protection to the crustaceans, which would otherwise be extremely vulnerable to predatory fishes, but the association holds no obvious benefit for the coelenterate.

Many instances of associations between hydroids and other

animals have been reported. The spiny, encrusting *Hydractinia* very often lives on shells inhabited by hermit crabs, but can live independently and sometimes does so in nature. More intimate is the association between the minute two-tentacled hydroid *Lar* and the polychaetes whose tubes they inhabit. Other hydroids are commensal with gorgonians, sponges, mollusks, and live epiphytically on floating *Sargassum* as well as on attached marine plants. One of the few cases of parasitic coelenterates is the hydroid *Hydrichthys*, which lives upon fishes (Figure 164). The colony is attached to the host by a hydrorhizal network that sends stolons into the tissues. The hydranths feed directly on the tissues of the fish where they have been injured by the stolons. Hydroids themselves are widely preyed upon by nudibranch mollusks, some of which are able to store the ingested nematocysts in unexploded condition and employ them in their own defense. As the nudibranchs may feed also on other organisms and are not limited to hydroids, they must be considered predatory browsers and not inseparably associated with hydroids.

Relationships involving medusae are quite similar to those among the Anthozoa. Crustaceans such as amphipods and larval lobsters have been observed to infest scyphomedusae. Fishes, particularly the young of certain carangids (amberjacks and relatives), commonly take shelter among the tentacles of large scyphomedusans and seemingly are immune to their poisons. Similar

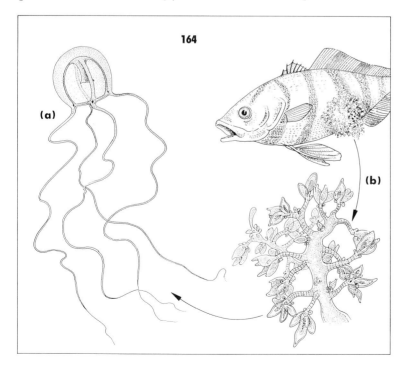

Figure 164. Parasitism in coelenterates. One of the few parasitic coelenterates is *Hydrichthys*, which has a free-swimming medusa (a). The colonial hydroid stage lives as an external parasite on fishes (b). [After Mayer, 1910, and Fewkes, 1888.]

is the association between the blue and silver fish *Nomeus* and the Portuguese man-of-war. Schools of the fish dart in and out among the trailing tentacles with impunity and are never found anywhere else. The pelagic community includes also the chondrophorans *Velella* and *Porpita* and the mollusks that prey on them, the prosobranch *Janthina* and the opisthobranchs *Fiona* and *Glaucus*. Some *Janthina* species as young snails ride on the coelenterates, feeding on the zooids, until they reach adult size when they form their own floats and assume an independent, predatory existence, whereas the common violet snail always floats independently, feeding on the *Velella* colonies that are thrown within reach by waves and currents.

The closest association between coelenterates and other organisms is the intracellular symbiosis of unicellular algae called zooxanthellae with a wide variety of shallow-water species. Virtually all reef corals, littoral gorgonians, sea anemones, zoanthids, and many medusae contain these plant cells which are now considered to be dinoflagellates. Although the classification of zooxanthellae is a neglected subject, it is evident that they do not all belong to the same species. Their size differs in various host animals, and there also are obvious structural differences which await interpretation. Zooxanthellae are spherical bodies about 7 to 10 μ in diameter, with a distinct cellulose cell wall. In virtually all coelenterates they are located only in the gastrodermis, where each plant cell occupies a special gastrodermal *carrier cell*. In the reef corals and sea anemones, the algae are concentrated in the gastrodermis of the oral disc, tentacles, and septal filaments. In alcyonarians, they may be generally distributed in the polyps and also in the walls of the gastrodermal solenia permeating the coenenchyme. In some cases, special solenial pouches filled with zooxanthellae lie in the mesogloea just beneath the epidermis, where light is at its maximal intensity.

This relationship between plant and animal is one of the most interesting physiological problems, as it varies greatly in its intimacy according to the species of coelenterates involved, as well as the ways in which it enters into the physiological processes of the host. The question of the role played by the zooxanthellae in the physiology of their hosts has been briskly debated by those who seek a neat theory to explain the phenomena observed. Some have held that the zooxanthellae serve only to supplement the oxygen supply and remove carbon dioxide, whereas others have argued that the algae also serve as a source of food. Both views may be correct. However, it is becoming increasingly clear that no one explanation fits all cases, and there are, in fact, many degrees of intimacy and complexity in this association. Some coelenterates that usually contain zooxanthellae are perfectly capable of living without them and may do so in nature, whereas others are not. It can be generalized that the algae produce oxygen during the daylight as a result of photosynthesis and require carbon dioxide which is produced by the animal. It is probable that the metabolic wastes produced by the coelenterate are utilized by the plant cells, and nutrient substances produced by the algae during photosynthesis are taken up by the animal. Some investigators have argued that the coelenterates obtain these nutrients by digesting the zooxanthellae, and others have suggested direct exchange. Whatever the route, and it undoubtedly varies with species, some coelenterates (for example, certain alcyonarians) are nutritionally dependent upon their algae and cannot survive without them, being incapable of feeding in the normal fashion, whereas others are not. In addition to entering into respirational and nutritional processes, the zooxanthellae have a bearing on calcification in coelenterates that produce a skeleton, hence are of utmost significance to theories of reef formation. In the case of reef corals, Dr. T. F. Goreau has found that zooxanthellae contribute to the process of skeleton formation, probably by assisting in the removal of H_2CO_3 resulting from the formation of $CaCO_3$ from calcium bicarbonate produced by the combination of calcium ions with metabolic bicarbonate. Below a depth of about 30 meters, coral skeletons become progressively weaker and less massive due to the lessened effectiveness of the zooxanthellae in skeletogenesis under conditions of reduced illumination. Below a depth of about 60 meters, calcification is so much reduced that corals are incapable of forming reef structures, although they are probably as healthy biologically as their massive brothers in shallow water. Thus the importance of depth to reef formation becomes clear, and accordingly the depth requirement of the "antecedent platform" for the successful establishment of reefs.

3

Phylum Ctenophora

Introduction

The ctenophores, or comb jellies, are planktonic animals of delicate, gelatinous consistency, generally resembling the coelenterates and grouped with them in some classifications. They do not have as long a recorded history as do the coelenterates. The first recognizable account in the literature dates only from 1671, but it is reasonable to assume that common forms were known to ancient people just as were the medusae, corals, and other invertebrates. Because of their jelly-like appearance they were probably grouped indiscriminately with the jellyfishes under the term "Acalephae" (or "nettles"), as they were in several of the early post-Linnean classifications. It was Eschscholtz (1829) who first recognized the ctenophores as a distinct group and gave them the name "Ctenophorae." Because their ephemeral nature makes ctenophores poor subjects for fossilization, there is no known fossil record and their origin is obscure, even on a conjectural basis. The discovery of a creeping ctenophore was regarded as evidence of the origin of flatworms from them, but careful study of these presumed "missing links" has shown that they are modified ctenophores, nothing more, and probably of no great phylogenetic import. Ctenophores have been used in various experimental work, but they have no direct economic value. It is possible that they have some effect upon oyster populations, as they are voracious carnivores feeding on plankton and could decimate populations of oyster larvae in areas of concentrated occurrence.

Morphology and Classification

GENERAL FEATURES

The ctenophores are like the coelenterates in their gelatinous consistency, composed of an outer and an inner epithelium, separated by a thick mesogloea which accounts for the greatest part of the animal's volume. The only body cavity is the gastrovascular system, and structures are tetramerously arranged in radial fashion around the oral–aboral axis. They differ from the coelenterates most conspicuously in the development of highly specialized ciliary swimming structures called *combs*, arranged in eight *comb rows* placed like the meridians of a globe (Figure 165), which are one of the most obvious external features of the ctenophore body. Moreover, the presence of mesenchymal muscle fibers in the mesogloea makes this layer a better developed ectomesoderm than is the coelenterate mesogloea. The gastrovascular tract is better organized as a complex system of canals with a large stomodaeum and two aboral anal pores. The subepidermal nerve plexus shows definite concentration in the region of the apical organ at the aboral pole and along the eight comb rows. Although the symmetry superficially appears to be radial, the flattening of the mouth, presence of only two tentacles, and arrangement of the comb rows and meridional canals of the gastrovascular system are such that the animal can be cut into identical halves along two planes, so that its symmetry is actually *biradial*. The halves cut along the sagittal plane (through the long axis of the mouth) are not like those cut along the transverse plane at right angles to it. Nematocysts are definitely known to be present in only one kind of ctenophore, thus pointing to a common origin with the coelenterates in the distant past, with subsequent loss of these structures during the evolutionary history of the group. The tentacles of ctenophores are provided with remarkable adhesive cells or *colloblasts*, quite different from nematocysts in structure and function. Gonads develop in the walls of the gastrovascular canals and in some species are provided with rudimentary genital ducts. Embryological development is strikingly different from that of coelenterates, and the usual larval form is called the *cydippid* after the most primitive ctenophores, which it resembles. Curious ciliated structures known as *cell rosettes* located in the canal walls have been interpreted as excretory structures, but their function is not established definitely and the presence of an excretory system in this phylum remains debatable. Ctenophores do not have medusoid and polypoid structural types so that each species has but a single form and is thus called *monomorphic*; there is no alternation of generations. No skeletal structures are developed in this phylum, and the animals are never colonial although some of the creeping, commensal forms may be gregarious. All species are marine and most are free-living, although a few are commensals and one is a parasite. In general, they are planktonic in habit, living in the open ocean as well as in coastal waters, but a few are adapted for an exclusively benthonic mode of life.

STRUCTURE

The fundamental body form is ovate or spheroidal (Figure 165), with the mouth at one pole (the *oral pole*) and the apical sense organ at the corner (*aboral pole*). The most striking external features are eight rows of combs or *ctenes*, which begin near the aboral pole and extend along equally spaced meridians almost to the oral pole.

The mouth, flattened or slit like, leads to a more or less elongated canal lying in the polar axis. Immediately within the mouth, this canal has plicated walls and is termed the *pharynx*; this leads into a wider space, the *stomach*, which is flattened at right angles to the flattening of the mouth and pharynx. The cavity in the main body axis continues upward from the stomach to the apical sense organ, around which it produces four short branches, the *anal canals*. Two opposite anal canals open to the outside as *anal pores*, whereas the two at right angles to these are blind sacs. The chief branches of the gastrovascular cavity are given off from the stomach. Two unbranched *pharyngeal canals*, one on each side, extend from the stomach along the two broad sides of the pharynx toward the mouth, near which they end blindly. At right angles to these, the stomach gives off two more canals, each with three main branches. The middle branch of each, the *tentacular canal*, terminates at the *tentacle sheath*, which is a deep pouch leading to the surface and containing a long, extensile tentacle. The two side branches of the tentacular canal diverge outward toward the body surface and bifurcate once, making a total of eight canals, one running toward each of the eight comb rows. Just beneath the comb rows, each canal extends upward toward the aboral pole and downward toward the oral pole, closely following the comb rows. These are the eight *meridional canals*.

Many adult ctenophores, as well as all larval forms, correspond

Figure 165. Anatomy of ctenophores. (a) Diagram of the polar field and sense organ. (b) General anatomy. Code: A, aboral sense organ; B, balancer; C, combs; D, mouth; E, pharynx; F, pharyngeal canal; G, stomach; H, transverse canal; I, interradial canal; J, meridional canal; K, tentacular canal; L, tentacle sheath; M, tentacle; N, statolith; O, anal canal; P, anal pore.

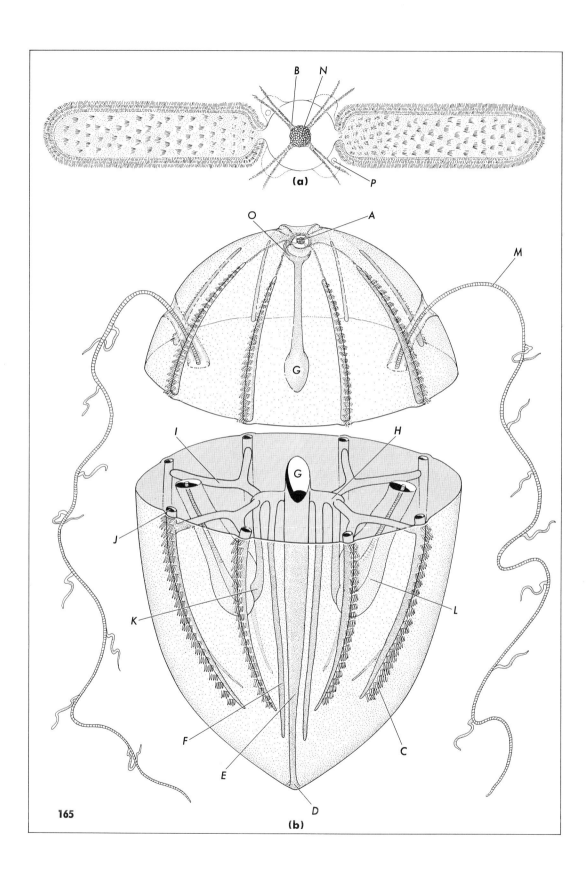

(a)

(b)

Phylum
Ctenophora

166

Figures 166 to 170. Histology of ctenophores. **166.** Ciliated basal cells of comb rows in *Eucharis*. [Redrawn from Chun, 1880.] **167.** Epidermis of *Coeloplana*. **168.** Pharyngeal epithelium of *Coeloplana*. **169.** Cell-rosette of *Coeloplana*. [Redrawn from Abbott, 1907.] **170.** Amoeboid cells of mesogloea of *Coeloplana*. [Redrawn from Abbott, 1907.] Code: A, epidermal nucleus; B, clear gland cell; C, granular gland cell; D, gastrodermal nucleus.

closely with this general plan, but some kinds depart from it more or less strongly in the adult stage, and these modifications will be mentioned briefly in the discussion of the principal subdivisions of the phylum.

HISTOLOGY

The epidermis (Figure 167) is syncytial in some forms, but usually consists of columnar or cuboidal cells, often interspersed with gland cells. Granular and mucous gland cells may be very numerous, and pigment cells and pigment granules sometimes occur. Sensory cells are present, some with one bristle, others with several. In some species, sensory cells are concentrated in sensory papillae. The combs are dense horizontal rows of long cilia arising from ridgelike thickenings of exceptionally tall epidermal cells (Figure 166). The epidermis between the bases of the combs is ciliated in some species but not in others.

Gastrodermis (Figure 168) lines stomach and the gastrovascular canals. In the canals, this epithelium is tall and vacuolated on the outer wall toward the combs, and low and ciliated on the inner wall toward the stomach. The ciliated portion circulates the fluid in the canals, and it is likely that the tall, vacuolated cells participate in intracellular digestion. The canal walls are perforated here

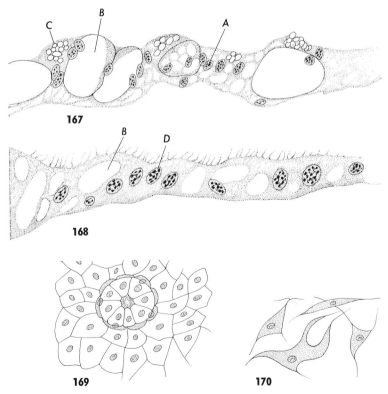

and there by small openings, leading into the mesenchyme, rimmed by ciliated gastrodermal cells called *cell rosettes* (Figure 169). One circle of cilia beats toward the mesenchyme and another beats toward the canal. Circumstantial evidence points to an excretory or regulatory function of the cell rosettes, as they can move fluids to or from the mesenchyme.

The great bulk of the ctenophore body consists of the gelatinous *mesenchyme* lying between epidermis and gastrodermis. This is made up of muscle, connective, and nerve fibers, and amoeboid cells (Figure 170). The muscle fibers develop from the amoeboid mesenchyme cells rather than from cells of the epidermis and gastrodermis as happens in the coelenterates. They are smooth, elongated, branching, and sometimes interconnecting (Figures 171, 172). Longitudinal and circular components are located under the epidermis and surround the pharynx, and radial elements course through the mesenchyme connecting the two. Sphincters are formed around the mouth and apical organ, and the oral lobes, if present, are particularly muscular.

Sensory cells (Figure 173) with one or several bristles have been reported, but the most general receptors of ctenophores are the

Morphology
and
Classification

Figures 171 to 173. Histology of ctenophores. **171.** Anastomosing muscle fibers around mouth of *Callianira*. **172.** Branched muscle bases from sensory papillae of *Eucharis*. **173.** Sensory epithelium. [All redrawn from Chun, 1880.]

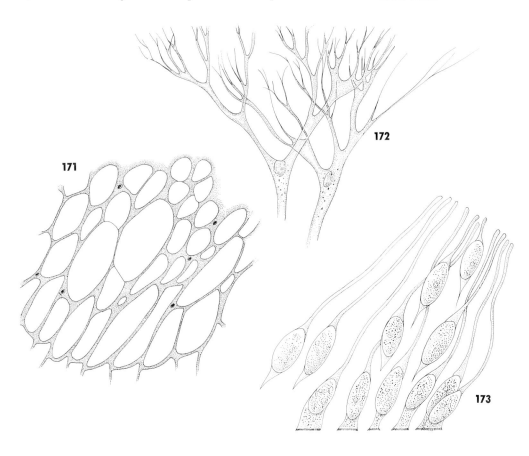

cilia. The nervous system consists of a subepidermal plexus of multipolar ganglion cells and neurites with synaptic connections. Fibers extend to the muscles in the mesenchyme. Under the comb rows the neurites are more closely set and thus form eight nerve strands (Figure 175) with extensions into the bases of the combs. The ganglion cells are not concentrated as ganglia and the system as a whole contains no localized control center. Thus, it is a diffuse system, just as in the coelenterates.

An outstanding anatomical peculiarity of the ctenophores is the aboral sensory organ (Figure 176). This consists of a pit or depression, the *statocyst*, lined with a tall, ciliated epithelium, located at the aboral pole. A tiny concretion of calcareous grains, the *statolith*, is supported within the statocyst by four tufts of stout cilia, the *balancers*. Tall cilia around the rim of the statocyst are fused over it as a domelike protective bell. Two *ciliated furrows* (Figure 165) extend from each balancer to the two comb rows of that quadrant of the animal. From two opposite sides of the statocyst a ciliated tract extends outward in the sagittal plane, serving an unknown sensory function. These are the *polar fields* (Figure 165). The aboral sensory organ enables the animal to detect changes in orientation through gravitational changes in pressure of the statocyst on the balancers.

The four short anal canals, two blind and two opening by pores,

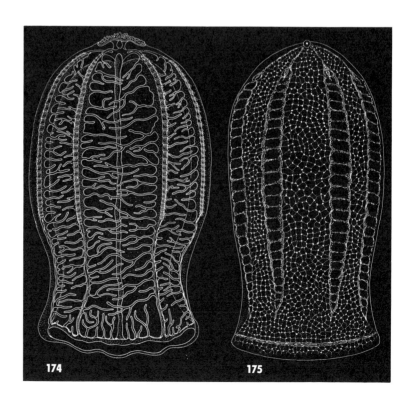

Figures 174 and 175. Anatmomy of ctenophores. **174.** Canal system of *Beroe*. [After Mayer, 1912.] **175.** Nerve plexus of *Beroe*. [Modified from von Heider, 1927.]

174   175

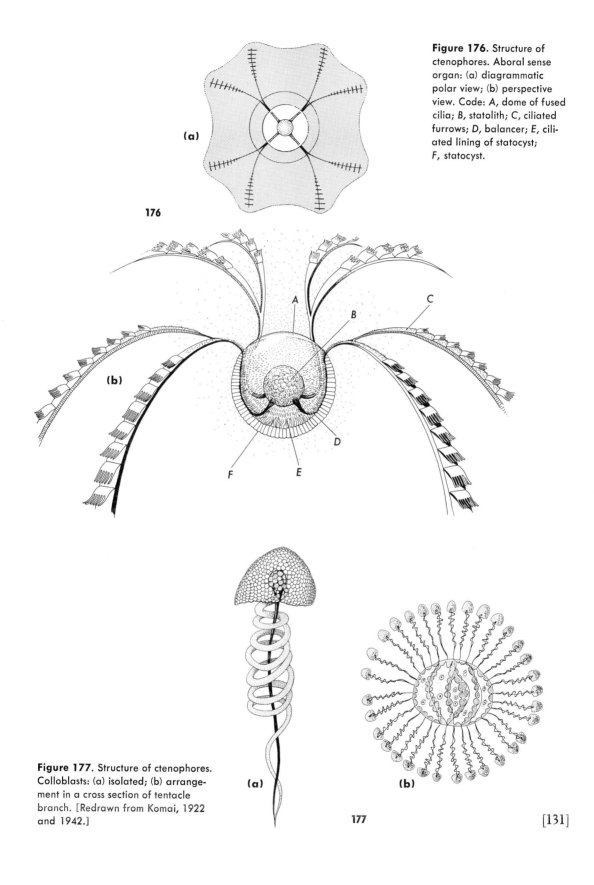

Figure 176. Structure of ctenophores. Aboral sense organ: (a) diagrammatic polar view; (b) perspective view. Code: A, dome of fused cilia; B, statolith; C, ciliated furrows; D, balancer; E, ciliated lining of statocyst; F, statocyst.

(a)

176

A

B

C

(b)

D

F   E

Figure 177. Structure of ctenophores. Colloblasts: (a) isolated; (b) arrangement in a cross section of tentacle branch. [Redrawn from Komai, 1922 and 1942.]

(a)   **(b)**

177   [131]

closely surround the sense organ, and the two pores open immediately adjacent to the statocyst. Strong musculature surrounding
the sensory organ functions as a sphincter to close off the statocyst.

The tentacles, present in most ctenophores, are extremely long,
highly contractile filaments with short lateral branches in a single
row. They can be pulled completely into the pitlike tentacle-
sheaths. They consist of a solid muscular core covered with epidermis made up of adhesive cells known as *colloblasts* (Figure
177), typical of the phylum. Although these cells function in the
capture of prey and thus correspond to the nematocysts of coelenterates, they are quite different structures. They are composed
of a hemispherical head covered with secretory granules that produce an adhesive substance, attached to the core of the tentacle
by a *spiral filament* coiled around a straight filament which originally was the nucleus of the cell. The colloblasts are incapable of
stinging as they have no mechanism for penetration, but by means
of their adhesive properties serve instead to hold prey fast while
it is pulled within reach of the mouth.

CLASSIFICATION, PHYLUM CTENOPHORA

I. Class Tentaculata. All species with tentacles, at least in larval
stages and usually throughout life (four orders).
   A. Order Cydippida (*Cydippe*; the sea gooseberries and sea
   walnuts). Globular forms with well-developed, retractile
   tentacles.
   B. Order Lobata (*Mnemiopsis*). Moderately compressed, ovate
   animals with tentacles more or less reduced in adult stage;
   two large oral lobes and four slender, flaplike ciliated auricles surrounding mouth.
   C. Order Cestida (*Cestum*; Venus' girdle). Body extremely
   compressed and laterally expanded to produce long, ribbon-
   like forms. Primary tentacles in sheaths but reduced in
   size; many small, simple tentacles along oral edge of animal.
   D. Order Platyctenea (*Coeloplana*, without comb rows in
   adult; *Ctenoplana*, with rudimentary comb rows). Sessile
   forms, compressed in oral–aboral direction, with pharynx
   widely expanded to form creeping surface. Comb rows rudimentary or completely absent in adults, present in cydippid larvae. Two primary tentacles present and usually well
   developed. Mostly commensals on coelenterates and echinoderms.
II. Class Nuda. All species lacking tentacles, even in larval stages
(only one order).

A. Order Beroida (*Beroe*). Body sac-like, laterally compressed, mouth widely gaping; walls filled with branching diverticula from meridional canals.

The phylum Ctenophora is divided into two classes and five orders on the basis of variations on the fundamental body plan as seen in the cydippids. As its name implies, all species of the largest class, Tentaculata, have two tentacles as noted in the general description just given, whereas the class Nuda, with only one order, contains only species completely devoid of tentacles.

Members of the tentaculate order Cydippida conform most closely to the described body plan, and the young of all orders resemble them, hence the name *cydippid larvae* for the young of all ctenophores. In our waters, the only cydippid seen commonly is *Pleurobrachia* (Figure 183), an oval or spheroidal animal with two long tentacles having short lateral branches in a single row. Striking modifications in form are found in *Callianira* (Figure 179), in which the aboral region of the body is drawn out into two tall, gracefully curving crests on each side of the sense organ, and in *Lampetia* (Figure 180), which can distend the pharynx enormously as a creeping surface whereby it walks on the sea floor.

In the order Lobata, the body is expanded on each side of the mouth to form a pair of broad *oral lobes* and is conspicuously flattened (Figure 181). Because of the oral lobes, the two comb rows on each broad side are longer than those on the narrow tentacular sides. The two comb rows flanking the tentacles on each side give rise to two flat, pointed flaps with ciliated edges, the *auricles* (Figure 181), which project around the mouth and assist in guiding food into it. In many lobate ctenophores the aboral pole of the animal is deeply sunken and the sense organ is situated at the bottom of the resulting pit. In young Lobata, the tentacles are situated in sheaths located as usual for cydippids, but as the animal matures, the tentacles migrate to a position near the mouth, losing their sheaths and remaining small in size. *Mnemiopsis*, one of the most abundant comb jellies of the Atlantic coast, is a typical lobate form. Its oral lobes are large and muscular, and although they are contractile they do not actively participate in swimming. In *Ocyropsis*, however, which has very weak and poorly developed combs, the lobes are exceptionally well developed and muscular and by their contractions help propel the animal through the water.

Although the Lobata are compressed, they retain a generally ovate form, but the Cestida, or Venus' girdles, are flattened almost to leaflike thinness (Figure 182). At the same time they are transversely expanded in the sagittal plane, resulting in a

[134]

Phylum
Ctenophora

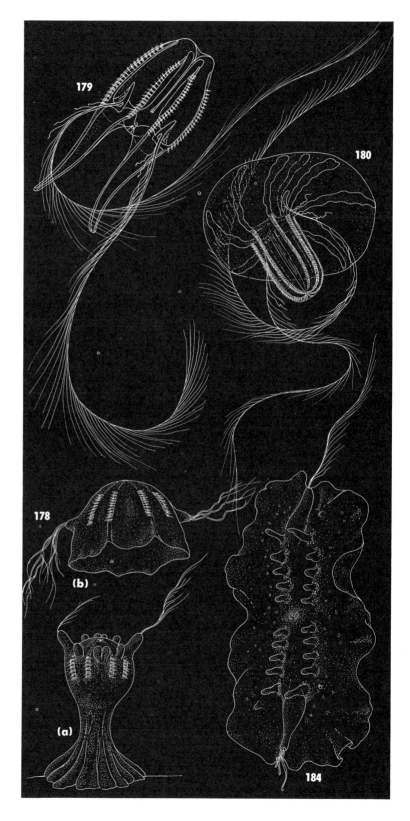

Figures 178 to 184. Diversity of body form in ctenophores. **178.** *Ctenoplana* (order Platyctenea) with vestigial comb rows in creeping (a) and swimming (b) attitudes. [After Dawydoff, 1938.] **179.** *Callianira* (order Cydippida) with aboral crests. [After Chun, 1880.] **180.** *Lampetia* (order Cydippida) with widely expansible pharynx. [After Chun, 1880.] **181.** *Mnemiopsis* (order Lobata), common comb-jelly with auricles A. [After Mayer, 1912.] **182.** *Folia* (order Cestida), one of the Venus's Girdles. [After Mayer, 1912.] **183.** *Pleurobrachia*, the sea gooseberry (order Cydippida). [After Mayer, 1912.] **184.** *Coeloplana* (order Platyctenea), completely devoid of comb rows. [After Dawydoff, 1939.]

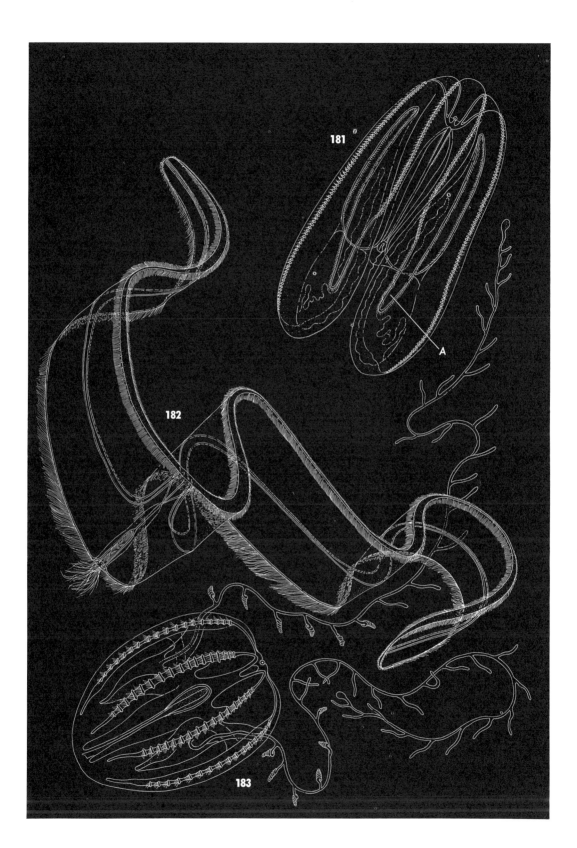

ribbon-like form sometimes exceeding a meter in length. In the adults, the tentacles are located in deep sheaths beside the mouth and are reduced to a rudimentary state. A row of small, simple tentacles extends along the whole of the narrow oral edge of the body. Because of the peculiar shape, the position of the comb rows and meridional canals differs from that found in spherical forms. Four of the rows are very long, two extending out on each side of the aboral sense organ and running along the upper edge of the band, whereas the other four are very short and confined to the vicinity of the sense organ. Correspondingly, four meridional canals follow the four long comb rows along the aboral edge of the animal. The canals of the four short comb rows extend down to the middle of the band and then run out to the ends. The two pharyngeal canals, which in cydippids stop near the mouth, in this case bifurcate and extend as two canals along the oral edge of the body on each side of the mouth. The well-known Venus's girdle, *Cestum veneris*, is one of the most striking of all ctenophores, swimming with graceful undulations. In sunlight it is resplendent with iridescent colors, and at night it is brilliantly luminescent. Although rarely seen, *Cestum* is common in warm seas around the world.

The final order of tentaculate ctenophores, the Platyctenea, also consists of extremely modified forms. Whereas the cestids are compressed laterally in the sagittal plane, the platyctenes are flattened in the oral–aboral axis. By great expansion and permanent eversion of the pharynx, with corresponding depression of the aboral pole, the body of these animals has taken on a flattened form and it creeps about on its enormously expanded pharyngeal surface. The margin of the whole animal actually represents the edge of the mouth, and the functional mouth is really the entrance to the stomach. Platyctenes of the genus *Ctenoplana*, known in the Pacific from New Guinea north to Japan, retain vestiges of the eight comb rows, which they use along with the two thin marginal lobes to swim in the plankton (Figure 178). They also can assume a creeping attitude by everting the pharynx and expanding the lobes. Two projecting chimney-like sheaths contain the long, unilaterally pinnate tentacles. Because of the thinness of the body in the oral axis, the gastrovascular system is greatly shortened. The canal system arises directly from the stomach, consisting of two short anal canals opening to the surface by pores, two tentacular canals leading to the tentacle sheaths, and eight meridional canals associated with the vestigial comb rows. These canals branch repeatedly and fuse to form a complicated vascular network. The gonads are located in the walls of the tentacular canals. The testes empty into ducts which open to the aboral surface by a pore, the first development of its kind in the Metazoa. The aboral sense organ, resembling that of other ctenophores, occupies the middle of the upper surface.

Other platyctenes have lost all traces of the combs in the adult state and their activities are thus limited to creeping or at most passively drifting in water currents. *Coeloplana* and *Vallicula*, both known from the coast of Florida and the West Indies, were overlooked for many years because of their inconspicuous appearance. In these very flattened forms, the tentacle sheaths project only slightly, but the upper surface may have several tuberculate projections containing extensions of the canals, arranged in a more or less symmetrical fashion (Figure 184). Pacific species of *Coeloplana* may be brightly colored, usually mottled, spotted or striped with red, brown, or green on a relatively translucent ground. Several other platyctenes have been discovered, some of bizarre appearance and brilliant coloration, others inconspicuous.

As already mentioned, the class Nuda, has only a single order, the Beroida, whose species completely lack tentacles and sheaths in all stages of development, even in the larva. Beroids are rather large, laterally compressed, sac-like animals up to eight inches in length. The opening of the sac is the mouth, and its interior is the capacious pharynx. The stomach is a small cavity lying near the aboral pole. It gives rise directly to four interradial canals which bifurcate to form the eight meridional canals. These produce an anastomosing system of lateral branches which form a complicated network through the mesenchyme. The aboral sense organ has a well-formed statocyst surrounded by polar fields fringed with branching papillae. *Beroe*, the best-known genus (Figure 174), has two species along the Atlantic coast, one southern, one chiefly northern. In both, individuals in the southern part of the range are dull milky or brownish in color, whereas those toward the north are beautifully tinted with pink or red.

Reproduction and Embryology

ASEXUAL REPRODUCTION

These fragile animals have a great capacity for regeneration, replacing or repairing any extirpated or wounded part, even the statocyst.

Budding does not occur nor is there any evidence that the planktonic species reproduce by fission. However, the benthic forms *Ctenoplana*, *Coeloplana*, and *Vallicula* rapidly multiply by a kind of fission which recalls pedal laceration in anemones.

Fragments of the margin of the body are pinched off and the entire margins of the fragment unite, thus closing the wound, the location of which establishes polarity in the developing bit of tissue. This grows into a complete representative of the species.

SEXUAL REPRODUCTION

So far as we know, all ctenophores are hermaphroditic; both ovaries and testes are located in the walls of the meridional canals. In planktonic species, the gametes are expelled through the mouth, and fertilization—probably commonly self-fertilization—takes place in the sea. Some of the platyctenes, however, brood their embryos, so fertilization evidently is internal. These animals (*Coeloplana* and *Ctenoplana*) are unusual in that their testes open to the aboral surface via a duct and pore, and moreover they have pocket-like *seminal receptacles* in which sperm is stored. Thus their reproductive structures are on a somewhat higher level than elsewhere in the phylum.

A very strange feature of the reproduction of ctenophores is the phenomenon of *dissogeny* shown by several species. Not only do the adults reproduce sexually, but in very warm weather their young, still in the cydippid larval stage, become sexually ripe and produce eggs that develop into perfect but miniature embryos. The sexually mature larvae then undergo regression until they reach the adult stage, in which they ripen again.

The pattern in which the cleavage planes divide the cells of the embryo is called *disymmetrical*. It is a unique cleavage as it is found only in ctenophores. The first and second furrows commence at the vegetal pole rather than the animal pole, which is usual in many other animals. These furrows are meridional, the second forming at right angles to the first, and the result is a four-celled embryo. The third cleavage is the disymmetrical one; each of the four cells divides by a diagonal furrow which extends obliquely from a point near the animal pole to the lateral part of the vegetal hemisphere (Figure 185). The eight cells thus formed lie in a saucer-like arrangement—that is, with a slight concavity on the animal side (Figure 185). The fourth cleavage is latitudinal and unequal, resulting in 8 *micromeres* on the concave animal side and 8 *macromeres* below. In the fifth cleavage (Figure 186), the micromeres divide, forming 16 micromeres, and the macromeres divide inequally into 8 macromeres and 8 micromeres. Thus the embryo now consists of a vegetal group of 8 macromeres on which lie 24 micromeres, a total of 32 cells. Thereafter the micromeres divide rapidly, forming a layer of ectodermal cells over the animal portion of the embryo (Figure 187), the apex of which will be the aboral pole of the adult. The macromeres divide equally into 16 large cells which will form the entoderm. This, then, is a determinate or mosaic cleavage in that the cells from which the two primary layers (ectoderm and entoderm) will form are designated very early in development.

Gastrulation is brought about by the growth of the micromeres down over the macromeres (*epiboly*) combined with *invagination* (Figure 188). Prior to invagination, the macromeres divide inequally once more, producing 16 micromeres, the fate of which has not been established. Some students believe that they give rise to the mesodermal cells of the mesenchyme. If so, the ctenophores have a mesoderm derived from the entoderm, or an *entomesoderm*. Others state that these 16 cells are entodermal, forming part of the gastrovascular system, and that the mesoderm is an *ectomesoderm* derived from inwandered ectoderm, as is usual in the coelenterates.

Reproduction
and
Embryology

Figures 185 to 190. Embryology of ctenophores. **185.** Embryo in eight-cell stage. **186.** Embryo undergoing fifth cleavage. **187 and 188.** Stages of gastrulation. **189.** Longitudinal section through the young cydippid larva; stomodaeum shown in fine stipple. [Redrawn from Chun, 1880.] **190.** Fully developed cydippid larva of *Bolinopsis*. [Redrawn from Mayer, 1912.]

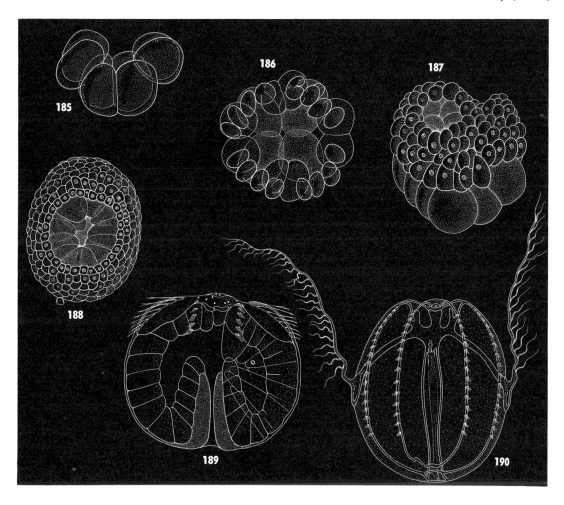

After gastrulation, four bands of ciliated ectoderm cells begin to differentiate, commencing near the aboral pole and extending downward. These are the *combs*, each of which will later divide into two. The *statocyst* develops as an ectodermal structure at the aboral pole, and at the oral pole ectoderm grows inward, forming the stomodaeum (Figure 189). The *tentacle sheaths* are also ectodermal invaginations. A tentacle develops from the base of each sheath and contains muscle cells from the mesenchyme. From the entodermal central gastric cavity, tubular outgrowths form the canal system.

The free-swimming larva, the *cydippid* (Figure 190), occurs in all of the class Tentaculata. It develops directly into the adult form in the order *Cydippida*, but in the other orders undergoes a gradual metamorphosis. For example, in the Lobata the tentacles move down toward the mouth, lose their sheaths and become very small, while the oral end expands into the large oral lobes. In the class Nuda, the beroid larva lacks tentacles and sheaths but otherwise resembles the cydippid.

Physiology

RESPIRATION

Intimate contact of extremely thin tissues with the surrounding sea water obviates the need for special respiratory mechanisms in the ctenophores, as is the case in coelenterates. Circulation of water in the gastrovascular passages serves to bring oxygen supplies to the tissues of the interior and to carry off carbon dioxide. Ciliary action and movement of the animals through the water results in constant renewal of oxygenated water, and gas exchange takes place directly across cell membranes. Consumption of oxygen is very low relative to the total weight of the animals but about normal with respect to dry weight.

NERVOUS REACTIONS

Abundant sensory cells in the epidermis result in general sensitivity to various types of stimuli—chemical, mechanical, and temperature. Response to light is minimal as receptors are absent, but dark adaption is necessary for the activation of bioluminescent properties, thus showing that the animals are affected by light physiologically even though direct response is not well defined. Sensitivity to chemical stimuli is greatest in the oral region. Reaction to food substances consists of feeding responses, such as alteration of the comb beats and secretion of mucus to entrap food particles. Mechanical stimulation may result in various kinds of response, such as contraction of the oral region, retraction of the combs into the mesenchyme, and alteration of the beat of the combs. Mechanical stimulation of the oral end causes the beat to reverse as well as the direction of the wave along the comb rows, so that the animal moves away from the irritant. Beating of the combs is appropriately adjusted to restore a normal position if the animal's orientation is changed. The beat of the combs of the two rows of each quadrant is synchronous, and the synchronization as well as the general coordination of beat is controlled by the statocyst, but not the beat itself. Combs continue to beat, but without coordination, in the absence of the statocyst. Thus it is clearly seen that the nervous system controls ciliary action in the ctenophores.

DIGESTION

Ctenophores are carnivorous, and digestion takes place very much as in the coelenterates. Extracellular phases of digestion occur in the pharynx and the resultant material is distributed throughout the canal system. There the cells of the outer canal walls ingest the food particles and digestion is completed intracellularly. Indigestible material passes from the body by way of the mouth as in coelenterates and also through the two anal pores. The anal canals slowly distend with water containing particles to be expelled, and periodically the pores open to discharge the accumulation.

BEHAVIOR

Ctenophores feed either by capturing small organisms with their exceedingly long, unilaterally pinnate tentacles, by trapping them in a mucous sheet which is moved into the mouth by ciliary action, or simply by ingesting such animals as are encountered while swimming with the oral end foremost. The large mouth of *Beroe* enables it to ingest larger animals including other ctenophores. In areas where currents bring together dense swarms of comb jellies, their voracious feeding upon smaller plankton may decimate the populations, including molluscan and crustacean larvae which may be of major economic importance. By their predation on baby herring, they may even influence the abundance of these fishes from year to year in European waters.

The creeping platyctenes repeatedly extend and withdraw their long tentacles in "fishing" activities, streaming them out in the passing currents to capture any small animals that may come into contact with the sticky colloblasts. Prey is then pulled within reach of the margin and the animal simply envelops it.

Only *Euchlora* has nematocysts; otherwise, ctenophores are lacking in defensive mechanisms aside from the colloblasts, whose significance from this standpoint is probably minor. In *Eurhamphaea*, a lobate genus, bright red globules occur in the meridional canals and are ejected through pores in the canal walls as a fluorescent red cloud when the animal is disturbed. Possibly this material is an excretory product which serves a secondary function as a defense cloud, but the matter has not been fully investigated. It is also known that at least some ctenophores contain a toxic substance, but the manner in which it functions, if indeed it does, is unknown.

Because of their very watery consistency, ctenophores may readily be damaged by strong wave action, and accordingly descend to the quiet of deeper water during periods of rough weather. The more delicate forms, such as *Leucothea ochracea*, *Ocyropsis crystallina* and *Bolinopsis vitrea*, are seen at the surface only in calm weather, and even the slightest rippling of the water causes them to sink to quieter levels. Some are so delicate that even a slight current of water suffices to injure them; the Venus' girdles may tear themselves to shreds by their own muscular contractions.

Some of the most spectacular examples of bioluminescence can be found in the ctenophores. If sufficiently dark-adapted, they produce brilliant flashes of blue-green light from the meridional canals when disturbed.

Ecology and Distribution

ECOLOGY

For the most part, ctenophores are planktonic animals, living in the open sea as well as in coastal waters. Although some species frequent brackish bays and estuaries where salinities may be much less than in the sea, they do not inhabit fresh water. They live chiefly in the upper layers of water, but have been found also at depths approaching two miles.

Action of the combs results in rather weak swimming movements. When in motion, the animals appear to drift sedately through the water. A few lobate forms with poorly developed comb rows employ the oral lobes to supplement the feeble activity of the combs. The ribbon-like cestids progress by serpentine undulations and by rolling and unrolling the body. Some normally planktonic cydippids and lobate ctenophores are able to crawl on the widely expanded pharynx, which functions as a creeping sole. This trend has been carried to the extreme by the benthic Platyctenea, which are exclusively creeping forms that only rarely change locations by reeling out the tentacles and rafting with the water currents. One of these benthic forms has become completely sessile. It has lost the use of the mouth through permanent attachment and takes food through the two tubular projections containing the tentacles.

Most species of Platyctenea are more or less definitely associated with other organisms upon which they live as commensals. Species of *Coeloplana* are chiefly commensals on gorgonians and soft corals, but some live on starfishes and sea urchins. One platyctene has even become a parasite. The strange *Gastrodes parasiticum* lives embedded in the mantle of the pelagic tunicate, *Salpa*. On the other hand, the common West Indian *Vallicula* lives indiscriminately on plants and encrusting animals such as bryozoans and tunicates and seems not to be definitely associated with any particular organism.

DISTRIBUTION

As is often the case with planktonic animals, the free-swimming ctenophores have a very wide distribution. They are found from Arctic to Antarctic seas and a number of species are cosmopolitan. Temperature seems to be an important factor influencing distribution; some forms are found chiefly in cold waters, others in warm. Although predominantly dwellers in surface waters, ctenophores have been found at depths of nearly 10,000 feet. Most species are abundant, and because of their generally passive nature they are frequently swept by currents into vast swarms. As would be expected, the sessile and benthic platyctenes have more limited ranges, although even these have been able to attain rather wide distribution through drifting, by trailing out the tentacles to catch water currents, and by virtue of their free-swimming cydippid larvae. Because many of them are commensals, their distribution may be limited by that of their hosts.

4

Phylum Platyhelminthes

Introduction

Under the general term "worms" or its Latin equivalent "Vermes" have been grouped at one time or another all of the elongated, wormlike invertebrates, both segmented and unsegmented, as well as many animals not in the least wormlike. The early concept of a major taxonomic group consisting of "worms" was based on vague external similarities resulting from vermiform shape or soft consistency and had no scientific foundation whatever. Much nomenclatural and zoological juggling was required over a period of more than a hundred years before the major fundamental groups were correctly recognized. This juggling continues even now, for the taxonomic arrangement of many of the vermiform invertebrates is still debated.

Members of this phylum have been known since ancient times, when the conspicuous parasitic forms such as the tapeworms were observed and reported. The notion of a distinct taxonomic unit for the flatworms as distinguished from roundworms and annelid worms is attributable to C. Vogt (1851), who treated them as a class "Platyelmia." Subsequent workers raised the flatworms to phylum rank, recognized the three classes, Turbellaria, Trematoda, and Cestoda, and altered the name from Platyelmia to the etymologically preferable Platyhelminthes, from the Greek words for "flat" and "worm." The concept of the phylum as now accepted dates from Minot's work of 1876.

The phylum is known to the layman chiefly through its parasitic members, the tapeworms and the flukes, which have tremendous economic and medical significance and thus have attracted much attention from medical and veterinary researchers. The free-living Turbellaria are extremely abundant in the sea but on the whole have been much neglected systematically, perhaps because of the difficulties of studying them, as well as experimentally, because of the ready availability of fresh-water forms. Fresh-water planarians are noted for their regenerative capacities and several forms have been used widely in experimental work, among them *Dugesia*, *Phagocata*, and *Polycelis*. Some of the polyclad turbellarians of tropical seas are noted for their large size and spectacular coloration, easily rivalling the colorful opisthobranch mollusks in brilliance.

Although the Platyhelminthes have figured prominently in speculations about the early ancestry of the Metazoa and origin of the Bilateria, all conclusions dealing with flatworms have been based upon theoretical considerations of their structure. Lacking a skeletal system, flatworms have left no fossil evidence to guide our theories.

The phylum is divided into three classes, the Turbellaria or free-living flatworms, the Trematoda or flukes, and the Cestoda or tapeworms. Because of the complexity of life cycles and morphology of the various parasitic groups, which in themselves form a special subject, this account will be limited to the more familiar, free-living Turbellaria. Those wishing information regarding the parasites are referred to Hyman (1951).

Morphology and Classification

GENERAL FEATURES

The Platyhelminthes are bilaterally symmetrical, usually flattened, more or less elongated animals, hence the name "flatworms." They lack coelom, circulatory, and respiratory systems, but an excretory system of protonephridia is present. The digestive cavity is generally blind, lacking a definite anus, although anal pores exist in some forms. A mesenchymal connective tissue occupies the spaces between organ systems, and no skeletal structures are formed.

Flatworms are the first of the bilateral animals, the first to show a centralization of the nervous system near the anterior end with attendant cephalization. A distinct constriction clearly delimits the head in many forms, and this may carry tentacles or other projections as well as eyespots. In free-living forms, the ventral surface acts as an organ of locomotion and bears genital and oral openings.

The body consists of an outer epidermis of one layer, syncytial or cellular, at least partially ciliated, beneath which there is a subepidermal muscle layer, separated from the digestive tract and other organs by a cellular mesenchyme. There is no internal space except the cavity of the digestive tract. Hence, these animals lack a coelom and are called acoelomate.

The reproductive system is generally more complicated than the other systems in the flatworms, but it has very simple beginnings in the acoel turbellarians, growing more complex in the higher groups. The animals are usually hermaphrodites but have elaborate copulatory structures whereby internal cross fertilization is accomplished. Asexual reproduction, by transverse fission and by fragmentation, is common in many terrestrial and fresh-water turbellarians.

Free-living flatworms may reach a length of two feet but usually are smaller, and many of them are minute. They occupy a variety of habitats, in some cases terrestrial but mostly aquatic, mainly marine. Aside from their habits, the Turbellaria differ from the flat-worms of the two other classes in having a cellular or syncytial epidermis wholly or partially ciliated, usually containing structures known as rhabdoids. In the parasitic classes the body is covered by a cuticle and is not ciliated, and rhabdoids are absent.

The body is usually dorsoventrally compressed, ventrally flattened as a creeping surface, and dorsally convex. In shape the flatworms range from very wormlike (Figure 191) to broadly oval or even nearly circular (Figures 192 to 195). Certain marine polyclads have a ruffled margin that is employed in swimming (Figure 197). Although a constricted neck may clearly delimit the head from the body, as in the familiar planarians, this is more often not the case and the sides taper toward the head end, which may be narrower than the rest of the body. It may bear tentacle-like structures (Figure 196) and contains a concentration of sensory organs and nervous tissue.

The nervous system, with its definite trend toward anterior

Figures 191 to 197. Body form in Turbellaria. 191. Elongate triclad *Bipalium costaricense*. [Redrawn from Hyman, 1939.] 192. Acoel *Amphiscolops*. [Redrawn from Hyman, 1939.] 193. Rhabdocoel *Maehrenthalia*. [Redrawn from von Graff, 1882.] 194. Triclad *Sorocelis*. [Redrawn from Hyman, 1939.] 195. Polyclad *Pseudoceros*. 196. Head region of *Pseudoceros*, showing marginal tentacles. 197. Very large tropical polyclad *Nymphozoon*. [Redrawn from Hyman, 1959.] Code: A, marginal tentacles; B, cerebral eyes; C, statocyst; D, mouth; E, testis; F, vas deferens; G, penis; H, ovary.

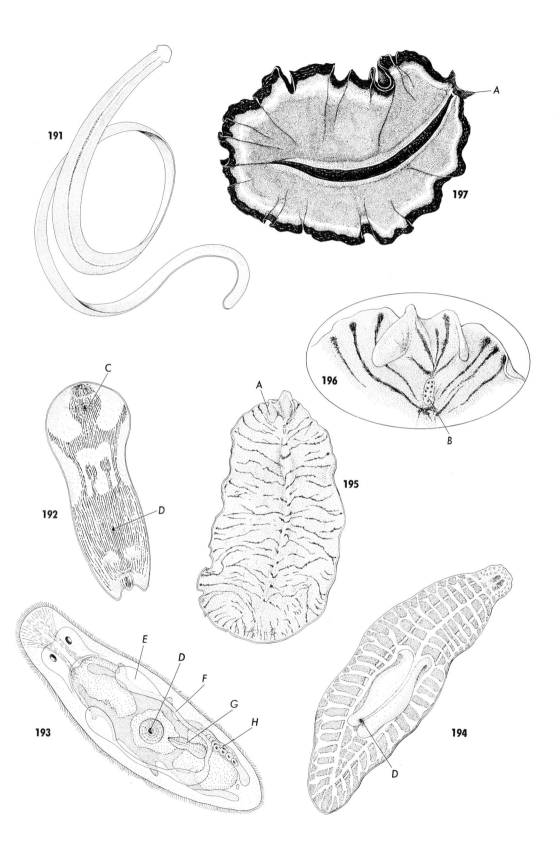

centralization, is a distinct advance over the coelenterate-cteno-phore condition but is definitely derivable from it via the most primitive flatworms. These have an epidermal nerve net weakly concentrated to form a ganglion in the head. In more advanced forms, the nerve plexus has moved to positions beneath the epidermis and beneath the muscle layer. The submuscular part of the system contains several longitudinal cords with ganglionic centers. Commonly, the two ventral cords are more prominent than the rest, and in some cases are the only nerve cords. A pair of cerebral ganglia at the anterior end is the principal nervous center and represents a brain. The longitudinal cords are joined by transverse connections and in forms with only one ventral pair results in a ladder-type nervous system. Sensory structures are numerous in the free-living Turbellaria. In most flatworms, the digestive cavity is blind, as in coelenterates; it may be richly branched in some, simple in others, or even completely absent.

An excretory system consisting of protonephridia with flame bulbs has arisen in the flatworms, but no special mechanisms for respiration and circulation have been developed.

HISTOLOGY AND STRUCTURE

The outer layer of free-living flatworms consists of an epidermis, more or less completely ciliated. In the small worms of the orders Acoela, Rhabdocoela, and Alloeocoela, the epidermis is wholly or partly a syncytium (Figure 198), but in larger animals such as triclads and polyclads, it consists of definite cells, polygonal in plan view and cuboidal or columnar in profile (Figure 199), which may be narrowed toward the base like many anthozoan epidermal cells. A remarkable feature of turbellarian epidermis is the location of the nuclei, which in some cases may descend through the sub-epidermal musculature, leaving the epidermal layer seemingly without nuclei. This condition, known as an *insunk epidermis* (Figure 200), is found in acoels and alloeocoels, and in some marine and terrestrial triclads.

Cilia may be developed over the entire epidermis (Figure 201), but often are limited to the ventral surface and absent from glandular and adhesive structures. Sensory regions may be richly ciliated, and the special tracts used in creeping are very strongly ciliated (Figure 202). A fibrillar system unites the epidermal cilia

Figures 198 to 201. Histology of Turbellaria. **198.** Syncytial epidermis of the rhabdocoel *Tetracelis.* [Redrawn from von Graff, 1908, after Luther, 1904.] **199.** Cellular epidermis of the terrestrial triclad *Geoplana.* [Redrawn from von Graff, 1899.] **200.** Insunk epidermis of the terrestrial triclad *Bipalium.* [Redrawn from von Graff, 1899.] **201.** Rhabdite-producing gland in epidermis of the acoel *Amphiscolops.* [Redrawn from von Graff, 1891.]

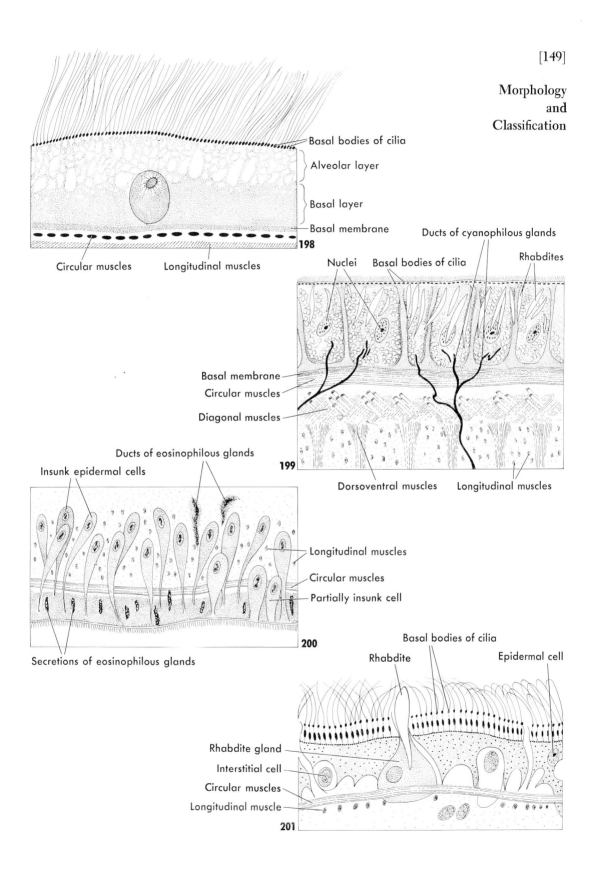

Basal bodies of cilia
Alveolar layer
Basal layer
Basal membrane

198

Circular muscles   Longitudinal muscles

Ducts of cyanophilous glands
Nuclei   Basal bodies of cilia   Rhabdites

Basal membrane
Circular muscles
Diagonal muscles

199

Dorsoventral muscles   Longitudinal muscles

Ducts of eosinophilous glands
Insunk epidermal cells

Longitudinal muscles
Circular muscles
Partially insunk cell

200

Secretions of eosinophilous glands

Basal bodies of cilia
Rhabdite   Epidermal cell

Rhabdite gland
Interstitial cell
Circular muscles
Longitudinal muscle

201

as in the ciliate protozoans. The turbellarians lack a cuticle such as is found in parasitic flatworms, although the epidermis of a few nonciliated forms having ectocommensal habits has a clear, cuticle-like outer zone.

The epidermis contains gland cells, sensory cells and inclusions known as *rhabdoids*. The latter are bodies of dubious function produced by gland cells. According to their form, they are called *rhabdites, rhammites,* and *chondrocysts*. Rhabdites (Figure 199) are secreted either by epidermal or by mesenchymal gland cells, but rhammites are produced only in the mesenchyme. Rhabdoids are minute capsules containing a fluid, which lie in the epidermis, sometimes in great numbers, at right angles to the surface. Under adverse conditions, the animal can expel the rhabdoids, where-upon they are thought to disintegrate into a mucus-like coating with protective properties, but facts are lacking as to their true function. Pseudorhabdites and sagittocysts are similar epidermal inclusions of even more indefinite nature. The epidermis of certain turbellarians may also contain nematocysts as the result of feeding upon hydras. These foreign bodies are resistant to digestion and ultimately pass to the epidermis of the worm, where they retain their ability to discharge upon mechanical stimulation. In the case of the rhabdocoel *Microstomum*, it is said that the nematocysts are used by the worm in capturing prey, and moreover that when their supplies are depleted, the worms will feed heavily upon hydras although they normally prefer other food.

Underlying the epidermis is a basement membrane which separates it from the mesenchyme below. Beneath this membrane are the subepidermal gland cells, connected to the surface by their long, necklike extensions. The subepidermal gland cells seem to be glands that are insunk from the superficial epidermis just as ordinary cells may in some cases be insunk. Two kinds of sub-epidermal glands can be recognized on the basis of staining reactions. Some take blue connective tissue stain and are called cyanophilous; others take eosin and are termed eosinophilous. The former are located abundantly in the anterior part of the ventral mesenchyme and discharge a slimy mucous secretion necessary for locomotion. A cluster of gland cells near the brain and discharging via tubules leading to pores at the anterior tip of the body is known as the *frontal gland* (Figure 204), evidently involved in food capture. It, too, is cyanophilous. The eosinophilous gland cells secrete a sticky substance and form the marginal adhesive zone, the adhesive disc, and the glandular margin surrounding the creeping sole. The necks of the eosinophilous cells terminate at the surface in adhesive papillae that enable the animals to cling very tightly to the substrate (Figure 205). A cluster of eosinophilous glands opens at the posterior tip of the body as a caudal gland, also adhesive in nature. The glands that produce the rhabdoids belong to this eosinophilous category, differing in that their secretion granules are rod-shaped rather than spherical.

Turbellarians are able to cling tightly to the substrate by virtue of the close adherence of the ventral surface aided by sticky secretions, but in many forms specialized adhesive structures are developed (Figure 206). One kind of adhesive organ consists merely of glandular areas of epidermis lacking cilia and rhabdites, located

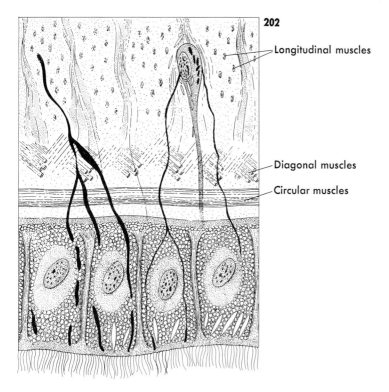

202
Longitudinal muscles

Diagonal muscles

Circular muscles

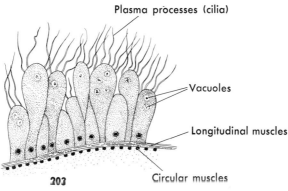

Plasma processes (cilia)

Vacuoles

Longitudinal muscles

203   Circular muscles

Figures 202 and 203. Histology of Turbellaria. **202.** Ventral epidermis of the terrestrial triclad *Geoplana*. [Redrawn from von Graff, 1889.] **203.** Intestinal epithelium of the rhabdocoel *Stenostomum*. [Redrawn from Ott, 1892.]

chiefly along the edge of the body. In a more complex type, these glandular areas are sunk in pits with lobulated rim and supplied with complex musculature permitting active protrusion and retraction. Finally, these structures may be distinctly cuplike, in some cases even stalked, and separated from the mesenchyme by a muscular septum. In such suckers, vacuum produced by the musculature is more important in adhesion than are the mucous secretions.

Flatworms receive information about their surroundings through a variety of receptors (Figure 207), more or less closely associated with the epidermis. These receptors may be unicellular or multicellular. Three kinds of primary sensory cells have been recognized: tangoreceptors, rheoreceptors, and chemoreceptors. Moreover, physiological evidence shows that photoreceptors must be distributed generally over the body, although these have not been recognized.

The tangoreceptors or tactile cells have a few widely diverging terminal branches with bristles of moderate length and are distributed generally over the body. The cells capable of detecting water currents, the rheoreceptors, are large, furnished with 20 to 100 long bristles extending beyond the cilia, and are situated in very specific locations. The cells that detect chemicals, the chemoreceptors, have a single dendrite and a short projecting process or peg, which penetrates the epithelial cells to reach the outside. From a few to as many as several hundreds of these sensory processes may pass through a single epithelial cell.

Sensory cells commonly are aggregated together as sense organs, in papillae, pits, depressions, epithelial patches, statocysts, and eyes. Examples of multicellular receptors are the chemoreceptors, mostly located near the head in grooves and pits with specialized epithelia lacking rhabdoids, gland openings, and having distinctive ciliation. Ciliary action is important in the directional function of such organs. It is possible to recognize a long-distance perception akin to smell, used as a warning, seeking, and detecting sense, and an immediate-contact perception similar to taste, used for testing substances and guiding the action of the mouthparts. Groups of

Figures 204 to 209. Histology and anatomy of Turbellaria. **204.** Frontal organ of *Hydrolimax*, composed of frontal glands and sensory fibers. [Adapted from Hyman, 1938.] **205.** Adhesive gland with papillae. [Redrawn from Wilhelmi, 1909.] **206.** (a) Enlarged view of adhesive organs (suckers) situated marginally on flatworm (b). [Redrawn from Korotneff, 1912.] **207.** Cross-sectional diagram of sensory cells at anterior end of *Mesostoma*. [Redrawn from von Gelei, 1930.] **208.** Pigment-spot ocellus of *Alaurina*. [Redrawn from Brinkmann, 1906.] **209.** Complex turbellarian eyes: (a) Inverse pigment-cup ocellus of triclad. [Redrawn from Hesse, 1897.] (b) Eye of land planarian with retinal clubs. [Redrawn from Hesse, 1902.]

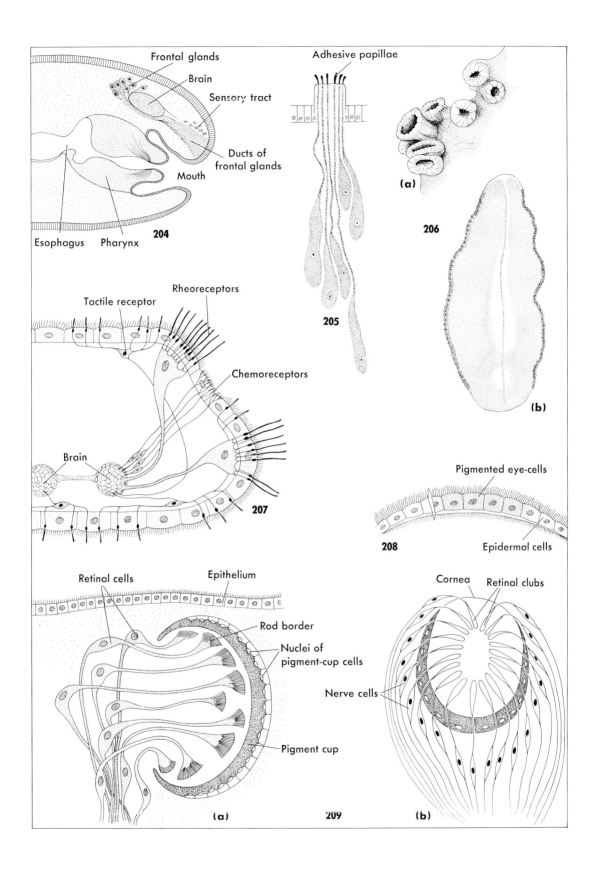

204

Frontal glands
Brain
Sensory tract
Ducts of frontal glands
Mouth
Esophagus
Pharynx

205

Adhesive papillae

206

(a)

(b)

207

Tactile receptor
Rheoreceptors
Chemoreceptors
Brain

208

Pigmented eye-cells
Epidermal cells

209

Retinal cells
Epithelium
Rod border
Nuclei of pigment-cup cells
Pigment cup

(a)

Cornea
Retinal clubs
Nerve cells

(b)

sensory cells are often associated with the openings of the frontal glands, together forming the *frontal organ* with chemoreceptive functions associated with perception of food.

Although the entire body of turbellarians is more or less sensitive to light, by virtue of unknown sensors, light perception is concentrated in special photoreceptors termed *ocelli*, or eyes. These are composed of neurosensory cells, pigment cells, supporting cells, and, in more advanced types, structures for the refraction of light. Two types of ocelli occur in turbellarians: the simple epidermal *pigment spot ocelli* and, usually, *pigment cup ocelli*. The former are epidermal spots consisting of retinal and pigment cells lying at the surface (Figure 208). Pigment cup ocelli are formed by the invagination of the pigment cells to form a pit in the epidermis, sometimes sunk into the mesenchyme into which the retinal cells project through the mouth of the cup or, in more complex eyes, between the pigment cells (Figure 209). The retinal cells are bipolar, with a clublike projection in the pigment cup and a fiber connecting the cell with the nervous system. In land planarians, the epithelium overlying the pigment cup forms a transparent cornea which may have the ability to focus light into a vague image. In the majority of forms, however, the ocelli certainly can do no more than distinguish light from dark. The retinal nerve fibers of eyes lying adjacent to the brain may form an optic nerve or join the brain directly. The fibers from eyes more distant ordinarily join the submuscular nerve plexus.

Many flatworms, notably the acoels, alloeocoels, and some rhabdocoels, have a statocyst (Figure 210) lying in close proximity to the brain. This structure is very similar to the statocysts of hydrozoans and may indeed be an ancestral reminiscence. It is made up of a lithocyte containing a statolith, encased in a vesicle-like cell. As in coelenterates, this is probably an organ of equilibrium, as it would enable the animal to detect changes of orientation through the effects of gravity upon the statolith.

The nervous sytem of turbellarians resembles that of coelenterates in that it is a net or plexus (Figure 211), but only in a few primitive forms is it located in the deep stratum of the epidermis as in the coelenterates. In most turbellarians, the main plexus is situated in the mesenchyme just within the subepidermal muscu-

Figures 210 to 213. Nervous system of Turbellaria. **210.** Statocyst of the alloeocoel *Hofstenia*. [Redrawn from Bock, 1923.] **211.** Nervous system of the acoel *Convoluta*. [Adapted from Delage, 1886.] **212.** Triclad nervous systems: (a) Brain of *Crenobia*. [Redrawn from Micoletzky, 1907.] (b) Cephalic neural plate of *Bipalium*. [Redrawn from von Graff, 1899.] 213. Nervous system of (a) the alloeocoel *Bothrioplana;* [Redrawn from Reisinger, 1925.] (b) The polyclad *Planocera*. [Redrawn from Lang, 1884.]

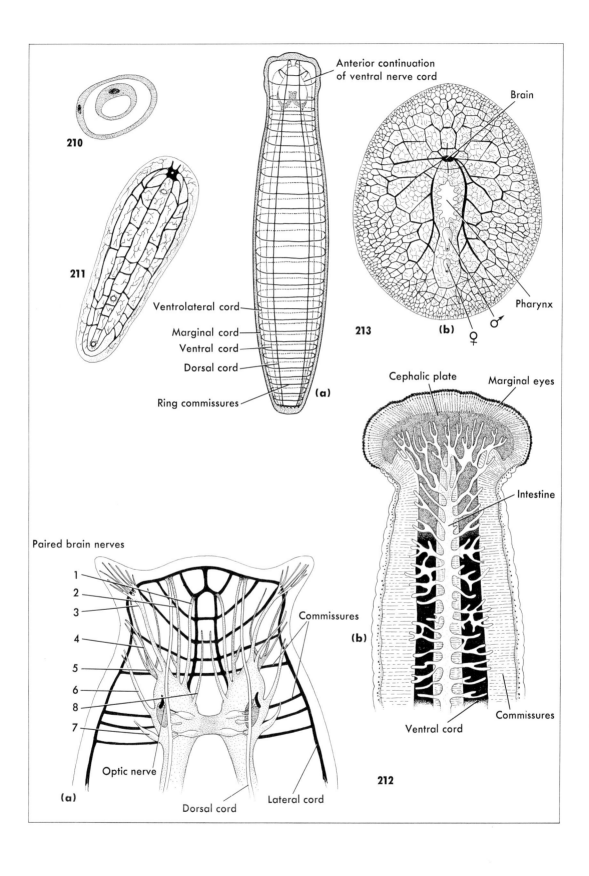

210

211

Anterior continuation
of ventral nerve cord

Ventrolateral cord

Marginal cord

Ventral cord

Dorsal cord

Ring commissures

(a)

Brain

Pharynx

213   **(b)** ♀ ♂

Cephalic plate   Marginal eyes

Intestine

(b)

Commissures

Ventral cord

212

Paired brain nerves

1
2
3

4

5
6
8
7

Optic nerve

(a)

Commissures

Dorsal cord   Lateral cord

lature and is called the *submuscular plexus*. Another, finer, net may lie just beneath the basement membrane of the epidermis and thus is called the *subepidermal plexus*. In many flatworms, some of the longitudinal components of the submuscular plexus are more strongly developed, usually in pairs and chiefly in the ventral part of the body. These are the *longitudinal nerve cords*. The anterior end of some of these cords may be somewhat thickened as primitive *cerebral ganglia*, and in some cases form a bilobed nerve center, called the *brain* (Figure 212), lying deeper in the mesenchyme of the head. Strong sensory nerves extend out from the brain to the cephalic sense organs and connect with the nerve cords and with the general plexus. The dorsal and ventral longitudinal cords may be joined by vertical commissures, and more or less regular transverse commissures join the longitudinal cords, sometimes forming evenly spaced rings around the body (Figure 213). The ventral submuscular plexus in terrestrial triclads may be strongly developed as a *ventral nerve plate*, a very dense mesh or solid nervous layer sometimes with traces of longitudinal thickenings. In forms with a ventral nerve plate, the extension of this layer in the head corresponds to the brain, but there are no definite cerebral ganglia. The nerve supplies of the pharynx and copulatory and adhesive structures are particularly strong.

Flatworms, like the coelenterates, have bipolar and multipolar nerve cells but show an advance in the presence, chiefly in the brain, of many unipolar neurons similar to those of higher invertebrates. In all, seven types of nerve cells have been recognized, as well as supporting glial cells, designated by the letters A to J (omitting I). Cells of the type designated F, found principally in the granular masses of the brain of some polyclads, are structurally identical with the globuli cells known from the brain of certain advanced nemerteans, polychaetes, mollusks, and arthropods. As in those groups, the globuli cells are located in one or two pairs of distinct masses of the brain and, as far as known, their processes terminate within the brain in association with the pathways leading from the higher sense organs. Some of the other types of nerve cells are of uncommon occurrence, being known in only one or a few types of flatworms.

The separation of the bodies of the nerve cells from the mass of fibers in the nerve cords and cerebral ganglia of the flatworms represents another important advance over the lower animals. This results in an outer rind of cells surrounding a core of fibers, and this development is accompanied by the differentiation of special supporting or glial cells.

Among the turbellarians there is a wide range of complexity in development of the brain, from no differentiation into special regions, to the extremely complex brains of certain marine polyclads which are on a level of histological differentiation equivalent to that of some nemerteans, mollusks, and arthropods.

In some primitive worms, the epidermis contains muscle fibers (Figure 214) just as in coelenterates, the outer ones longitudinal, the inner ones circular. However, in most turbellarians the musculature is complex and divided into subepidermal and mesenchymal components. The *subepidermal musculature* consists of a circular outer layer and a longitudinal inner layer of fibers lying immediately beneath the epidermis, separated from it by the basement membrane (if there is one). The longitudinal fibers may be in a uniform layer or grouped in bundles, and diagonal fibers, often in several layers, may separate the longitudinal and circular layers. This part of the musculature is thought to correspond with the muscular system found in coelenterates, and together with the epidermal muscle fibers of the primitive forms, is a suggestion of the origin of the flatworms from coelenterate stock.

The mesenchyme is traversed by muscles running in longitudinal, transverse, and dorsoventral directions, becoming very complicated in large flatworms. The muscle fibers are long, homogeneous, or fibrillar strands, sometimes cross-striated, surrounded by a nucleated protoplasmic sheath. Slender processes ramify out from the sheath and may perform nutritive functions. The very complex musculature of the turbellarians, with its multiple layers extending in every conceivable direction throughout the body, affords the extraordinary mobility of form that these animals have attained.

A mesenchymal connective tissue, specially termed *parenchyma*, surrounds the organs in the body of flatworms, solidly filling in all spaces except for some fluid-filled lacunae interpreted as blastocoel remnants. The mesenchyme may consist solely of separate, rounded cells but more commonly is a nucleated syncytium in which amoebocytes wander freely. The mesenchyme is not merely connective in nature but has important nutritive and excretory functions.

214

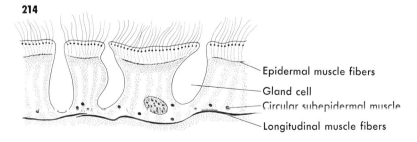

Epidermal muscle fibers
Gland cell
Circular subepidermal muscle
Longitudinal muscle fibers

Figure 214. Anatomy of Turbellaria. Epidermal muscle fibers in *Acoela*. [Redrawn from Luther, 1912.]

Figure 215. Anatomy of
Turbellaria. Diagrammatic
longitudinal section of the
alloeocoel *Hydrolimax* showing general organization.
[Adapted from Hyman,
1938.]

The coloration of turbellarians may be due to pigment, symbiotic algae, or food material in the digestive tract. Pigmentation is
located both in epidermal and mesenchymal cells. Pigment cells
as such are rare; instead, the color is contained in ordinary epidermal cells, dissolved in fluid contained in vacuoles, or in granular or rodlike forms in the cytoplasm. In the mesenchyme,
granular pigment may be scattered through the syncytium, dissolved in the fluid in syncytial spaces, or located in cells, chiefly
in dissolved form. Greenish and brownish colors may result from
the presence of zoochlorellae and zooxanthellae, the algae living
symbiotically in the mesenchyme of the worms. The color of
ingested food commonly is visible through the intestinal wall and
body of the animal to which it imparts a foreign hue.

The digestive system (Figure 215) consists of three parts:
mouth, pharynx, and intestine, sometimes with a short esophagus
connecting pharynx and intestine. Except for worms in one family
of rhabdocoels with parasitic habits, all turbellarians have a
mouth, located on the ventral surface in the midline, often about
the middle of the body. It is typically capable of considerable
distension to encompass large food items. In most turbellarians,
the mouth leads into a muscular tube or pharynx. In its simplest
form (Figure 216) the pharynx is no more than a tubular invagination lined with epidermis, without any special development of
the subepidermal muscles. In many forms, however, the inner end
of the pharyngeal wall is greatly thickened and muscular, forming
a bulb distinctly separated from the surrounding mesenchyme.
Because of this muscular bulb, such a pharynx is called *bulbous*
(Figure 217). The pharyngeal wall between the bulb and the

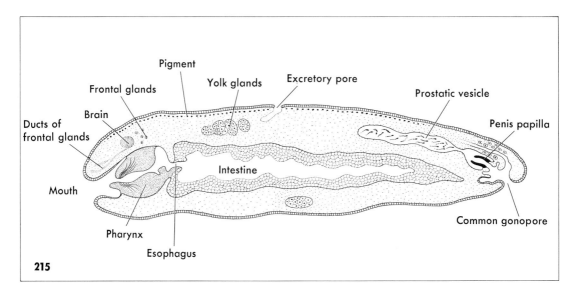

mouth is not thickened and forms the pharyngeal cavity. Its flexibility allows the bulbous portion to be everted through the mouth. The bulbous type of pharynx may lie at right angles to the body axis or parallel with it. Numerous gland cells are located between the muscle fibers in the pharynx, and the bulb contains a nerve plexus derived from the nerves leading from the ventral nerve cords or direct from the brain.

The most complex type of pharynx, general in triclads, polyclads, and a few others, is the *plicate pharynx* (Figure 218), which has the form of a pleated cylinder hanging down from the roof of the pharyngeal cavity or projecting into it from either before or behind. It varies from a simple cylinder to a ruffled circular curtain. Some species of flatworms may have several pharynges, either in a common pharyngeal cavity with one mouth, or with several mouths. This type of pharynx is structurally complex, consisting of several muscular layers interspersed with gland cells, a nerve plexus, and radial muscle fibers. The epithelium has the construction described as *insunk*—that is, the nuclei are separated from the bodies of the epidermal cells by the intervening subepidermal muscle layer. The pharyngeal nerve plexus arises from the

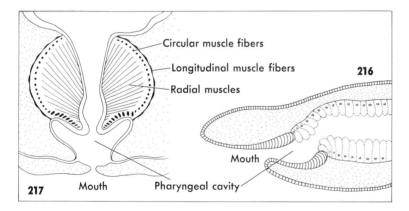

Figures 216 and 217. Anatomy of Turbellaria. 216. Pharynx of the pharynx simplex type in the rhabdocoel *Macrostomum*. [Redrawn from von Graff, 1882.] 217. Bulbous pharynx of the rosulate type. [Adapted from von Graff, 1904; and Hyman, 1951.]

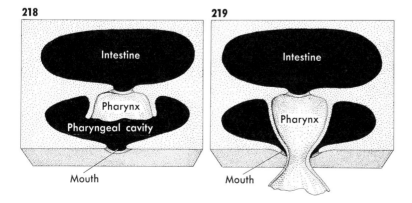

Figures 218 and 219. Diagram of action of plicate pharynx. 218. In retracted position. 219. Everted in feeding position.

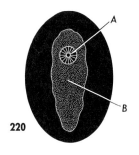

220

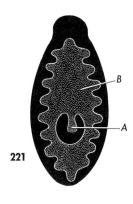

221

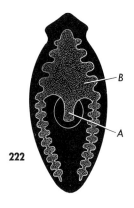

222

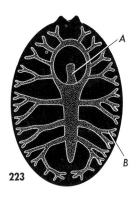

223

ventral nerve cords and in some worms reaches such complexity, with all the necessary components, that the experimentally isolated pharynx can act independently. In worms with a plicate pharynx, food is not ingested through the mouth, but through the opening of the pharynx protruded through the mouth (Figure 219).

The digestive cavity or *intestine* ranges in form from a simple chamber to a complex system of branching or even anastomosing diverticula (Figures 220 to 223). The acoels do not have any permanent intestine, but temporary spaces form around food in the mesenchyme during digestion. Other types of turbellarians regularly have an intestine. It is lined with gastrodermis (Figure 203) composed of phagocytic cells and sometimes granular clubs in addition, and may be ciliated or not depending upon taxonomic group. The complexity of the intestine differs in the various orders of Turbellaria and provides one of the bases for their recognition.

The fundamental unit of the turbellarian excretory system is the *protonephridium*. This is made up of a nephridial tubule which gives off many small branchlets or capillaries, terminating in bulblike tips enclosing a tuft of long cilia. Each capillary and its terminal bulb is a single cell, the *flame cell*, so called because of the flickering, flamelike beating of the cilia in the flame bulb. Sometimes, one flame cell may have several flame bulbs (Figure 224). The number and arrangement of protonephridia varies among the turbellarian orders, as does their connection with the outside. They may empty by way of one or more nephridiopores (Figure 225), located either dorsally or ventrally on the animal, or into the pharyngeal cavity or the genital antrum. All turbellarians except the acoels have a protonephridial excretory system, and it is usually better developed in the fresh-water flatworms than in those of other habitats.

The reproductive system (Figure 226) of turbellarians contains complete male and female components, as these animals are hermaphroditic. Thus, each individual has both *ovaries* and *testes* and both male and female copulatory appurtenances (Figure 227).

Except for the acoels, in which the sex cells occur freely in the mesenchyme, the turbellarians have gonads that are clearly delimited from the general mesenchyme (Figure 226). In the majority of free-living flatworms, there is a small number of gonads, one or a few pairs of testes, and one pair of ovaries, sometimes a single one, but in the polyclads both testes and ovaries are numerous.

Figures 220 to 223. Shape of intestine in turbellaria. **220.** Rhabdocoel. **221.** Alloeocoel. **222.** Triclad. **223.** Polyclad. Code: A, pharynx; B, intestine.

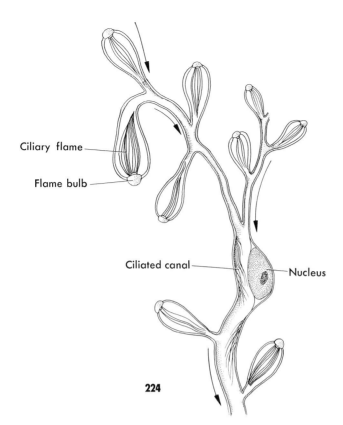

Ciliary flame

Flame bulb

Ciliated canal — Nucleus

224

Figure 224. Excretory system in Turbellaria. Diagram of part of nephridial cell with multiple flame bulbs. [Adapted from Reisinger, 1923.]

In the male portion of the system, the testes lead, via sperm ductules if there are many testes or a sperm duct if there are few, to the copulatory apparatus. A sperm-storage area, the *spermiducal vesicle*, may precede the final ejaculatory duct. The copulatory complex includes seminal vesicle, prostatic apparatus, and penis.

The *seminal vesicle*, also a sperm-storage area, participates in sperm transport by means of its muscular walls. The *prostatic glands* commonly empty into a *prostatic vesicle*, likewise a vessel with thick muscular walls, then to the *ejaculatory duct*. The prostatic glands secrete a granular material that is mixed with the sperm and discharged with it during copulation. The distal part of the male canal is modified as an intromittent organ called *penis*, or can be everted to form a copulatory structure called *cirrus*. At rest, the penis lies retracted within a chamber, the *male antrum*, into the lumen of which it projects as a conical penis papilla. The male antrum may open directly to the outside by a *male gonopore*, or join the *female antrum* to form a common antrum with a *common gonopore*, or even enter the pharyngeal cavity. During copulation, muscular action elongates the penis to its functional position outside the body.

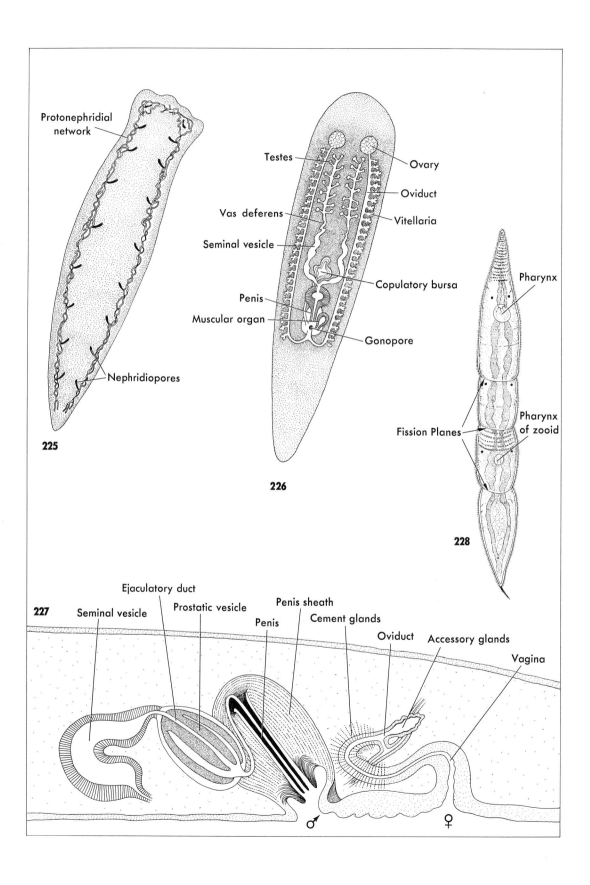

225

Protonephridial network

Nephridiopores

226

Testes

Ovary

Vas deferens

Oviduct

Seminal vesicle

Vitellaria

Copulatory bursa

Penis

Muscular organ

Gonopore

228

Pharynx

Fission Planes

Pharynx of zooid

227

Ejaculatory duct

Seminal vesicle

Prostatic vesicle

Penis

Penis sheath

Cement glands

Oviduct

Accessory glands

Vagina

♂

♀

The female system has a wide diversity of form, varying from the condition in acoels, in which there are no female structures except the sex cells loose in the mesenchyme, to that of the more advanced flatworms in which there is a complex system including, besides the ovaries, special glands to produce the yolk cells, canals for the passage of eggs, uteri for storage of eggs, chambers for the receipt and storage of sperm, and a cavity to accommodate the penis of the partner during copulation.

In flatworms without a female genital tract, the eggs reach the outside either via the mouth or through rupture of the body (resulting in death of the parent). More often there is an *oviduct* leading toward a *gonopore*. Because the eggs of many flatworms do not have intrinsic yolk their food supplies are stored in separate *yolk cells*. The latter are formed either in a special yolk-producing region of the ovary or in completely separate *yolk glands* which discharge into the oviducts. During oviposition, numerous yolk cells are encased with the eggs in the egg capsule. In some turbellarians, notably the marine forms which have a swimming larval stage, the yolk supply is incorporated in the egg in conventional manner, and yolk glands are absent.

The oviduct leads into the female copulatory apparatus (Figure 227). This includes a chamber to receive sperm, which is given different names depending upon the length of time that sperm are retained in it. In many instances it is called a bursa: a *copulatory bursa* if sperm remain in it only a brief time, or a *seminal bursa* if they remain for a longer time. A short canal connects the bursa with the antrum, which opens to the exterior via the gonopore.

A part of the oviduct may be enlarged as a storage area for ripe eggs awaiting oviposition, or a special blind canal may lead off from the antrum for this purpose. Such egg storage structures are called *uteri*. In their passage from the body, the eggs usually receive their capsular investment from glands in the antrum, and then are smeared with adhesive secretions of the cement glands as they leave the genital pore.

Even though the turbellarians are mostly hermaphroditic, they do not fertilize themselves. Definite cases of self-fertilization are extremely rare. Sperm transfer is achieved between individuals by means of hypodermic impregnation or copulation. In the former method, one animal forces its armed penis through the epidermis

Figures 225 to 228. Excretory and reproductive systems in Turbellaria.
225. Diagram of triclad nephridial system. [Redrawn from Wilhelmi, 1906.]
226. Diagram of triclad reproductive system. [Redrawn from Steinmann, 1911.] **227.** Diagram of triclad copulatory apparatus. [Redrawn from Lang, 1884.] **228.** The catenulid rhabdocoel *Alaurina* producing a chain of zooids by transverse fission. [Redrawn from Ivanov, 1955.]

of another and deposits sperm in the mesenchyme. More often, mutual copulation resulting in sperm exchange takes place. The protruded copulatory organ of each partner is inserted into the female or common gonopore or into the bursal pore of the other, permitting mutual insemination.

CLASSIFICATION, PHYLUM PLATYHELMINTHES

I. Class Turbellaria. Free-living unsegmented flatworms having a definite, usually ciliated epidermis, not a cuticle; a digestive tract is present in all orders but one, and in that one temporary digestive spaces form around ingested food (five orders).
   A. Order Acoela. Minute flatworms with mouth but no intestine; no definite excretory system or genital tract.
   B. Order Rhabdocoela. Small flatworms with definite but simple digestive tract without branches or diverticula; excretory and genital systems usually present (four suborders).
   C. Order Alloeocoela. Small flatworms with digestive tract sometimes having short diverticula; excretory and reproductive systems well developed (four suborders).
   D. Order Tricladida. Flatworms of moderate size, with three-branched intestine, one branch extending forward from the pharynx, two posteriorly (three suborders).
   E. Order Polycladida. Mostly large flatworms with intestine having many branches, often anastomosed (two suborders).
II. Class Trematoda. Parasitic unsegmented flatworms usually known as flukes; body covered with cuticle, lacking epidermis; digestive system complete (three orders).
III. Class Cestoda. Parasitic flatworms known as tape worms, in which body is usually segmented, often very long; epidermis lacking, surface covered with cuticle; digestive system absent (nine orders).

The nature of the digestive tract and related structures forms a major feature in distinguishing the five turbellarian orders. In the order Acoela (*a*, without; *coela*, cavity), all of which are small animals one or a few millimeters in length, there is no digestive cavity at all, and the mouth opens via a simple tubular pharynx into the interior mesenchyme. Ingested food is digested by phagocytic cells scattered through the mesenchyme or by a central digestive syncytium in which temporary digestive spaces form around food particles. Acoels are oval in shape, varying from rather stout to elongate (Figure 192). Those containing symbiotic algae are brown or green but otherwise they are dull in color. Some have caudal lobes or a tail filament, but projections from the head region are lacking. When present, there are two to four eyes. The nervous system is an epidermal plexus in the simpler acoels but has moved to a position below the muscle layer in the majority of forms. Three to six pairs of longitudinal nerve strands may be differentiated. No excretory system is present in this order.

Acoels are hermaphroditic flatworms with a relatively simple reproductive system. Mesenchyme cells give rise directly to eggs and sperm, which migrate in longitudinal bands toward the tail. The sperm accumulate in single or paired seminal vesicles leading to two or four simple penes. The latter may have prostatic glands opening into their bases, and sometimes a muscular penis-papilla armed with stylets is present. The female system is extremely simple, lacking oviducts and sometimes all other female parts, hence the eggs must be discharged either by way of the mouth or through rupture of the body wall. In some forms a vagina is present, opening separately in front of the male pore or via a common gonopore. In the simplest method of sperm transfer, the penis armed with stylets is forced through the epidermis of the partner in any available place and sperm is injected into the mesenchyme. Usually, however, impregnation is effected by mutual copulation, in which each partner inserts the protruded copulatory organ into the female orifice or common gonopore of the other, and sperm is exchanged. One or more seminal bursae receive the sperm and pass it along to the eggs. The eggs are deposited, either through the gonopore, mouth, or a rupture in the body wall, depending upon the complexity of the female system. They may be enclosed in a capsule or in a mass of gelatinous material and stuck to solid objects.

Flatworms of the order Rhabdocoela are small, similar in size to the acoels (Figure 193). However, they have a definite digestive cavity of simple nature, consisting of a rounded or elongate sac, as well as an excretory system of one or two protonephridia. Some kinds known as Kalyptorhynchia have at the anterior end a curious food-catching organ called a *proboscis* although the mouth does not open through it. This eversible structure snares small organisms by rapid action and sticky secretion and conveys them to the mouth. In rhabdocoels, the sex cells are concentrated in definite gonads, a pair of testes, and one or two ovaries. The male copulatory structures include a penis of various form and seminal and prostatic vesicles. The female structures consist of seminal or copulatory bursa, seminal receptacle, uteri, yolk glands, and other gland cells. These worms achieve mutual fertilization by a process of copulation and deposit encapsulated eggs singly. They may be attached by a stalk or unattached. Some families produce two kinds of eggs, one with thin shells which hatch without undergoing a dormant period, and one with thick shells, called dormant eggs, which are adapted for overwintering under adverse conditions. Self-fertilization, very unusual in turbellarians, is known to occur in some rhabdocoels. The order is divided into four suborders, in some of which asexual reproduction is characteristic. Commensal and, rarely, parasitic habits are prevalent in several groups.

A third order is the Alloeocoela, which occupy an intermediate position between the acoels and the triclads, to be considered next. Even the simplest are distinguishable from acoels by the presence of a definite intestine (Figure 215) which ranges in complexity from a simple cavity to a lobulated structure approaching the form of a triclad digestive tract. They are slender or stout cylindrical worms, some with statocysts, and with or without eyes. The nervous system has three or four pairs of longitudinal cords joined by commissures. The protonephridia are branched and open by multiple nephridiopores. The gonads are well formed and consist of several testes and a pair of ovaries, and the copulatory apparatus conforms with the general structure already mentioned but differs in details in the various taxonomic subdivisions.

As their name implies, the Tricladida are turbellarians with a three-branched digestive cavity (Figure 194). They are worms of moderate size, ranging in length from a few millimeters up to several centimeters, of distinctly flattened, elongate form. In some familiar types, such as the common planarians, the head is well defined and furnished with lateral projections called *auricles*, but in many there is no boundary between head and body. The epidermis is ciliated on the ventral creeping surface and is kept moist by a mucous coating throughout. The ventral surface, and sometimes also the edge of the body, is provided with glandulomuscular adhesive organs. The nervous system is generally composed of a subepidermal and a submuscular plexus with three or four pairs of longitudinal cords developed in the latter. These are connected by commissures and by the reticulations of the nerve plexus. In some kinds, only the ventral cords are present and in others these are replaced by a ventral *nerve plate*, a thick layer of nervous tissue in the mesenchyme, which joins the submuscular plexus laterally. The ventral cords may be thickened anteriorly to form a brain, but there is no brain in species with a nerve plate. Eyes may be well developed as in the planarians or totally absent as in cave-dwelling species and a few others. A characteristic feature is the plicate pharynx, which leads to the three-branched digestive cavity (Figure 222); one branch extends forward and two to the rear. The excretory system consists of a network of nephridial tubules along each side of the body, opening by way of numerous nephridiopores. Reproductive organs include two ovaries, usually more than two testes, and the copulatory apparatus. The eggs, encased in a capsule or cocoon, pass out through the common gonopore, and are attached to stones by a sticky substance. The triclads are further divided into three suborders, each with special ecological requirements. One group is wholly marine, another is limited to fresh waters, and the third is terrestrial (Figure 191), living in the leaf mold and other moist situations in tropical jungles but intolerant of submersion.

The fifth and last order of turbellarians is the Polycladida, characterized by the highly complicated branchings of the digestive tract (Figure 223). Flatworms of this order are of moderate to considerable size and, in some families, brilliant coloration (Figure 195). They are generally of a very flattened, ovate shape, with a pair of tentacles located either on the dorsal surface in the vicinity of the brain or on the anterior margin. They glide about on the ventral surface of the body, but some are able to swim by graceful undulations of the margin (Figure 197) and a few are pelagic. Organs of attachment or adhesion are not of general occurrence in this order, although a ventral adhesive disc is present in some forms and adhesive cells in others. Eyes are numerous on the anterior part of the body, often concentrated in clusters near the tentacles and brain, and sometimes along the margins. The nervous system consists of a close subepidermal plexus and a wide submuscular net, strongest in the ventral part of the body. The only indication of nerve cords are the large strands of the ventral plexus extending from the brain posteriorly beside the pharynx. The pharynx is ruffled or plicated and leads into the principal intestinal cavity, lying in the midline. Numerous intestinal branches extend outward from this toward the margins, commonly branching and anastomosing to form a complicated system. Strangely enough, the excretory system is poorly known in this order of flatworms, although they are known to have flame bulbs as in the other groups. The reproductive system consists of many ovaries and testes and complicated copulatory structures sometimes with either the male or the female apparatus repeated. As in virtually all other flatworms, cross fertilization is the rule, and this is achieved mutually by copulation or by hypodermic impregnation. The polyclads are divided into two suborders on the basis of a ventral adhesive disc—the Acotylea (without) and the Cotylea (with). With the exception of one fresh-water species, the entire order is marine.

Reproduction and Embryology

ASEXUAL REPRODUCTION

Multiplication by *transverse fission* occurs in some rhabdocoels and fresh-water and terrestrial triclads. In the rhabdocoels, the body first develops lateral indentations and then the fission plane becomes evident. Successive fission planes appear so that the worm eventually consists of an anterior region followed by a series of zooids, or incipient worms each of which becomes well differentiated before it separates from the chain (Figure 228). The worms reproduce repeatedly by fission until they become sexually mature, at which time fission ceases and their powers of regeneration may be lost as well.

Certain triclads regularly divide transversely into two individuals. Usually the fission plane is physiological rather than morphological and located posterior to the pharynx, although it may cut through the pharynx or anterior to it. The worm attaches firmly to the substrate at the posterior end while continuing to move forward. The body is thus stretched to the breaking point. The posterior portion regenerates an anterior and the anterior, a new tail. This type of reproduction commonly occurs when the worms are not sexually active. Another type of multiplication, by *fragmentation*, occurs in some triclads. These worms break into numerous small pieces which encyst in mucus, undergo a reorganization within the cyst, and some weeks later emerge as tiny worms indistinguishable from natural young hatched from eggs.

Turbellarians are famous for their regenerative powers and have been used experimentally to study the processes of regeneration. However, this capacity is not universal, some species being capable only of wound-healing. Those which reproduce asexually, the rhabdocoels and triclads, regenerate readily, and in some, a piece from any part of the body except that anterior to the cerebral ganglia will grow into a new worm. The polarity of the anteroposterior axis strongly influences regeneration: anterior structures will form from the anterior part of a piece, and posterior structures from the posterior cut surface. Physiological axial gradients have been studied extensively in experiments on planarian worms in an effort to illuminate their role in determining the path of development. The interested reader is referred to Child (1941) and Hamburger (1966).

SEXUAL REPRODUCTION

The consideration of embryology will be limited to the primitive, relatively unmodified development of worms in which the yolk is contained within the egg (*entolecithal eggs*), not produced separately by yolk glands. Acoels, some rhabdocoels and alloeocoels, and all polyclads have entolecithal eggs. Of these, the embryology of the polyclads is best known and will be summarized here.

The eggs are laid in capsules which may have special structures ("escape hatches") through which the young emerge when intracapsular development is complete. Most species hatch as miniature adults which may swim for a time close to the bottom but soon commence creeping and feeding. Others, such as *Hoploplana*, *Thysanozoon*, and *Pseudoceros*, emerge in a free-swimming planktonic form known as Müller's larva (Figures 235, 237).

Cleavage is the inequal determinate type known as *spiral cleavage*, which also occurs in annelids and molluscs. The first two meridional cleavages result in four cells, often of different sizes, and are followed by a latitudinal third cleavage in which four *micromeres* are divided from the four large cells or *macromeres* (Figure 229). The micromeres, located around the animal pole, are often virtually yolkless, the yolk being concentrated in the macromeres. The cleavage pattern is called spiral because in this third and in several succeeding divisions, the axis of the spindles of the dividing cells is tilted, with reference to the animal–vegetal axis. In a view of the animal pole of the embryo, the spindles of the four cells dividing in the third cleavage will be inclined in a clockwise (*dexiotropic*) direction. Then, in the fourth cleavage,

Figures 229 to 231. Embryology of Turbellaria. **229.** Embryo of *Notoplana* in eight-cell stage. **230.** same in twelve-cell stage. **231.** Same in twenty-four-cell stage. [All redrawn from Kato, 1940.] Code: A, micromere; B, macromere.

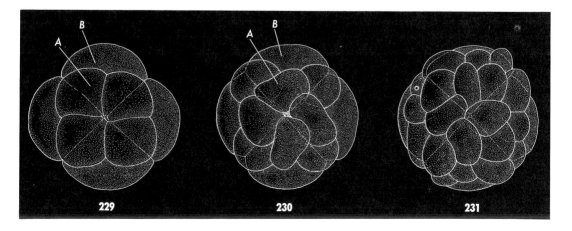

229   230   231

the spindles will be oriented in the opposite or counterclockwise (*laeotropic*) direction (Figure 230). This alternation continues until divisions of the macromeres have produced four groups (quartets) of micromeres. Rarely the spindles will first be tilted in a counterclockwise direction.

Spiral cleavage is described as determinate because careful studies of *cell lineage* have shown that each group of cells will form a particular part of the larval or adult worm. For example, the first quartet of micromeres, those formed in the third cleavage, and all the cells produced by their divisions, will form the *ectoderm* of the anterior dorsal part of the body, the pigment cells of the eyes, the nervous system with cerebral ganglia, and also the frontal glands. The descendants of the second and third quartets form more ectoderm as well as ectomesoderm from which the muscles and mesenchyme of the pharynx will arise. The fourth quartet of micromeres are larger and yolkier than the other micromeres. Three of these cells, together with the four yolky macromeres, are used to nourish the growing embryo. The fourth micromere, designated as *4d*, has a tremendous potentiality, for from its descendants will develop all of the *entoderm* and *entomesoderm*. In the first division of 4d, the lines of cells which will give rise to these two germ layers are segregated. The descendants of one cell, 4d^1, will form the intestine (entoderm), while those of 4d^2 will differentiate into mesenchyme, muscles, glands, and the reproductive system (entomesoderm).

The blastula has an inconspicuous blastocoel or none at all. Gastrulation comes about largely through epiboly, the micromeres gradually covering the macromeres and the fourth quartet micromeres. Since these yolky cells then occupy the center of the embryo, there is no *archenteron* and the stage is a *stereogastrula*. A blastopore is present for a short time and then closes, owing to multiplication of the micromeres. Nearby, close to the vegetal pole where the blastopore was, an invagination of ectoderm commences. It leaves an opening, the mouth, and forms a tube which will become the lining of the pharynx and will connect with the intestine developing from the entodermal descendants of 4d^1 (Figure 232). The frontal glands are in apical position, and in some species a tuft of stiff sensory flagella extends out from them. The epidermis is ciliated.

The embryo next begins a period of differential growth in which the principal body axis, until now animal-vegetal, is altered to anteroposterior. The result is that the animal pole, with frontal glands and developing cerebral ganglia, is gradually moved to one side, the future anterior end, while in the vegetal area, which will be ventral, the mouth is pushed in the opposite direction posteriorly (Figures 233, 234). This elongation has begun a dorsoventral flattening of the body which continues. Development henceforth consists of further differentiation, and most acotylean species soon hatch as miniature flatworms.

Others (the Cotylea and some Acotylea) develop four, six, or eight posteriorly directed, heavily ciliated lobes, after flattening and the shift to anteroposterior orientation have begun. The lobes are paired. In those with eight lobes, there is an anterior ventral pair between frontal glands and mouth, a pair by the mouth, another pair posterior to these, and another near the future posterior end of the body (Figure 235). Sometimes the lobes are mere buds when the larva hatches. If there are eight or six lobes, it is known as *Müller's larva* (Figures 235, 236); if four, as in *Stylochus*, *Götte's larva*. After a brief planktonic period, the larva commences to resorb the lobes as it further elongates and flattens, and it soon settles on the bottom.

Physiology

As flatworms, particularly planarians, have been used extensively in experimental work, a substantial amount of information is known about their biology. Small species mostly are short-lived, succumbing to adverse conditions at the onset of winter, leaving behind dormant eggs to produce a new generation the next spring. Some can encyst as adults and thus survive unfavorable conditions for a longer time. Some of the larger planarians have a greater life span, as much as two or three years, but little is known of the longevity of the large marine forms. Laboratory-reared colonies of species that specialize in asexual reproduction may remain healthy for several years under proper conditions, propagating freely by fission.

Activities may have a distinctly cyclic pattern usually related to outside forces. Asexual as well as sexual reproduction occur periodically, sometimes alternately, but many asexual generations can be produced without intervention of a sexual period. In some forms, asexual worms will develop sex organs and reproduce after exposure to a period of low temperature. In nature, the seasons provide these temperature changes, inducing sexuality with the increase in temperature in spring, but an inherent cycle is lacking as the animals can be experimentally made to breed at intervals of much less than a year.

Deterioration and general senescence often follows upon periods of sexual activity or results from extended laboratory cul-

Phylum
Platyhelminthes

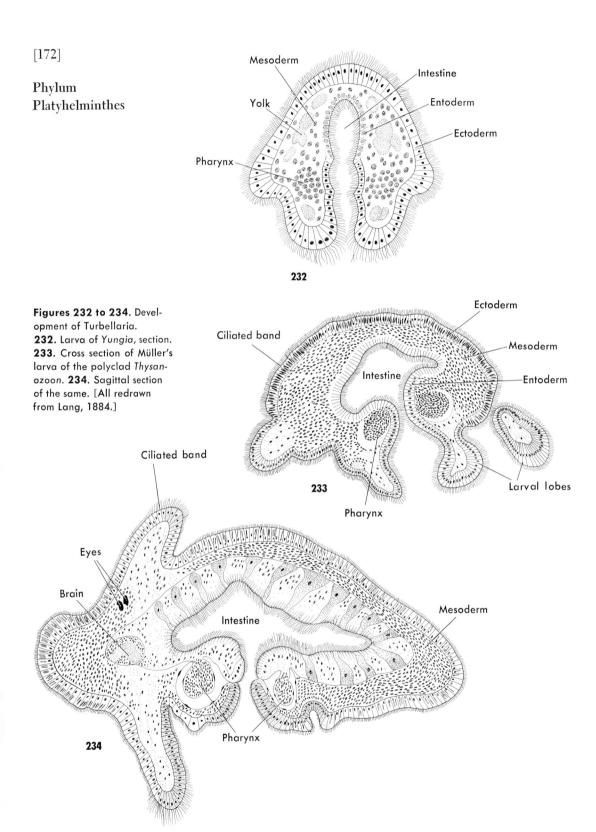

Figures 232 to 234. Development of Turbellaria.
232. Larva of *Yungia*, section.
233. Cross section of Müller's larva of the polyclad *Thysanozoon*. **234.** Sagittal section of the same. [All redrawn from Lang, 1884.]

ture. The end result may be disintegration and death, or fragmentation of the animal into small pieces which then encyst and subsequently emerge as new individuals. This process is a natural result of sustained satisfactory conditions and it can be forestalled experimentally by preventing growth by underfeeding. Such starved animals do not grow and thus never get "old."

RESPIRATION

The metabolism of turbellarians requires oxygen just as does that of all other metazoans. However, the flatworms have developed no transport mechanism to convey it because their tissues are in direct contact with the oxygen-rich medium or removed from it by only a very small distance. Thus it is possible for them to take up oxygen and give off carbon dioxide by diffusion through the surface of the body. There is no oxygen carrier such as the hemoglobin of vertebrates. In the metabolic process, the flatworm obtains energy from food substances through oxidation by a dehydrogenase enzyme which reduces cytochrome, a respiratory pigment present in practically all aerobic animal cells. To regain its potency, the cytochrome reduces an oxidase enzyme which in turn obtains its oxygen from the surrounding medium.

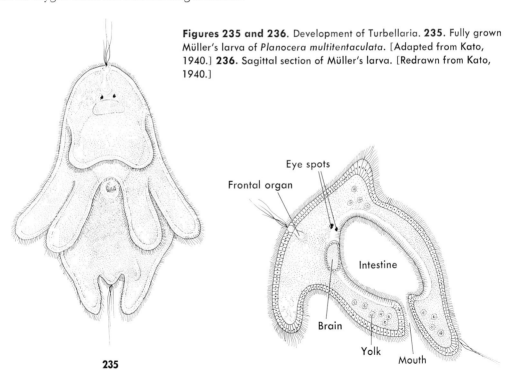

Figures 235 and 236. Development of Turbellaria. **235.** Fully grown Müller's larva of *Planocera multitentaculata.* [Adapted from Kato, 1940.] **236.** Sagittal section of Müller's larva. [Redrawn from Kato, 1940.]

Eye spots

Frontal organ

Intestine

Brain

Yolk

Mouth

235

236

OSMOREGULATION

Aquatic animals in general maintain a constant balance between the salt content of their tissues and that of the surrounding medium. As long as the animal remains in water with a relatively constant salt content the balance remains undisturbed. A marine flatworm placed in fresh water becomes bloated by uptake of water by its tissues under reduced osmotic pressure. Conversely, a fresh-water worm placed in sea water loses water to the surrounding medium and so shrinks. They have no efficient means of controlling the passage of salts and water into and out of the tissues. Thus, they tend to inhabit either fresh water or sea water, but very few venture into brackish situations because fluctuations of salinity may be large there. However, there are species that live in habitats undergoing great changes in salinity daily, due to fresh-water runoff into marine situations, or from evaporation of water from tide pools. As they can survive and show less disruption of osmotic balance than the environmental change calls for, it follows that they have some osmoregulatory mechanism. This is also borne out by the fact that the tissues of marine turbellarians have a distinctly lower concentration of salts than in the sea, and fresh-water forms have a higher concentration of salts than does fresh water.

Although many fresh-water organisms are quite sensitive to the hydrogen-ion concentration of the water, turbellarians seem able to tolerate almost any condition in this respect.

NERVOUS AND SENSORY REACTIONS

Even though many workers have studied various kinds of turbellarians from the standpoint of their neurophysiology, our knowledge is still very fragmentary in this area. The turbellarians are particularly interesting in this connection because they are the lowest animals in the phylogenetic sequence to have a brain. Many activities are under nervous control, among them ciliary locomotion, muscular motions including various types of looping and leech-like actions, muscular waves along the ventral surface, avoidance reactions, searching movements by the anterior end, feeding, swimming, and many more.

Experiments on various turbellarians show that locomotion is not dependent upon the brain, as decerebrated worms remain active and responsive to stimuli. Damage done to the chemoreceptors in such experiments diminishes the ability to recognize food to varying extent depending upon species. Some are only moderately affected whereas others cannot recognize food at all, but when it is encountered by the pharynx by chance, swallowing

is normal in all. Negative responses to touch persist in decerebrated animals but positive responses are obliterated.

Polyclads have been experimentally conditioned to cease crawling when stimulated by light, and this conditioning requires the
brain. However, once acquired, a conditioned response can be
retained by the worm following decapitation.

Regeneration in the absence of the brain varies among the
turbellarians. Many polyclads are unable to regenerate but may
survive in a quiescent state for long periods. A few will respond
to strong stimulation by crawling or swimming, but others remain
inert. However, headless pieces of triclads readily regenerate new
heads, as is well known. It appears that there is some justification
for the notion that the turbellarian brain is necessary chiefly to
maintain a general level of excitability or nervous tone rather than
for the control of specific activities, but it is also certain that the
various turbellarian groups differ widely in this regard.

The effects of various taxes and the action of other stimuli upon
them have been extensively investigated in triclads.

LOCOMOTION

The epidermis of turbellarians is largely, if not completely
ciliated, but the locomotion of only the small species, and probably the young of others, is due to the cilia. The triclads and
polyclads progress by means of muscular action, either gliding or,
less frequently, swimming. Waves pass from front to rear, either
across the whole lower surface or separately along the two halves
in an alternating step-wise action. When annoyed, many turbellarians hurry in inch-worm style by rapid extension and contraction
of the body, alternately clinging and releasing the adhesive organs. Some of the large marine polyclads can swim vigorously by
graceful muscular undulations of their ruffled margins, and some
smaller species swim by flexing the body alternately dorsally and
ventrally or by very rapid flittering motions of their edges. Young
flatworms can also swim by ciliary action, and small individuals
are a frequent component of the inshore plankton of tropical
regions.

FEEDING AND DIGESTION

Turbellarians, even the acoels which lack a digestive cavity,
are carnivorous animals. Small species feed on a variety of micro-
organisms, including rotifers, nematodes, minute crustaceans, and
the like, whereas the polyclads can successfully attack larger prey
such as mollusks, annelid worms, insect larvae, and even other
flatworms. Many kinds will also feed upon dead or dying animals

or upon pieces of flesh. Some of the larger species prey upon defenseless sedentary animals. One Atlantic species is a pest among oyster beds where it slithers between the valves of the mollusk and nibbles away the flesh. Active prey may become entangled in mucus from the worms and so immobilized and devoured. It has been suggested that the mucus is toxic, at least in some species, which may assist in subduing prey, but the effectiveness of this action has not been well demonstrated.

Flatworms with a protrusible, ruffled pharynx can encompass prey of some size, ingesting it whole, but those with a nonexpansive cylindrical pharynx either insert it into the food and suck in the contents, or take only small prey that can be accommodated readily. Some types of pharynx are not protrusible and worms so provided ingest their food whole. In most cases, the glandular nature of the pharynx provides lubricating mucus to facilitate ingestion.

The food, reduced to small particles by the pharynx during ingestion, fills the gastric cavity where digestion takes place. Cells of the gastrodermis phagocytize the particles, forming food vacuoles. These are gradually concentrated and their contents eventually broken down into soluble form. Fats and proteins are digested, and part of the latter is converted directly to fats for storage. Carbohydrates apparently cannot be digested, and glycogen storage is scanty or nonexistent. Food reserves are retained in the gastrodermis, but it is not known how these are moved to other tissues and utilized.

When deprived of food for long periods, some turbellarians can call upon their own tissues as a source of energy. The reproductive system may be consumed except for vestiges of the gonads, the mesenchyme disappears, and the food reserves and phagocytic cells of the gastrodermis break down.

Ecology and Distribution

The great majority of the Turbellaria are aquatic, comparatively few having invaded terrestrial habitats. Those that have done so are restricted to moist situations by their limited defense against desiccation, living in leaf mold or under objects on the floor of humid tropical jungles, rarely in temperate regions. Terrestrial flatworms are best known through introduced tropical species now widely distributed in greenhouses where warm, damp conditions are maintained for the culture of exotic plants.

Turbellarians are fundamentally marine animals and evidently have migrated from the sea into fresh-water habitats. Polyclads and acoels are marine; the triclads, rhabdocoels, and alloeocoels inhabit marine, fresh-water, and terrestrial situations. Turbellarians are found in a wide variety of habitats but are absent from the oceanic abysses and from dry terrestrial habitats. The large polyclads and triclads are mostly benthic animals, dwelling under rocks, amongst the rubble of coarse bottoms, and on coral reefs where spectacularly colored species are found. Muddy and sandy situations are inhabited mostly by the acoels and rhabdocoels which are especially adapted to interstitial existence by their small size and slender form, strong development of sensory bristles and adhesives structures, and several other features.

Intertidal turbellarians may tolerate wide fluctuations in temperature and salinity such as are encountered in tide pools, whereas some tropical marine forms are so sensitive that they may disintegrate under even moderately adverse conditions.

Rather few turbellarians are planktonic—notably acoels and polyclads—but certain of these groups are characteristic members of the *Sargassum* community to which their brown coloration is especially adapted. The planktonic Müller's larvae of polyclads are typical components of the tropical plankton.

The fresh-water turbellarians are typically dwellers among the debris in lakes, ponds, and slow-flowing streams in temperate regions. Some, however, occur only in springs or swift mountain streams. A few, such as the stream-dwelling forms at high altitude, require cold water, but most kinds can endure a wide range of temperatures. Some extend even into hot springs with temperatures up to 116°F, but in general flatworms are not well represented in the warm fresh waters of tropical regions.

237

Figure 237. Development of Turbellaria. Living Müller's larvae of polyclad.

5

Phylum Nemertea

Introduction

The nemerteans, commonly called ribbon worms or bootlace worms, are the highest of the acoelomate bilateral phyla—that is, they are the most complex animals in the phylogenetic sequence to have a solid construction without coelomic spaces between the organ systems.

Nemerteans undoubtedly had been observed from rather early times by people familiar with the seashore and its life, but they escaped the attention of scientists until the mid-eighteenth century. Then, because of the inadequate means of observation and the poor level of discrimination then prevalent, they were not recognized as being much different from elongated flatworms. More than a hundred years elapsed before they were studied with enough care and detail to show that they are, indeed, quite distinct from turbellarians with which they had been grouped. The first species was recorded by Baron Cuvier, the giant of French zoology, who recognized in it a most peculiar animal deserving a special order of its own but who nevertheless classified it in a heterogeneous grouping of worms called "intestinaux cavitaires."

The first name above family rank used for these worms was "Nemertea." Other investigators used various permutations of this word, such as Nemertina, Nemertinea, and Nemertini, and through ignorance of the anatomical features distinguishing nemerteans included with them a variety of other wormlike forms such as the hairworm *Gordius* (phylum Aschelminthes), the acornworm *Balanoglossus* (phylum Chordata), and various flatworms. Because of this lack of precise limits of the old group called Nemertea, some recent authors have discarded that name in favor of Rhynchocoela, proposed by Schultze, the first investigator who really achieved a grasp of their anatomical peculiarities. However, hardly one of the major phyla and classes was originally constituted with exactly its present-day limits and no erroneous inclusions, and practically all would have to take later names were this practice followed. Thus, we prefer to retain the earliest name, Nemertea, for the ribbon worms, recognizing that originally there were some animals incorrectly attributed to this group just as there were to almost every other group of animals.

Ribbon worms have essentially no economical or medical significance. They are not used by man as food or for any other purpose. Parasitism is virtually unknown among them, and they are not known to be predators on any commercially valuable marine products. They have been used for experimental work but not nearly to the extent that planarians have been.

The origin and place of nemerteans in the phylogenetic scheme of the Metazoa are dependent upon interpretation of their structure as seen in modern representatives. Like the flatworms, they are devoid of skeleton and have thus left no useful fossil record behind them. There is one fossil, preserved under extraordinarily favorable conditions, believed to be a nemertean. That is *Amiskwia,* a finned, two-tentacled creature with a shape much like some pelagic nemerteans of the present day, and evidently with some median structure, either gut or rhynchocoel, running the whole length of the body from head to tail (Figure 241). As *Amiskwia* is found in sedimentary rocks laid down in Cambrian geological time, 500,000,000 or more years ago, it suggests that nemerteans had already evolved at that early period and had developed free-swimming pelagic or planktonic forms.

The nemerteans are bilaterally symmetrical, flattened, exceedingly elongate animals (Figure 238) not unlike the longer flatworms but showing some distinct advances over the platyhelminth organization. Although they lack a coelom around the digestive tract, they do have a coelomic space, the rhynchocoel, holding an eversible proboscis. Very important is the development in this phylum of a "straight-through" gut with anterior mouth and posterior anus (Figure 239). A circulatory system appears for the first time. The excretory system consists of protonephridia with flame bulbs not very different from those of flatworms.

Although the anatomy of all nemerteans is very similar, certain variations in anatomical relationships have been used to divide the phylum into two large groups usually ranked as classes. In the class Anopla, the proboscis is not armed, the brain lies in front of the mouth, and the nervous sysytem is subepidermal or in the muscle layers of the body wall. In the Enopla, the proboscis may have little toothlike stylets, the brain is behind the mouth, and the nervous system lies below the musculature of the body wall.

Ribbon worms are of extremely elongate form as their common names suggest, some reaching a length of over 100 feet. With this enormous length, however, goes an extremely narrow diameter, a quarter of an inch or less. On the whole, most kinds are of moderate size, usually two feet or shorter, but even these are remarkable for their extensibility. A worm two feet long at rest may stretch to six feet and assume almost hairlike thinness. In form, the bottom-dwelling nemerteans show little diversity, the various species differing externally chiefly in size, proportions of the body, shape of the anterior end (Figure 240), including position of the mouth, and, most conspicuously, in color. The planktonic species, with their adaptations for flotation and swimming, have developed a greater variety of body forms (Figures 242 to 246) which, for the most part, are related to their way of life. Moreover, both hermaphroditism and sexual dimorphism have arisen in these free-swimming forms. Indeed, in some cases the males (Figure 242) may be so unlike the females (Figure 243) that they can be recognized as belonging to the same species only by a specialist in their systematics.

Many nemerteans are drab in color, white, yellowish, or various shades of brown, but others are orange, pinkish, red, or even green, not uncommonly with longitudinal stripes. In the tropics, many species have brilliant colors, usually deployed in patterns of transverse bands or longitudinal stripes. The bathypelagic forms are translucent, colorless, or tinted with pink, red, orange, green, or gray.

As a rule nemerteans do not have a differentiated head, although some have an anterior expansion, called the *cephalic lobe* (Figure 240) rather than head as the brain is usually located behind it. Sensory organs in the form of *cephalic slits* or *grooves*, eyes, and, in a few pelagic kinds, tentacles are located at or near the anterior end. An opening for the proboscis is situated near the anterior tip on the ventral side and the mouth lies just behind it, never midventrally as is often the case in flatworms.

Figures 238 and 239. Form and structure of Nemertea. **238.** Body form of *Cerebratulus,* common benthic ribbon worm. **239.** General organization of nemertean. [Adapted from Joubin, 1893.]

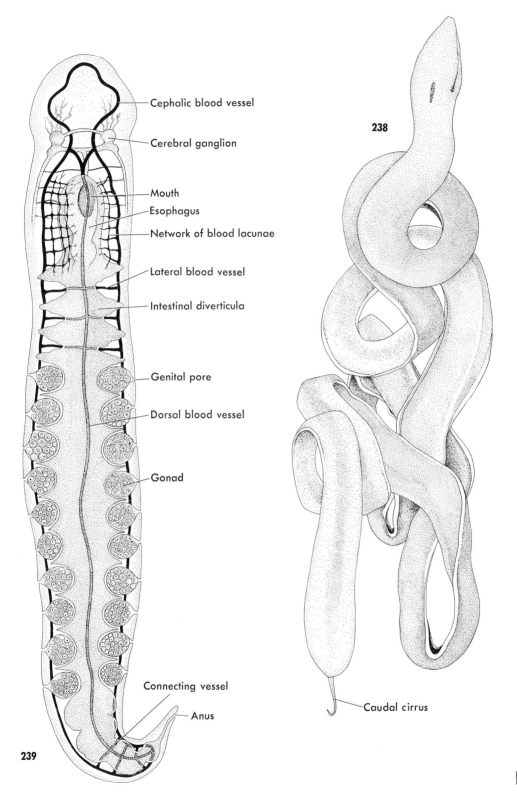

Cephalic blood vessel

Cerebral ganglion

Mouth

Esophagus

Network of blood lacunae

Lateral blood vessel

Intestinal diverticula

Genital pore

Dorsal blood vessel

Gonad

Connecting vessel

Anus

238

239

Caudal cirrus

[181]

A tail-like *caudal cirrus* (Figure 238) forms the posterior tip of the body in some benthic species, and in pelagic kinds there may be a fanlike caudal fin of one or two lobes (Figures 242, 245). The swimming species are generally broad and flattened in form and some have lateral fins as well as a tail. A posterior adhesive disc is present in the species that live commensally in clams. In all, the anus is posterior, at or just dorsal to the tip of the body, or at the base of the caudal cirrus.

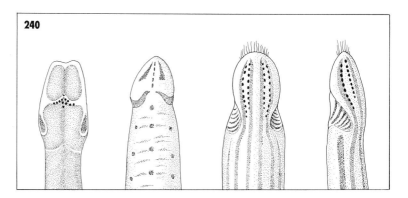

Figure 240. Cephalic lobes of various shapes in benthic nemerteans. [Redrawn from Joubin, 1893.]

Nemertean structure, fundamentally similar to that of flatworms, is more highly organized and differentiated into a body wall composed of epidermal, dermal, and muscular layers. The epidermis (Figure 247) consists of a complex ciliated epithelium with associated gland, interstitial, and sensory cells. This is underlain by the *dermis*, a layer of hyaline connective tissue, sometimes very thick and fibrous. The muscular layer beneath the dermis is much better developed than it is in flatworms and merits the term *body-wall musculature* (Figures 253 to 256). This consists of two or three strong layers, depending on taxonomic group. Proceeding inward, the layers may be either circular–longitudinal–circular, or longitudinal–circular–longitudinal. Thin strata of diagonal fibers may lie between the two outer layers, and radial fibers run through all these layers into the epidermis. Mesenchyme, corresponding to that of flatworms, is distributed between the muscle layers and fills the space between the musculature and the digestive tract. Consequently, the circulatory, nervous, and

Figures 241 to 246. Shapes of pelagic Nemertea. **241.** Fossil *Amiskwia*, presumed pelagic nemertean. **242.** Male *Nectonemertes mirabilis*. [Redrawn from Coe, 1943.] **243.** Female *Nectonemertes mirabilis*. [Redrawn from Coe, 1943.] **244.** *Pelagonemertes moseleyi*. [Redrawn from Moseley, 1875.] **245.** *Balaenanemertes lobata*. [Redrawn from Coe, 1926.] **246.** *Proarmaueria pellucida.* [Redrawn from Coe, 1926.] Code: A, dorsal ganglion; B, testes; C, lateral nerve; D, proboscis; E, ovary; F, proboscis sheath; G, brain; H, intestinal diverticulum; I, lateral vessel.

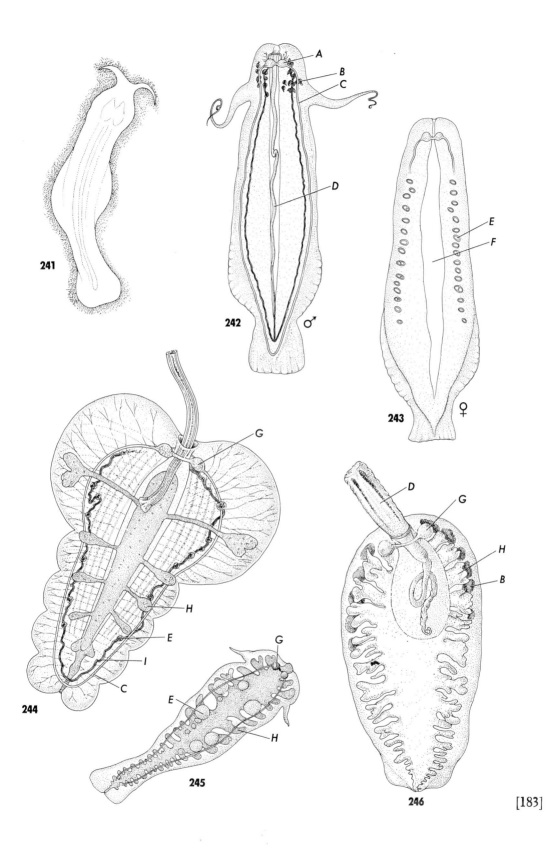

241

242 ♂

243 ♀

244

245

246

excretory systems are surrounded by it and the gonads are derived from it. Elaborate copulatory structures, so conspicuous in flatworms, are not developed in nemerteans. The digestive tract is closely paralleled by the proboscis in its sheath.

Morphology and Classification

MORPHOLOGY

The outer layer of nemerteans is a ciliated epidermis composed of tall, columnar epithelial cells interspersed with sensory, interstitial and gland cells (Figure 247). The ciliated cells are very tall, narrowing basally to slender filaments embedded in a syncytium of interstitial cells. Gland cells are of great diversity and limited distribution. They, too, are very long, some tapered basally like the epithelial cells, some flask-shaped and tapered distally. Others are aggregated into clusters opening to the outside by a common duct, and are termed *packet glands* (Figure 250). These are, in fact, compound glands and they may lie either wholly within the epidermis or in the dermis beneath. The epidermis of some nemerteans contains structures resembling the rhabdites of flatworms and, like them, secreted by glands.

The epidermis lies on a layer of connective tissue belonging to the mesenchyme and usually called *dermis*. It is hyaline, nucleated, and more or less fibrous.

The sense organs of nemerteans are concentrated in the anterior end and consist of the *cephalic grooves* or *slits*, the *frontal organ, eyes, statocysts*, and the *cerebral organs*.

The *cephalic grooves* generally run diagonally around the sides of the head (Figure 240) and may be either continuous or a series of pits. The epithelium in the grooves is unpigmented and lower than elsewhere, ciliated but without gland cells. *Cephalic slits*, which run longitudinally along each side of the head, are deeper than the grooves, with a similarly modified epithelium underlain by ganglion cells. The function of both slits and grooves is assumed from the structure to be of chemoreceptive and tactile nature.

Also thought to serve similar purposes is the *frontal organ*, a ciliated pit without gland cells, situated at the anterior tip of the animal. The pit may be protrusible, and ducts of the frontal glands (Figure 252) may open into it. Abundant nerve connec-

Figures 247 to 250. Histology and anatomy of Nemertea. **247.** Ciliated epidermis. [Redrawn from Coe, 1943.] **248.** Lateral organ. [Redrawn from Coe, 1943.] **249.** Cerebral organ. [Redrawn from Coe, 1943.] **250.** Epidermis with packet glands. [Redrawn from Bürger, 1895.]

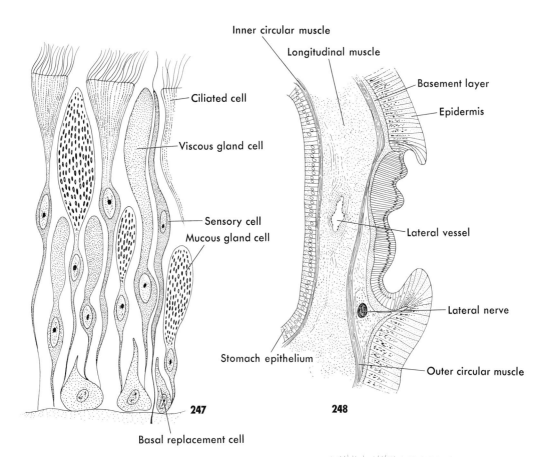

Ciliated cell

Viscous gland cell

Sensory cell

Mucous gland cell

247

Basal replacement cell

Inner circular muscle

Longitudinal muscle

Basement layer

Epidermis

Lateral vessel

Lateral nerve

Stomach epithelium

Outer circular muscle

248

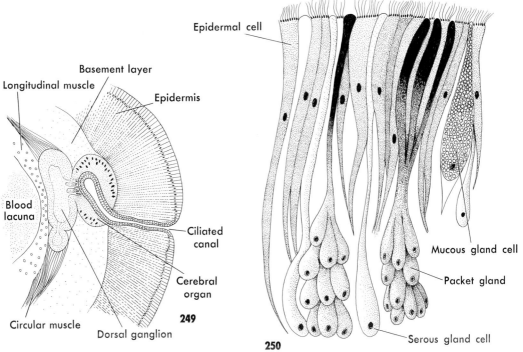

Epidermal cell

Basement layer

Longitudinal muscle

Epidermis

Blood lacuna

Ciliated canal

Cerebral organ

Circular muscle

Dorsal ganglion

249

Mucous gland cell

Packet gland

Serous gland cell

250

tions lead from the frontal organ to the brain. A pit of special epithelium furnished with muscles for protrusion and supplied by nerves occurs near the excretory pore on each side of the body in certain species and is termed the *lateral organ* (Figure 248). It apparently has chemotactile properties.

The *eyes* are pigment-cup ocelli like those of flatworms, situated in the dermis, muscle layers, or mesenchyme, sometimes directly on the brain. They are located only in the head region, and their number and distribution differs according to species. Often there are only one or a few pairs, but in some cases there may be median or lateral clusters or short rows of many ocelli, never very far from the brain. General distribution of eyes over the whole body or around the margins does not occur as it may in flatworms.

Statocysts are not of general occurrence in nemerteans, having been found in only one genus. They are vesicles with nonciliated lining containing one or several statoliths, located in the ventral cerebral ganglia.

Of wide occurrence among nemerteans are the characteristic *cerebral organs*, which are apparently of chemosensory and possibly endocrine function (Figure 249). These vary in complexity from a tubular pit in the epidermis or dipping into the dermis, to a long *cerebral canal* passing through the musculature of body wall and into the mesenchyme. The canal is lined with a strongly ciliated epithelium and its inner end is surrounded by a cluster or larger mass of gland and nerve cells. This glandular-nervous body is connected by nerves to the dorsal cerebral ganglion or may even be attached to it.

Epithelial sensory cells are of general distribution over the body and evidently serve primarily tactile functions. They are more densely concentrated near the head and tail ends, and their sensory bristles can sometimes be seen in the living animals. Clusters of sensory cells slightly sunk into the epithelium form sensory pits, generally distributed over the surface of the body in pelagic

Figure 251. Structure of Nemertea. Nervous system in anterior part of *Tubulanus.* [Redrawn from Burger, 1895.]

251

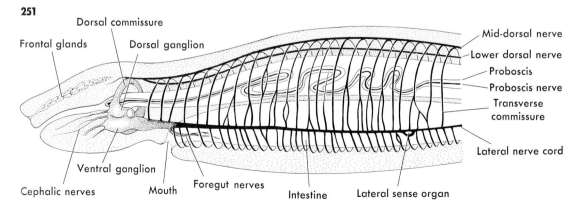

Dorsal commissure

Frontal glands

Dorsal ganglion

Mid-dorsal nerve

Lower dorsal nerve

Proboscis

Proboscis nerve

Transverse commissure

Lateral nerve cord

Ventral ganglion

Cephalic nerves

Mouth

Foregut nerves

Intestine

Lateral sense organ

and some benthic species. Sensory cells also may be clustered in small papillae, especially in the proboscis, where they send bundles of axons to the proboscis nerves.

The nervous system (Figure 251) is structurally similar to that of flatworms, being fundamentally a plexus with nerve cords and definite cerebral ganglia forming a brain. However, with the greater complexity of the body musculature, there arise more possibilities for the distribution of the nervous system with respect to other tissues. Thus, in the Nemertea, there is a transition from the epidermal location found in flatworms to a deeper position within the mesenchyme. There may be either one plexus or two. In the paleonemertines, the body-wall plexus lies either in the epithelium or in the dermis outside the muscle layers. In the heteronemertines, if only one nerve layer is present it lies between the outer longitudinal and the circular muscle layers; if there are two, the outer plexus has the position just mentioned and the inner one lies between the circular muscles and the inner longitudinal layer, with radial connections linking the two. Very little is known of the function of the plexi, but the evidence at hand suggests that they are not diffusely conducting nerve nets of the coelenterate type.

The brain consists of four ganglia, one dorsal and one ventral on each side, more or less fused. Dorsal and ventral commissures join the lobes of the two sides, encircling the rhynchodaeum. The ventral ganglia give rise to a pair of large nerve cords, the lateral nerves, which extend along the sides to the posterior extremity where they are connected by the *anal commissure*.

Smaller ganglionated cords proceed from the cerebral ganglia into the head region (the cephalic nerves), from the dorsal com-

Figure 252. Structure of Nemertea. General anatomy shown in sagittal section of anterior end of *Nemertopsis*. [Redrawn from Burger, 1895.]

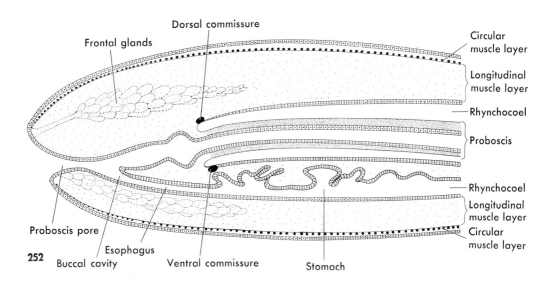

252
Proboscis pore
Buccal cavity
Esophagus
Ventral commissure
Stomach
Frontal glands
Dorsal commissure
Circular muscle layer
Longitudinal muscle layer
Rhynchocoel
Proboscis
Rhynchocoel
Longitudinal muscle layer
Circular muscle layer

missure backward in the midline (the middorsal nerve), from the middorsal nerve to the proboscis sheath (the lower dorsal nerve), a midventral nerve, proboscis nerves, and many others. Transverse commissures may connect the lateral and middorsal nerves both dorsally and ventrally around the body, resulting in an irregular series of rings. One of the pelagic nemerteans, *Neuronemertes*, is peculiar in having a rather regular series of ganglia along the median dorsal nerve, but their functions and connections remain unknown. The ganglia and nerve cords may lie in the epidermis, dermis, body musculature or mesenchyme, according to taxonomic group. The major ganglia and nerve cords are made up of an inner core or mass of nerve fibers surrounded by a layer of ganglion cells. The ganglion cells are unipolar and some, known as *neurochord cells*, are remarkable for their large size and are, in fact, giant nerve cells. The large fibers of the neurochord cells may form distinct bundles in the lateral nerve cords. Each of the dorsal lobes of the brain contains a lateral cluster of small cells, rich in chromatin, which have been recognized as equivalent to the masses of *globuli cells* in the cerebral ganglia of higher annelids, arthropods, and mollusks. As already has been mentioned, corresponding structures have been detected in some of the polyclad flatworms also. Their function has not been experimentally demonstrated, but they are thought to participate in more complex associative processes.

The body-wall musculature (Figures 253 to 256) is more complex than it is in flatworms and consists of two or three main layers of muscle fibers of the smooth type. If the musculature is two-layered, the outer stratum is circular and the inner is longitudinal, but in three-layered forms, the outer and inner layers may be circular, separated by a longitudinal stratum, or just the reverse, outer and inner longitudinal, separated by circular. In addition, there are usually thin diagonal layers between the two main outer strata, radial fibers traversing all the layers, and dorsoventral bundles running through the mesenchyme may join the dorsal and ventral body walls. For functional reasons the dorsoventral bands are strongly developed in swimming forms, and in the passively floating types the musculature is generally weak.

Mesenchymal connective tissue occurs between the layers of muscles and surrounds all the organ systems. It is a gelatinous material containing cells of various types according to location. Around the internal organs they are rounded and vesicular, but in the dermis they may be branched or syncytial and the matrix is more fibrous.

Clusters of glands homologous with the *frontal glands* of flatworms lie in the cephalic region and open by a pore in front of the proboscis pore or into a sensory pit that corresponds to the *frontal organ* of flatworms. Submuscular glands in the ventral mesenchyme are probably equivalent to the glands that produce the slime trails for locomotion in flatworms.

A very curious structure which plays an important role in feeding yet is not a part of the digestive system is the proboscis (Figures 246, 252). This is a blind, tubular organ, often longer than the body, attached at the bottom of a short cavity, the *rhynchodaeum*, and lying inverted in a *proboscis sheath* whose lumen extends the length of the body dorsal to the digestive tract. The rhynchodaeum opens to the outside by way of the *proboscis pore*,

Morphology
and
Classification

Figures 253 to 256. Body musculature in major groups of Nemertea. **253.** Paleonemertini. **254.** Heteronemertini. **255.** Hoplonemertini. **256.** Bdellonemertini. [All adapted from Coe, 1943.]

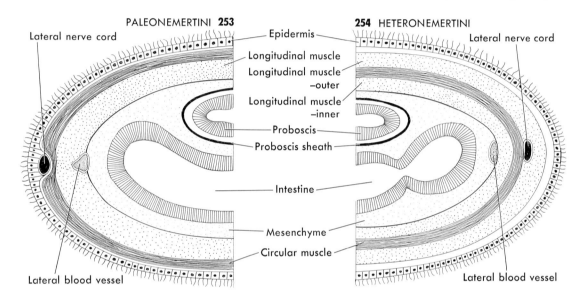

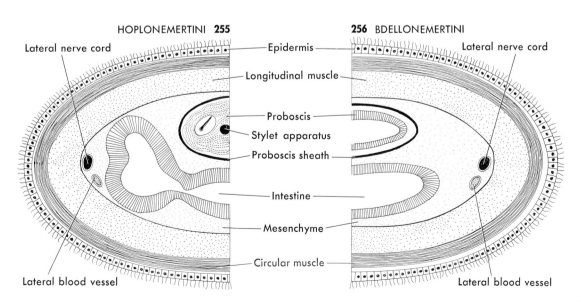

situated just anterior to the mouth. The inverted proboscis is lined with a glandular, nonciliated epithelium containing rhabdites, sometimes localized in special areas or in papillae. This epithelium is turned to the outside when the proboscis is everted. The wall of the tube consists of circular and longitudinal muscular layers which partly duplicate the sequence of layers in the body wall. The inturned surface of the proboscis is covered with a low endothelium of the same kind that lines the proboscis sheath. The wall of the sheath contains layers of muscles which complete the duplication of the body-wall musculature. The complete musculature of the proboscis apparatus—proboscis and sheath—thus represents a tubular invagination of the body wall which has become separated into two layers by a split. This results in two tubes, one lying inside the other. The inner tube is the proboscis, enclosed in an outer tube, the proboscis sheath; the space between them is the rhynchocoel.

The rhynchocoel is filled with a fluid containing elongate or discoidal amoeboid lymphocytes. When the muscles of the proboscis sheath compress the fluid in the rhynchocoel, hydraulic pressure causes the proboscis to turn inside out and protrude through the proboscis pore, bringing it into functional position. Retractor muscles attached to the posterior end of the proboscis sheath extend to the distal end of the proboscis and serve to retract it by pulling it back inside the sheath.

The proboscis is unarmed in some nemerteans and armed with small, toothlike *stylets* (Figure 257) in others. The unarmed type is a simple tube that narrows toward its posterior end (the tip when everted) and is completely eversible. The armed type has a thick-walled anterior part separated from the narrower, shorter terminal part by an intermediate bulbous region which bears the stylets on a partition, the *septum*, communicating with the blind terminal portion by a narrow canal. The armed proboscis everts only as far as the septum, thus exposing the stylet which is used to puncture prey. Glandular secretions, possibly toxic, from the terminal part may be discharged upon the prey through the pore near the base of the stylet. The stylet may be damaged or lost during use, in which case one of the *accessory stylets* contained in two pockets in the septum moves into functional position. A constant reserve of stylets is therefore maintained for use as needed.

The proboscis apparatus of nemerteans is one of the most characteristic features of the phylum and at the same time one of the means of relating it to the Platyhelminthes. The proboscis apparatus of nemerteans could be derived from the simple, eversible proboscis found in the kalyptorhynch rhabdocoels. The flat-worm proboscis is a simple invagination which is everted for use. A division of its wall into two layers separated by a space would produce sheath, rhynchocoel, and proboscis as seen in nemerteans.

In lower metazoans such as coelenterates and ctenophores, a combination of ciliary action and body contraction suffices to circulate fluids through the ramifications of the gastrovascular system. The fluids consist of the surrounding water and partially digested food. The intimate contact of all tissues with the water and with the source of nutrition obviates any need for a circulatory system. The Platyhelminthes have no internal spaces except the digestive cavity, and the very flat construction of the body assures close enough contact between tissues and medium not to require any special means of circulation, although a system of protonephridia has developed to regulate the passage of salts and water into and out of the tissues and possibly to eliminate some waste products. In the nemerteans, however, increasing complexity of the organ systems and musculature and greater separation of tissues from the surrounding water has resulted in the development of a definite circulatory system consisting of blood enclosed in true vessels. It is a simple system, without any centralized pump, but it is the first blood-vascular system in the Metazoa (Figures 258 to 260).

The simplest arrangement consists of two *lateral vessels* following the digestive tract, connected above the rhynchodaeum by a *cephalic lacuna* and below the anus by an *anal lacuna*. It is a simple loop without main branches. With increasing complexity, lacunae appear in the vicinity of the foregut, vessels extend to the rhynchocoel from the lateral vessels, a ventral connective under the rhynchodaeum joins the lateral vessels and gives rise to a mid-dorsal vessel. Regular transverse connections join the lateral and middorsal vessels especially in the intestinal region, partly encircling the body, and numerous other ramifications extend out from the lateral and other large vessels.

The lacunae are spaces in the mesenchyme lined with only a thin membrane, but the vessels have definite walls. The smaller vessels consist of an endothelial lining separated from the epithelial coat by a gelatinous membrane. The larger vessels are rendered contractile by the addition of a layer of circular muscles outside the gelatinous connective layer.

The blood fluid is colorless but contains nucleated corpuscles containing pigments, among them hemoglobin. They impart a red, orange, yellow, or green color to the blood. As many as four

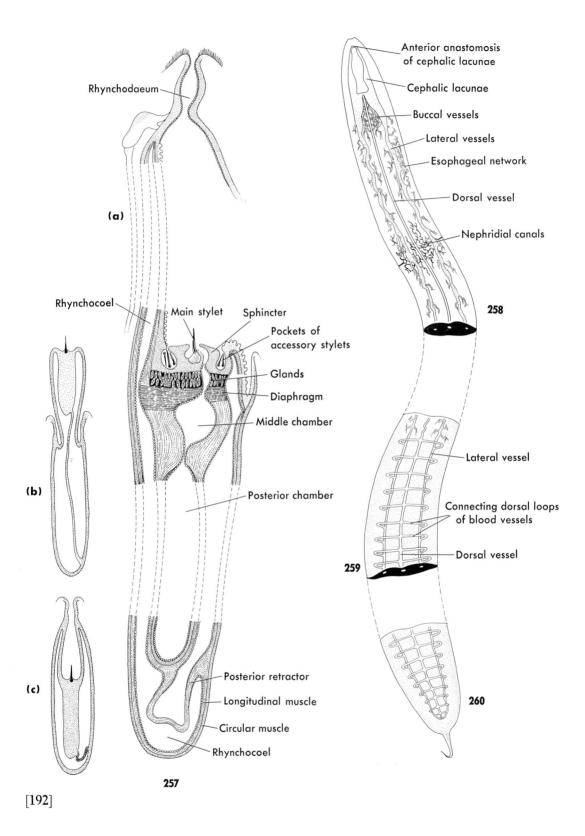

Rhynchodaeum

(a)

Rhynchocoel

Main stylet

Sphincter

Pockets of accessory stylets

Glands

Diaphragm

Middle chamber

(b)

Posterior chamber

(c)

Posterior retractor

Longitudinal muscle

Circular muscle

Rhynchocoel

257

Anterior anastomosis of cephalic lacunae

Cephalic lacunae

Buccal vessels

Lateral vessels

Esophageal network

Dorsal vessel

Nephridial canals

258

Lateral vessel

Connecting dorsal loops of blood vessels

Dorsal vessel

259

260

kinds of amoeboid lymphocytes may be present in addition to the discoidal corpuscles.

The digestive tract (Figure 239) is a tube, open at both ends, divided into two main regions, *foregut* and *intestine*, the latter usually provided with lateral diverticula. The foregut may be simple or divided into more or less distinct regions having their own histological peculiarities: buccal cavity, esophagus, and stomach (Figure 252). The mouth generally opens a little behind the proboscis pore, but in a number of species the esophagus joins the rhynchodaeum so there is no separate mouth. The posterior part of the foregut often has a layer of longitudinal muscle fibers, but this is the only part of the digestive tract supplied with its own musculature. Elsewhere the digestive tube and proboscis sheath may be closely enveloped by the inner layer of body-wall musculature, or they may be embedded in mesenchyme. The intestinal part of the digestive tube has lateral diverticula, often branched, to increase the digestive surface. These may disappear a short distance ahead of the anus, forming a simple rectum.

The external epithelium continues virtually unchanged into mouth and buccal cavity, but in the esophagus it becomes lower and gland cells disappear. In the stomach, numerous granular gland cells appear, evidently secretory in function, and in the intestine the epithelium becomes very tall, composed of ciliated cells and eosinophilous gland cells.

The excretory system (Figure 258) of nemerteans consists of protonephridia much as in the flatworms except that here they are closely associated with a circulatory system. Basically, there is one pair of nephridia in the vicinity of the foregut (Figure 261). The terminal flame bulbs are generally multicellular or multinucleate, although they may be unicellular as in flatworms. They indent the walls of the blood vessels and sometimes are directly immersed in blood, but there is no direct communication between blood and capillary fluid. The capillaries collect into a nephridial tubule consisting of ciliated epithelium, which runs posteriorly for some distance in close contact with the lateral blood vessel before opening to the surface by a nephridiopore.

In some cases, the capillaries lack flame bulbs and are closely crowded together to form a ridge projecting into the blood vessel. These are then called nephridial glands. The nephridia of some species are repeatedly branched (Figure 262), forming a complex

Figures 257 to 260. Anatomy of Nemertea. **257.** Diagram of proboscis apparatus of armed nemertean; middle part of (a) shows stylet in everted position on the right and retracted on the left. [Modified from Joubin, 1893.] Position of proboscis everted is shown in (b), retracted in (c). **258** to **260.** Circulatory and excretory systems of *Cerebratulus*. [Redrawn from Coe, 1943.]

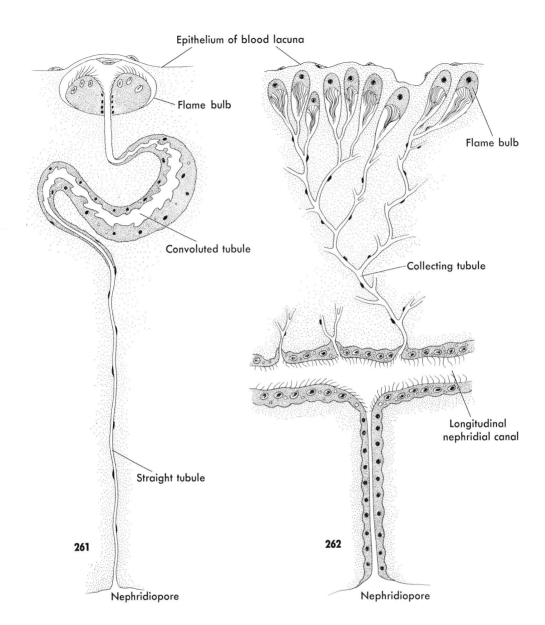

Epithelium of blood lacuna

Flame bulb

Convoluted tubule

Flame bulb

Collecting tubule

Straight tubule

Longitudinal
nephridial canal

261

262

Nephridiopore

Nephridiopore

Figures 261 and 262. Excretory system of Nemertea. **261.** Simple nephridium. **262.** (Complex nephridium emptying into nephridial canal. [Redrawn from Coe, 1943.]

system in close connection with the lateral vessels and the foregut lacunae. The two original nephridia may then be broken up into many separate nephridia, each with its own duct and nephridiopore.

In its simplicity, the reproductive system of nemerteans contrasts sharply with the complicated arrangements prevalent in flatworms. A few kinds are hermaphrodites but most are dioecious. The gonads are rounded sacs (Figure 263) that usually occur in a regular row along each side of the body in the intestinal region, but in a few species they are irregularly scattered through the mesenchyme. In certain pelagic species the testes occur in the head and adjacent regions, but the ovaries are situated as usual. Such species may also show external sexual dimorphism by the presence of a pair of cephalic tentacles in the males but not in the females.

The sex cells are derived from mesenchyme cells which cluster together in thin-walled sacs. When the sex cells are ripe, each gonad develops a short gonoduct to the surface, where a gonopore opens (Figure 263). In the hermaphroditic species, some of the gonads may be male and some female, or both sexes may be combined in ovotestes (Figure 264). The male cells tend to ripen well in advance of the female, showing even here a tendency

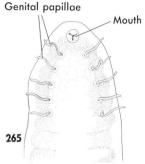

265

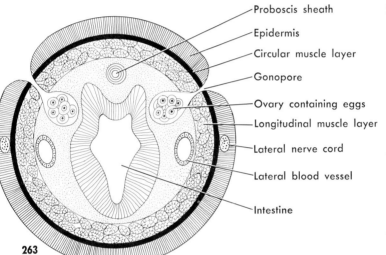

Proboscis sheath
Epidermis
Circular muscle layer
Gonopore
Ovary containing eggs
Longitudinal muscle layer
Lateral nerve cord
Lateral blood vessel
Intestine

263

Figures 263 to 265. Structure and reproduction of Nemertea. **263.** Diagrammatic cross section of *Procarinina* showing ovaries in relation to other structures. [Redrawn from Nawitzky, 1931.] **264.** Ovary (a) and hermaphroditic gonad (b) of *Pelagonemertes*. [Redrawn from Coe, 1926.] **265.** Head of *Phallonemertes* showing multiple penes or genital papillae. [Redrawn from Coe, 1943.]

264

(a)

(b)

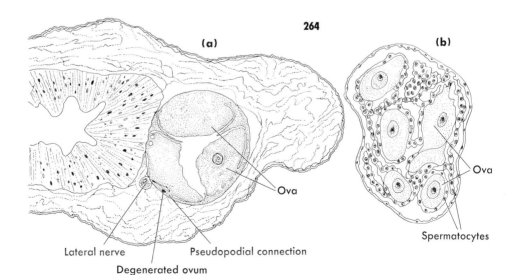

Ova

Ova

Spermatocytes

Lateral nerve
Degenerated ovum
Pseudopodial connection

toward separation of the sexes. Copulatory structures are generally lacking in nemerteans, and the adults may spawn without physical contact or while encased in a mucous sheath into which the gametes are discharged. In some cases the male discharges sperm while creeping over the female, and in a very few pelagic forms the male openings are set at the end of digitate projections termed penes (Figure 265). Fertilization can be either external or internal, the sperms making their way into the ovaries, and some species retain the eggs through development to produce young worms alive (Figure 266). Usually, however, eggs are deposited in gelatinous masses, either scattered singly or clustered in groups within enclosing capsules.

Classification, Phylum Nemertea

I. Class Anopla (the unarmed nemerteans). Mouth is located behind cerebral ganglia, and nervous system lies close to surface, either just below epidermis or in body-muscle layers (two orders).
   A. Order Paleonemertini. Two or sometimes three layers of body muscles and gelatinous dermis.
   B. Order Heteronemertini. Always with three layers of muscles and fibrous dermis.
II. Class Enopla (the armed nemerteans). Usually (not always) have stylets in proboscis; mouth is placed at tip of body anterior to cerebral ganglia, and nervous system has sunk to a position in mesenchyme below muscle layers (two orders).
   A. Order Hoplonemertini. With straight intestine giving off paired lateral diverticula; some have only one stylet in proboscis and are grouped as suborder Monostylifera, others have many stylets and comprise suborder Polystylifera.

Figure 266. Structure and reproduction of nemertea. Section of *Geonemertes* showing ovaries, testes, hermaphroditic glands, and internally developing embryos. [Redrawn from Coe, 1943.]

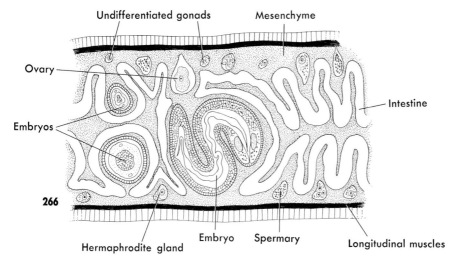

Undifferentiated gonads   Mesenchyme

Ovary

Intestine

Embryos

266

Hermaphrodite gland   Embryo   Spermary   Longitudinal muscles

B. Order Bdellonemertini. Leechlike commensals of clams and other invertebrates; they have a sinuous intestine lacking diverticula, and proboscis is without stylets.

Reproduction and Embryology

ASEXUAL REPRODUCTION

Nemerteans are rather intolerant of continued mechanical irritation and other unsatisfactory conditions and commonly respond by fragmentation of the body in the intestinal region. In most species, the anterior piece containing the foregut is able to regenerate all the lost posterior structures. Some, however, regularly reproduce asexually by *fragmentation*, each piece regenerating a complete new worm. As would be expected, such species show extensive regenerative capacities under experimental conditions. Any piece is capable of forming a complete worm as long as it includes part of the lateral nerve cords. Regenerative processes are accomplished by mesenchyme cells which migrate to the site of injury, forming a regeneration blastema. Phagocytic cells supply nutrition for the process by ingesting old tissue cells and then disintegrating for utilization by the regenerative mesenchyme cells. Special clumps of cells aggregate to become ganglion cells, others regenerate lost parts of the proboscis apparatus and gut.

SEXUAL REPRODUCTION

As in the Turbellaria, cleavage is spiral and determinate. Three or four quartets of micromeres are formed. In some species the "micromeres" are actually as large or even larger than the macromeres. Eventually a ciliated *coeloblastula* develops and this gastrulates through invagination, sometimes combined with epiboly (Figure 267). Polar ingression, resulting in the formation of a stereogastrula, is also known to occur.

The origin of the mesoderm is variable. In *Malacobdella* and *Cephalothrix*, it is derived entirely from the ectoderm and is thus an *ectomesoderm*. In others, it apparently is nearly all an *entomesoderm* which develops either from an irregular proliferation of entoderm cells into the blastocoel or else from the descendants of 4d, or its equivalent. In still other genera, some descendants of the second quartet of micromeres give rise to ectomesoderm while entomesoderm develops from one of the macromeres or 4d. The blastocoel becomes filled with a mesenchyme from which muscles, connective tissue and reproductive structures eventually will differentiate.

The invaginated archenteron is, of course, an entodermal structure. From the ectoderm are derived the epidermis, cerebral organs, nervous system, perhaps the excretory system, and the epidermal lining of foregut and proboscis. At the aboral pole, an apical sense organ consisting of flagellated columnar cells (Figure 267) forms.

In the hoplonemertines—for example, *Cephalothrix* and *Malacobdella*—development after gastrulation is direct, with small worms hatching out of the capsules. The heteronemertines, however, characteristically have an indirect development with a free-swimming larva, the *pilidium*.

The gastrula of those with the direct mode of development gradually attains a bilateral symmetry through a movement of the aboral sense organ toward the future anterior end, just as described for the Turbellaria. The blastopore closes, and near it an ectodermal invagination forms *stomodaeum* and *foregut* which will become continuous with the entodermal midgut. The intestine grows posteriorly from the midgut (Figure 268), and the anus appears either where the intestine grows out, making contact with the ectoderm, or at a *proctodaeal invagination*. The nervous system and the lining of the proboscis likewise arise as ectodermal invaginations. In the mesenchyme, muscles, connective tissue, and the circulatory vessels differentiate. A small worm with a ciliated epidermis hatches.

In those forms with an indirect mode of development, the ciliated gastrula grows a pair of oral lobes, one on each side of the spacious stomodaeum, and at the opposite pole there is an *aboral sense organ* with a tuft of flagella. This is the *pilidium* larva (Figures 269, 271). Its digestive system consists of a stomodaeum and foregut of invaginated ectoderm which has become continuous with the entodermal midgut. The commodious blastocoel contains amoeboid mesenchyme cells in a gelatinous fluid. Some of these differentiate into larval muscle.

Figures 267 to 269. Development of the pilidium larva. **267.** Invaginating coeloblastula. **268.** Young pilidium. **269.** Pilidium larva. Code: A, apical sense organ; B, ectoderm; C, blastocoel; D, mesoderm; E, entoderm; F, blastopore. [After Coe, 1899.]

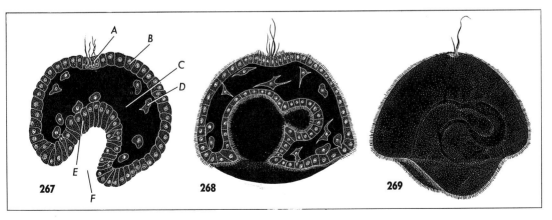

Not all heteronemertines have a free-swimming pilidium—for example, *Lineus ruber* in which a postgastrula stage called *Desor's larva* occurs. This stage takes place within the capsule and it is especially interesting because, although it develops and even metamorphoses as the pilidium does, the Desor's larva lacks all those structures which particularly fit the pilidium for pelagic existence—that is, the oral lobes, ciliated oral band, and the aboral sense organ and tuft. This fact suggests that those structures missing in Desor's larva are special adaptations for a planktonic phase in the life cycle and have no particular phylogenetic significance.

Curious growth phenomena precede the metamorphosis of the pilidium and Desor's larva into miniature nemertean worms. In six to eight places on the larval body, a plate of ectoderm sinks below the larval ectoderm, forming an *ectodermal disc*. The larval ectoderm which forms a thin covering over each ectodermal disc is called the *amnion*. Usually there is a pair each of anterior *cephalic discs*, lateral *cerebral discs* and posteroventral *trunk discs*,

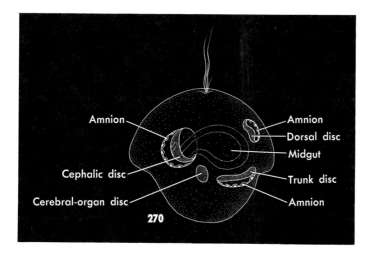

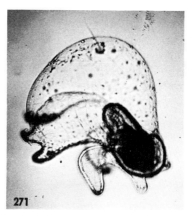

Figures 270 and 271. Development of pilidium larva. **270.** Pilidium larva showing embryonic discs. [Adapted from Salensky, 1912.] **271.** Metamorphosing pilidium.

and an unpaired posterior *dorsal disc* (Figure 270). A single *proboscis disc* may lie between the cephalic discs. The discs grow and eventually fuse with one another forming the ectoderm of the young worm and surrounding the larval gut and some of the mesenchyme. The amnia also unite so that the developing worm is enclosed in a delicate embryonic membrane.

From the cephalic discs will form the epidermis of the anterior end and the cerebral ganglia from which the nerve cords will sprout. The cerebral discs give rise to the cerebral canals of the cerebral organs, and from the proboscis disc or the region between the cephalic discs the proboscis epithelium will originate. The epidermis of most of the body is derived from trunk and dorsal discs. The digestive system is completed by a proctodaeal invagination, and differentiation of ectodermal and mesodermal structures occurs generally as in direct development. Finally the external framework, in the case of the pilidium including apical organ and oral lobes, is shed with the amnion and a small nemertean emerges.

Physiology

RESPIRATION

Like flatworms, the nemerteans respire through the epithelium by diffusion, having no special mechanisms for respiration. Those that have abundant blood lacunae in the walls of the foregut and take water into this area for respiratory purposes show a trend toward development of a respiratory system. Blood flow in the main vessels can be in either direction but usually proceeds forward in the middorsal vessel and backward in the laterals.

The close proximity of the protonephridia to the blood vessels in many species indicates their probable excretory nature but nothing is known of their manner of function or their excretory products.

NERVOUS AND SENSORY REACTIONS

Sensory functions in the nemerteans are very poorly known and are in the main deduced from observations upon reactions of the animals and upon the structure of presumed sense organs. The anterior end, normally the part of the active worm that meets the surrounding environment first, is the principal site of such organs. The animals quickly react in a negative way toward chemicals and other obnoxious stimuli, and they are able to detect food substances over considerable distances by chemoresponse. The cephalic grooves and slits, cerebral organs, and lateral organs are presumed to be the chemotactile sensors responsible for such abilities. Although the entire surface of the nemertean body is sensitive to touch, the head, tail, and proboscis are particularly endowed in this respect. Photosensitivity is most highly developed in the eyes and living prey can be detected to a distance up to 2 cm. The general epithelium is also sensitive to light, and response is negative in most species. The animals make every effort to regain concealment when exposed, although the adults of at least one species, as well as the larvae and young of most others, are photopositive. Strong positive thigmotaxis results in the widespread habit among nemerteans of burrowing under objects or into muddy bottom.

Experimental evidence shows that general nervous control is maintained by the cerebral ganglia, which are responsible for coordinated spontaneous movements. The peripheral nervous system, which controls ciliary action and peristaltic waves in the body musculature, is largely automatic and is inhibited by the cerebral ganglia.

The cerebral ganglia exert their influence in several different ways. In some species, loss of the brain stops the action of the cilia by permitting the nerve cords and plexi to impose an inhibitory effect. Stimulation of the decapitated animals causes resumption of ciliary gliding in the normal directions—forward if stimulated from the rear and vice versa. In some cases, continued strong stimulation is necessary to restore activity, whereas mild and intermittent stimulation is effective in others. Loss of the brain does not stop the cilia in a few nemerteans that have been studied, which shows that locomotion is independent of the brain. So little work has been done that we cannot for the moment say whether under different conditions one species could react in all the ways that have been observed.

Gliding and crawling locomotion in nemerteans seems largely due to ciliary action rather than to muscular waves, as can be shown experimentally by blocking ciliary action with lithium salts, which abolishes gliding, whereas the animals continue to move if their muscles are paralyzed but their cilia are not immobilized. The glandular lower surface exudes a thick cushion of mucus in which the cilia beat, driving the animal forward. Peristaltic waves of the body musculature propel burrowers through mud, and the proboscis may be employed to initiate penetration or even to pull the animal along the surface by grasping objects, after which the body is contracted and the process repeated. The swimming forms use the strong dorsoventral musculature to produce bodily undulations which propel the worm through water.

The production of mucus by the epidermal glands varies greatly under different conditions and nervous control may be suspected. Moreover, epidermal gland cells appear to account for the brilliant luminescence of a species of *Emplectonema*. As general stimuli such as temperature changes, chemicals, and electric shock elicit brilliant overall bioluminescence and local mechanical stimulation produces only local luminescence, some nervous control is suggested but by no means proved.

FEEDING AND DIGESTION

Nemerteans are chiefly predatory animals feeding mainly on other invertebrates small enough to be overcome. The use of the proboscis in capture of prey has been observed infrequently but is assumed to be of general occurrence. The rapid action of this structure, together with its prehensile ability, sticky mucus, rhabdites, and (in armed forms) stylet render it an efficient raptorial organ. The blind terminal end of the proboscis has been reported to secrete toxic substances that may be jabbed into the prey by the stylets, and the abundant mucous secretions of the body have been shown in some species to contain poisonous substances. These may function in overcoming prey as well as in defense against enemies.

Nutrition in the nemerteans is not well known, as is true of most other aspects of the physiology of these animals. However, the common European species *Lineus ruber* has been investigated in some detail. The animals prey upon small annelids and crustaceans and also ingest dead organic material that is not badly decomposed. The proboscis everts immediately upon detection of the prey, around which it coils in a tight spiral. No stylets for stabbing prey are present in this species, but the sticky secretions of the proboscis epithelium insure a firm grip. As the proboscis pulls the prey toward the mouth, the anterior tip of the body reaches out and curls down over the food, bringing it to the mouth. The proboscis slowly releases its grip and the prey is taken through the mouth into the buccal cavity by muscular contractions. The lining of the buccal cavity is ciliated and contains numerous gland cells whose secretions probably aid in the passage of food into the foregut. The entire process may take less than half a minute if the prey is small, but ingestion of a large animal may require half an hour. Small animals succumb almost immediately upon ingestion, presumably killed by acid secretions of the gland cells of the foregut. When the food enters the intestine, glandular secretions begin its disintegration and the gastrodermal cilia circulate the acid medium containing fragmenting food into

the intestinal diverticula. Within thirty minutes the prey is reduced to a heterogeneous mass of tissue fragments and material
released from the gut of the prey. The gastrodermal cilia now
perform the astonishing feat of fusing together into pseudopodial
processes which reach out into the semidigested mass to engulf
particles of food. An hour after feeding, the gastrodermal cells
are filled with spheres of food undergoing intracellular digestion
and the gut contains only a homogeneous fluid with indigestible
remains such as setae. The intracellular phase of digestion continues in an acid medium and is completed about six hours after
feeding. In nine hours, the cilia have reverted from the pseudopodial condition back to their normal shape and they then sweep
the indigestible material into the terminal unpouched part of the
intestine, from which it is ejected by muscular contractions of
the posterior body wall.

The chief food reserve in *Lineus* is fat, which exists as intracellular globules mostly in the mesenchyme and to some extent in
the columnar cells of the intestinal wall. Minute granules of glycogen are also scattered throughout the mesenchyme, muscles,
and gastrodermis, but there are no protein reserves. Starvation
results in gradual resorption and utilization of tissues by phagocytic action of the mesenchyme cells, with attendant dedifferentiation. Tissues of the various organ systems are gradually broken
down in a more or less orderly sequence, first the pigment cells
and granules, then the digestive tract, muscles, and gonads, with
the nervous system lasting the longest time. Experiments have
shown that this process of dedifferentiation ultimately results in
the return to a condition strongly resembling a larval animal, and
finally to masses of rounded cells suggestive of an egg in the
morula stage. Thus, the entire process of growth and differentiation can be reversed by starvation, resulting in a return to embryonic condition.

Ecology and Distribution

Most nemerteans are marine, although a few species have invaded fresh-water and terrestrial habitats. Some of the fresh-water
forms inhabit caves and seem to be restricted to this habitat, and
one of the terrestrial species frequents the moist leaf axils of
Pandanus, a monocotyledonous tree, and thus may be found high
above the ground. However, nemerteans have in general not pro-
liferated out into as many ecological niches as have the Turbellaria.

Some of the marine nemerteans are planktonic or pelagic, but the majority are benthic animals, burrowing in muddy bottom, hiding under stones, or crawling through clumps of algae such as the calcareous *Halimeda*, which offer ample shelter and at the same time harbor many food organisms.

In general, the benthic forms are inhabitants of shallow coastal regions, but a few have been found at moderate or considerable depths, down to 700 to 800 fathoms. A substantial number of species have bathypelagic habits and these characteristically dwell at great depths, down to 1,500 fathoms or more. Here the weak, soft-bodied forms passively drift, and the more muscular types with expanded tail and sometimes lateral fins actively swim in search of prey.

Geographically the species are concentrated chiefly in temperate and arctic regions and a number of them are widely distributed, even circumpolar. There are fewer species in warmer latitudes. In such regions they develop gaudy coloration as do the flatworms and many other kinds of animals.

A number of species have entered into commensal relationships with other animals, such as tunicates, clams, and sea anemones, with which they live for protection and concealment. Although they may intercept ciliary currents to obtain food and water for respiration, they are not evidently deleterious to their hosts. One species, *Carcinonemertes carcinophila*, lives among the gills and egg masses of crabs, feeding upon the eggs and thus approaching a parasitic existence.

Selected References

BULLOCK, T. H., and G. A. HORRIDGE. *Structure and Function in the Nervous Systems of Invertebrates*, Vol. 1. London: W. H. Freeman & Co., 1965, 798 pp.

CHILD, C. M. *Patterns and Problems of Development*. Chicago: University of Chicago Press, 1941, 811 pp.

CROWELL, SEARS (ed.). "Behavioral physiology of coelenterates." *American Zoologist*, 5:335–589, 1965.

DOUGHERTY, ELLSWORTH C. (ed.). *The Lower Metazoa: Comparative Biology and Phylogeny*. Berkeley: University of California Press, 1963, 478 pp.

HAMBURGER, V. "Regeneration." In *Encyclopedia Britannica*, 1966, Vol. 19, pp. 73–81.

HYMAN, LIBBIE H. *The Invertebrates: Protozoa through Ctenophora*. New York: McGraw-Hill Book Co., 1940, 726 pp.

——— *The Invertebrates: Platyhelminthes and Rhynchocoela*. New York: McGraw-Hill Book Co., 1951, 550 pp.

JONES, W. C. "Is there a nervous system in sponges?" *Biol. Review*, 37:1–50, 1962.

REES, W. J. (ed.). *The Cnidaria and Their Evolution*. London and New York: Academic Press, Inc., 1966, 449 pp.

ROTHSCHILD, LORD. *A Classification of Living Animals*. New York: John Wiley & Sons, Inc., 1961, 106 pp.

Sources of Illustrations

Abbott, James Francis
    1907. "The morphology of *Coeloplana*." *Zoologische Jahr-
        bücher* (Abt. Anat.), 24:41–70, pls. 8–10.

Agassiz, Alexander
    1888. "Three cruises of the U.S. Coast and Geodetic Survey
        steamer 'Blake' in the Gulf of Mexico, in the Caribbean
        Sea, and along the Atlantic Coast of the United States
        from 1877 to 1880." *Bulletin of the Museum of Com-
        parative Zoölogy*, 14:1–314, figs. 1–194; 15:1–220, figs.
        195–545.

Agassiz, Louis
    1860. *Contributions to the Natural History of the United
        States of America.* Second monograph. Parts: I, "Aca-
        lephs in general"; II, "Ctenophorae"; III, "Disco-
        phorae"; IV, "Hydroidae"; V, "Homologies of the
        Radiata"; with forty-six plates. Boston: Little, Brown
        and Company, vol. 3, 339 pp., 19 pls.
    1880. "Report on the Florida Reefs." *Memoirs of the Museum
        of Comparative Zoölogy*, 7(1):1–61, pls. 1–23.

Allman, George James
    1872. *A monograph of the gymnoblastic or tubularian hy-
        droids.* London: The Ray Society, publications 46–47,
        461 pp., pls. 1–23.

Bayer, Frederick M.
    1958. "Les octocoralliaires plexaurides des côtes occidentales
        d'Amerique." *Mémoires du Muséum National d'His-*

toire Naturelle, nouvelle série, Paris (A, Zool.), 16(2):41–56, pls. 1–6.

Berger, Edward William
    1900. "Physiology and histology of the Cubomedusae, including Dr. F. S. Conant's notes on the physiology." Johns Hopkins University: *Memoirs of the Biological Laboratory*, 4(4):1–84, 3 pls.

Bock, Sixten
    1923. "Eine neue marine Turbellariengattung aus Japan." *Uppsala Universitets Årsskrift* (Mat. Naturvet.), 1:1–55.

Bouillon, J.
    1955. "Le cycle biologique de *Limnocnida tanganyicae*." *Bulletin de l'Académie royale des Sciences coloniales*, nouvelle série, 1(3):229–246, figs. 1–10.
    1957. "Étude monographique du genre *Limnocnida* (Limnomeduse)." *Annales de la Société Royale Zoologique de Belgique*, 87(2):253–500, figs. 1–114.

Brinkmann, August
    1906. "Studier over Danmarks rhabdocøle og acøle Turbellarier." *Videnskabelige Meddelelser fra Dansk Naturhistorisk Forening i Kjøbenhavn*, 58:1–159, 5 pls.

Bürger, O.
    1895. "Die Nemertinen des Golfes von Neapel und der angrenzenden Meeres-Abschnitte." *Fauna und Flora des Golfes von Neapel*, Monograph 22:759 pp., pls. 1–31.

Cervigón, Fernando
    1958. "Contribución al estudio de los sifonóforos de las costas de Castellón (Mediterráneo Occidental)." *Investigación Pesquera*, Barcelona, 12:21–47, figs. 1–39.
    1961. "Descripción y consideraciones sobre los sifonóforos de las costas occidentales de Africa, recogidos en las campañas del 'Costa Canaria'," *Investigación Pesquera*, Barcelona, 18:9–31, figs. 1–21.

Chester, Wayland M.
    1913. "The structure of the gorgonian coral *Pseudoplexaura crassa* Wright and Studer." *Proceedings of the American Academy of Arts and Sciences*, 48(20):737–774, pls. 1–4.

Chun, Carl
    1880. "Die Ctenophoren des Golfes von Neapel und der angrenzenden Meeres-Abschnitte. Eine Monographie." *Fauna und Flora des Golfes von Neapel*, Monograph 1:331 pp., pls. 1–18.

Clark, Henry James

1878. "Lucernariae and their allies. A memoir on the anatomy and physiology of *Haliclystus auricula*, and other Lucernarians, with a discussion of their relations to other acalephae; to beroids, and polypi." *Smithsonian Contributions to Knowledge*, 23(2): 138 pp., pls. 1–11.

Coe, Wesley R.

1899. "On the development of the pilidium of certain nemerteans." *Transactions of the Connecticut Academy of Arts and Sciences*, 10:235–262, pls. 31–35.

1926. "The pelagic nemerteans." *Memoirs of the Museum of Comparative Zoology*, 49:246 pp., pls. 1–30.

1943. "Biology of the nemerteans of the Atlantic coast of North America." *Transactions of the Connecticut Academy of Arts and Sciences*, 35:129–328, pls. 1–4.

Corrêa, Diva Diniz

1964. "Corallimorpharia e Actiniaria do Atlântico oeste tropical." Universidade de São Paulo, Faculdade de Filosofia, Ciências e Letras, 139 pp., 16, pls., maps, tables.

Dawydoff, Constantin

1938a. "Les coeloplanides indochinoises." *Archives de zoologie expérimentale et générale*, 80:125–162, figs. 1–16, pl. 1.

1938b. "Les *Gastrodes* de l'Indochine." *Travaux de la Station Zoologique de Wimereux*, 13:131–145, figs. 1–12.

Dejdar, E.

1934. "Die Süsswassermeduse *Craspedacusta sowerbii* Lankester in monographischer Darstellung." *Zeitschrift für Morphologie und Ökologie der Tiere*, 28:595–691, 41 figs.

Delage, Y.

1886. "Etudes histologiques sur les planaires rhabdocoeles acoeles." *Archives de zoologie expérimentale et générale*, (2)4:109–160, pls. 6–7.

Dendy, Arthur

1890 "Observations on the West-Indian chalinine sponges, with descriptions of new species." *Transactions of the Zoological Society of London*, 12(10):349–368, pls. 58–63.

1893. "Studies on the comparative anatomy of sponges. 5. Observations on the structure and classification of the Calcarea Heterocoela." *Quarterly Journal of Microscopical Science* (n.s.), 138:159–257, pls. 10–14.

1915. "Report on the non-calcareous sponges collected by Mr. James Hornell at Okhamandal in Kattiawar in 1905–1906." *Report to the Government of Baroda on the*

Marine Zoology of Okhamandal in Kattiawar, part 2: 93–146, pls. 1–4.

1916.   "Report on the Homosclerophora and Astrotetraxonida collected by H.M.S. 'Sealark' in the Indian Ocean." Percy Sladen Trust Expedition, vol. 6. *Transactions of the Linnean Society*, London (2d series, Zoology), 17(2):225–271, pls. 44–48.

Dubosc, O., and Odette Tuzet

1937.   "L'ovogenèse, la fécondation et les premiers stades du développement des éponges calcaires." *Archives de zoologie expérimentale et générale*, 79(2):157–316, pls. 6–19.

Duerden, J. E.

1901.   "Report on the actinians of Porto Rico." *Bulletin of the U.S. Fish Commission*, 20(part 2):323–374, pls. 1–12.

Evans, R.

1900.   "A description of *Ephydatia blembingia*, with an account of the formation and structure of the gemmule." *Quarterly Journal of Microscopical Science* (n.s.), 44(1):71–109, pls. 1–4.

Fewkes, J. Walter

1879.   "The tubes in the large nectocalyx of *Abyla pentagona*." *Proceedings of the Boston Society of Natural History*, 20:318–324.

1880.   "Contributions to a knowledge of the tubular jellyfishes." *Bulletin of the Museum of Comparative Zoology*, 6(7):127–146, pls. 1–3.

1881.   "Report on the acalephae. Reports on the results of dredging, under the supervision of Alexander Agassiz, in the Caribbean Sea, in 1878, 1879, and along the Atlantic coast of the United States, during the summer of 1880, by the U.S. Coast Survey steamer 'Blake,' Commander J. R. Bartlett, U.S.N. commanding." *Bulletin of the Museum of Comparative Zoology*, 8(7):127–140, pls. 1–4.

1888.   "Studies from the Newport Laboratory. 19. On certain medusae from New England." *Bulletin of the Museum of Comparative Zoology*, 13(7):209–240, pls. 1–6.

Friedemann, O.

1902.   "Untersuchungen über die postembryonale Entwicklung von *Aurelia aurita*." *Zeitschrift für wissenschaftliche Zoologie*, 71:227–267, pls. 12–13.

von Gelei, J.

1930.   " 'Echte' freie Nervenendigungen. (Bemerkungen zu den Receptoren der Turbellarien)." *Zeitschrift für*

Morphologie und Ökologie der Tiere, 18:786–799, 8 figs.

Gohar, Hamed A. F.
1948. "A description and some biological studies of a new alcyonarian species *Clavularia hamra* Gohar." *Publications of the Marine Biological Station Al Ghardaqa (Red Sea)*, Egypt, No. 6:3–33, pls. 1–3.

Gosse, P. H.
1857. "On a new form of corynoid polypes." *Transactions of the Linnean Society*, London, 22:113–116, 1 pl.

Goto, S.
1903. "The craspedote medusa *Olindias* and some of its natural allies." *Mark Anniversary Volume*, New York, pp. 3–22, pls. 1–3.

von Graff, L.
1882. "Rhabdocoelida." *Monographie der Turbellarien*, Leipzig, 454 pp., 20 pls.
1899. "Tricladida Terricola (Landplanrien)." *Monographie der Turbellarien*, Leipzig, 588 pp., 58 pls.
1904–1908. "Turbellaria," in *Dr. H. G. Bronn's Klassen und Ordnungen des Thier-Reichs, wissenschaftlich dargestellt in Wort und Bild*, vol. 4, Vermes, part I, c: 1733–2599, pls. 1–30.

Günther, R. T.
1893. "Preliminary account of the freshwater medusa of Lake Tanganyika." *Annals and Magazine of Natural History* (series 6), 11:269–275, pls. 13–14.

Haeckel, Ernst
1872. *Die Kalkschwämme*. Eine Monographie. Berlin: Verlag von Georg Reimer, vol. 1, 484 pp.; vol. 2, 418 pp.; vol. 3, viii, 60 pls.
1888. "Report on the Siphonophorae collected by H.M.S. Challenger during the years 1873–76." *Report on the Scientific Results of the Voyage of H.M.S. Challenger*. Zoology, 28 (part 77): 380 pp., pls. 1–50.

Hammer, E.
1908. "Neue Beiträge zur Kenntniss der Histologie und Entwicklung von *Sycon raphanus*." *Archiv für Biontologie*, Berlin, 2:289–334, 6 pls.

Hand, Cadet
1960. "The systematics, affinities, and hosts of the one-tentacled, commensal hydroid, *Monobrachium*, with new distribution records." *Journal of the Washington Academy of Sciences*, 47(3):84–88, figs. 1–2.

Hedgpeth, Joel W.

1954. "Anthozoa: the anemones," in *Gulf of Mexico—its origin, waters and marine life*, P. S. Galtsoff (ed.). *U.S. Fishery Bulletin*, 89:285–290, figs. 60–61.

von Heider, K.

1927. "Vom Nervensystem der Ctenophoren." *Zeitschrift für Morphologie und Ökologie der Tiere*, 9:638–678.

Hesse, R.

1897. "Untersuchungen über die Organe der Lichtempfindung bei niederen Thieren. II. Die Augen der Plathelminthen, insonderheit der tricladen Turbellarien." *Zeitschrift für wissenschaftliche Zoologie*, 62:527–582, pls. 27–28.

1902. "Untersuchungen über die Organe der Lichtempfindung bei niederen Tieren. VIII. Weitere Thatsachen. Allgemeines." *Zeitschrift für wissenschaftliche Zoologie*, 72:589–652, pl. 35.

Hickson, Sydney J.

1891. "The medusae of *Millepora murrayi* and the gonophores of *Allopora* and *Distichopora*." *Quarterly Journal of Microscopical Science*, 32(3):375–407, 2 pls., 2 figs.

Hyde, Ida H.

1894. "Entwickelungsgeschichte einiger Scyphomedusen." *Zeitschrift für wissenschaftliche Zoologie*, 58:531–565, 6 pls.

Hyman, Libbie Henrietta

1938. "North American Rhabdocoela and Alloeocoela. II. Rediscovery of *Hydrolimax grisea* Haldeman." *American Museum Novitates*, 1004:1–19, 16 figs.

1939a. "Acoel and polyclad Turbellaria from Bermuda and the sargassum." *Bulletin of the Bingham Oceanographic Collection*, Peabody Museum of Natural History, 7(1):1–26, pls. 1–9.

1939b. "New species of flatworms from North, Central, and South America." *Proceedings of the U.S. National Museum*, 86(3055):419–439, figs. 47–51.

1940. *The invertebrates: Protozoa through Ctenophora.* New York: McGraw-Hill Book Company, 726 pp., 221 figs.

1951. *The invertebrates: Platyhelminthes and Rhynchocoela. The acoelomate Bilateria.* New York: McGraw-Hill Book Company, 550 pp., 208 figs.

1959. "A further study of Micronesian polyclad flatworms." *Proceedings of the U.S. National Museum*, 108(3410): 543–597, figs. 1–17.

Иванов, А. В.

1955. Тип плоские черви — Plathelminthes. Атлас беспозвоночных Дальневосточных морей СССР. Издатель-

ство Академии Наук СССР, Москва — Ленинград.
69-73, табл. XII.

Iwasa, Masao

1953. In *Nihon Dobutsu Zukan* (Kaitei Zoho). *Illustrated Encyclopedia of the Fauna of Japan*, rev. ed., Tokyo: Hokuryukan, Ltd., 2,133 pp., 5,213 figs.

Johnston, George

1847. A *history of the British zoophytes*, 2d ed. London: John van Voorst, vol. 1, 488 pp.; vol. 2, 74 pls.

Joubin, Louis

1893. "Les némertiens," in *Faune Française*, Raphaël Blanchard, and Jules de Guerne (eds.), Soc. d'Éditions Scientifiques, Paris, 235 pp., pls. 1–4.

Kato, Kojiro

1940. "On the development of some Japanese polyclads." *Japanese Journal of Zoology*, 8:537–573, pls. 50–60.

Kölliker, Albert

1870–1872. "Anatomisch-Systematische Beschreibung der Alcyonarien. Erste Abtheilung: Die Pennatuliden." *Abhandlungen der Senckenbergischen Naturforschenden Gesellschaft*, 7:111–255, 487–602; 8:85–275; pls. 1–24.

Komai, Taku

1922. "Studies on two aberrant ctenophores, *Coeloplana* and *Gastrodes*." Kyoto, Japan: author, 102 pp., 9 pls.
1935. "On *Stephanoscyphus* and *Nausithoë*." *Memoirs of the College of Science, Kyoto Imperial University* (series B), 10(5):289–339, pls. 21–22.
1939. "On the enigmatic coelenterate *Tetraplatia*." *Japanese Journal of Zoology*, 8(2):231–250, pl. 31.
1942. "The structure and development of the sessile ctenophore *Lyrocteis imperatoris* Komai." *Memoirs of the College of Science, Kyoto Imperial University* (series B), 17(1):1–63, pls. 1–3.

Korotneff, A. A.

1912. "Die Planarien des Baikalsees (Trikladen) systematisch, anatomisch, und zoogeographisch bearbeitet." *Wissenschaftliche Ergebnisse einer Zoologischen Expedition nach dem Baikal-See unter Leitung des Professors Alexis Korotneff in den Jahren 1900–1902. 5. Lief.* Berlin & Kiev, 1912. 28 pp., 7 pls., 13 textfigs.

Lang, Arnold

1884. "Die Polycladen (Seeplanarien) des Golfes von Neapel und der angrenzenden Meeresabschnitte." *Fauna und*

Flora des Golfes von Neapel, Monograph 11:688 pp., pls. 1–39.

Leloup, E.

1929. "Recherches sur l'anatomie et le développement de *Velella spirans* Forsk." *Archives de Biologie,* 39:397–478, pls. 10–12.

Lentz, Thomas L.

1966. *The cell biology of Hydra.* Amsterdam: North-Holland Publishing Co., 199 pp., 151 figs.

Lévi, Claude

1956. "Étude des *Halisarca* de Roscoff. Embryologie et systématique des démosponges." *Archives de zoologie expérimentale et générale,* 93(1):1–181, figs. 1–62.

1957. "Ontogeny and systematics in sponges." *Systematic Zoology,* 6(4):174–183, figs. 1–4.

Luther, A.

1912. "Studien über acöle Turbellarien aus dem finnischen Meeresbusen." *Acta Societatis scientiarum Fennicae, Fauna et Flora Fennica,* 36(5):1–60, pls. 1–2.

Mayer, Alfred Goldsborough

1900. "Some medusae from the Tortugas, Florida." *Bulletin of the Museum of Comparative Zoology,* 37(2):13–82, pls. 1–44.

1910. *Medusae of the world.* Carnegie Institution of Washington, publication 109. Vol. 1, *The Hydromedusae,* pp. 1–230, pls. 1–29; vol. 2, *The Hydromedusae,* pp. 231–498, pls. 30–55; vol. 3, *The Scyphomedusae,* pp. 499–735, pls. 56–76.

1912. *Ctenophores of the Atlantic coast of North America.* Carnegie Institution of Washington, publication 162, 58 pp., pls. 1–17.

Metschnikoff, Elias

1874. "Studien über die Entwickelung der Medusen und Siphonophoren." *Zeitschrift für wissenschaftliche Zoologie,* 24:15–83.

1881. "Vergleichend-Embryologische Studien." *Zeitschrift für wissenschaftliche Zoologie,* 36:433–444.

1886. "Embryologische Studien an Medusen." *Ein Beitrag z. Genealogie der primitiv Organe,* Wien: Hölder. 159 pp., 12 pls.

Micoletzky, H.

1907. "Zur Kenntniss des Nerven- und Excretionssystems einiger Süsswassertricladen nebst anderen Beitragen zur Anatomie von *Planaria alpina.*" *Zeitschrift für wissenschaftliche Zoologie,* 87:382–434, pls. 21–23.

Minchin, E. A.

1908. "Materials for a monograph of the ascons. The formation of spicules in the genus *Leucosolenia*, with some notes on the histology of the sponges." *Quarterly Journal of Microscopical Science*, 52(3):301–355, pls. 17–21.

Moseley, H. N.

1876. "On the structure and relations of the alcyonarian *Heliopora coerulea*, with some account of the anatomy of a species of *Sarcophyton*, notes on the structure of species of the genus *Millepora*, *Pocillopora* and *Stylaster*, and remarks on the affinities of certain Palaeozoic corals." *Philosophical Transactions of the Royal Society*, London, 166(1):91–129, pls. 8-9.

1880. "Report on certain hydroid, alcyonarian, and madreporarian corals procured during the voyage of H.M.S. Challenger, in the years 1873–1876." *Report on the Scientific Results of the Voyage of H.M.S. Challenger.* Zoology, 2 (part 7):248 pp., pls. 1–16.

Наумов, Донат Владимирович

1960. Гидроиды и гидромедузы морских, солоноватоводных и пресноводных бассейнов СССР. Определители по Фауне СССР, издаваемые Зоологическим Институтом Академии Наук СССР, № 70: 1-585, Табл. I-XXX.

1961. Сцифоидные медузы морей СССР. Определители по Фауне СССР, издаваемые Зоологическим Институтом Академии Наук СССР, № 75: 1-95.

Nawitzky, W.

1931. "*Procarinina remanei*. Eine neue Paleonemertine der Kieler Fiorde." *Zoologische Jahrbücher* (Abt. Anat.), 54:159–234, 29 figs.

Ott, H. N.

1892. "A study of *Stenostoma leucops* O. Schm." *Journal of Morphology*, 7:263–304, pls. 14–17.

Parker, Thomas Jeffery and William A. Haswell

1940. *A text-book of zoology*, 6th ed., vol. 1. London: Macmillan & Co., Ltd., 770 pp., figs. 1–733.

Prenant, M.

1925. "Observations sur les porocytes de *Clathrina coriacea* Mont." *Travaux de la Station Zoologique de Wimereux*, 9:198–204.

Rasmont, R.

1959. "L'ultrastructure des choanocytes d'éponges." *Annales des Sciences Naturelles*, Zoologie (12th series), 1(2):253–262, pls. 1–2.

Reisinger, E.

1923. "Untersuchungen über Bau und Funktion des Exkretionsapparates bei rhabdocölen Turbellarien." *Zoologischer Anzeiger*, 56.

1926. "Untersuchungen am Nervensystem der *Bothrioplana semperi* Braun." *Zeitschrift für Morphologie und Ökologie der Tiere*, 5:119–149.

Salensky, W.

1912. "Entwicklungsgeschichte der Nemertinen im Inneren des Pilidiums." *Mémoires de l'Académie Impériale des Sciences de St.-Pétersbourg*, 30:1–74.

Schulze, F. E.

1887. "Report on the Hexactinellida collected by H.M.S. Challenger during the years 1873–1876." *Report on the Scientific Results of the Voyage of H.M.S. Challenger. Zoology*, 21 (part 53):513 pp., 104 pls.

Schulze, P.

1922. "Der Bau und die Entladung der Penetranten von *Hydra attenuata* Pall." *Archiv für Zellforschung*, 16:383–438, 1 pl.

Sollas, W. J.

1888. "Report on the Tetractinellida collected by H.M.S. Challenger during the years 1873–1876." *Report on the Scientific Results of the Voyage of H.M.S. Challenger. Zoology*, 25 (part 63): 458 pp., 44 pls.

Southcott, R. V.

1956. "Studies on Australian cubomedusae, including a new genus and species apparently harmful to man." *Australian Journal of Marine and Freshwater Research*, 7(2):254–280, figs. 1–23, pls. 1–3.

1959. "Tropical jellyfish and other marine stingings." *Military Medicine*, 124(8):569–579, 6 figs.

Steinmann, Paul

1911. "Revision der schweizerischen Tricladen." *Revue Suisse de Zoologie*, 19(7):175–234, 3 figs.

Tuzet, Odette, and Max Pavans de Ceccatty

1953a. "Les lophocytes de l'éponge *Pachymatisma johnstonni* Bow." *Compte Rendu Hebdomadaire des Séances de l'Académie des Sciences*, Paris, 237:1447–1449, figs. 1–3.

1953b. "Les cellules nerveuses et neuro-musculaires de l'éponge: *Cliona celata* Grant." *Compte Rendu Hebdomadaire des Séances de l'Académie des Sciences*, Paris, 237:2342–2344, figs. 1–4.

Uchida, Tohru

    1953. In *Nihon Dobutsu Zukan* (Kaitei Zoho), *Illustrated Encyclopedia of the Fauna of Japan*, rev. ed., Tokyo: Hokuryukan, Ltd., 2,133 pp., 5,213 figs.

Verrill, Addison Emery

    1922. "Alcyonaria and Actiniaria." *Report of the Canadian Arctic Expedition 1913–1918*. Vol. 8, part G: 164 pp., pls. 1–31.

Wilhelmi, J.

    1906. "Untersuchungen über die Excretionsorgane der Süsswassertricladen." *Zeitschrift für wissenschaftliche Zoologie*, 80:544–575, 2 pls.

    1909. "Tricladen." *Fauna und Flora des Golfes von Neapel*, Monograph 32:405 pp., 16 pls.

Wilson, H. V.

    1894. "Observations on the gemmule and egg development of marine sponges." *Journal of Morphology*, 9(3):277–406, pls. 14–25.

Wulfert, J.

    1902. "Die Embryonalentwicklung von *Gonothyraea lovenii* All." *Zeitschrift für wissenschaftliche Zoologie*, 71:296–327, pls. 16–18.

Zimmermann, W.

    1925. "Die ungeschlechtliche Entwicklung von *Volvox*." *Naturwissenschaften*, 13:397–402.

Index

The page numbers in *italic* type refer to illustrations.

Abylopsis, 59
Acalephae, 26
Acoela, *147*, *164*, *165*
Acotylea, *168*, *171*
Actiniaria, *75*, *81*, *83*, *85*, *86*, *87*, *94*
  acontia, 85
  acrorhagi, 85
  gonads, *86*, *87*
  muscles, *86*, *87*
  septa, *86*, *87*
  septal filaments, *75*, *85*
  symmetry, 30, 78, 86
Actinula larva, 100, *101*, *100–102*
Adocia, 15
Agalma, *60*, *61*
Aglaophenia, 44
Aglaura, life cycle, *101*, *102*
Alaurina, *153*, *162*
Alcyonacea, 81, 82, 93
Alcyonaria, 76–80, 81, 82, 83, 84, 85
Alcyonium, 82
Alloeocoela, *164*, *166*
Allopora, *48*, *49*
Amiskwia, 179, *183*
Amoebocytes, Porifera, 9, *10*, 15 16
Amphiblastula, 17, *18*, *19*
Amphidiscophora, 14
Amphiscolops, *147*, *149*
Ampullae, *47*, *49*, *50*

Anopla, 180, 196
Anthomedusae, 44, *45*, 92
Anthozoa, 93
  general features, 74
  histology, 76
  life history, 104, *106*
  nematocysts, 76
  polyps, *74*, *75*
  septa, 74, 87
  sexual reproduction, 105, *106*, 107
  siphonoglyph, *75*
  skeleton, 76
  structure, *75–77*
  symmetry, 30, 76–78
Antipatharia, 83, 90, *91*, 94
Archaeocytes, 9, *16*, 17
Aristotle, 25, 26
Ascetta, 2
Asexual reproduction, Coelenterata, 94–96, *94*, 103, *105*
  Ctenophora, 137
  Nemertea, 197
  Porifera, 15–17
  Turbellaria, *162*, 168, 169, 171, 173
Associations, Coelenterata, 119–123, *121*
  Ctenophora, 143
  Nemertea, 204
  Porifera, 22, 23

Atolls, 117, 118
Aurelia, 66, 73, 74, 96, 105
Auricles, Ctenophora, 133, 135
    Tricladida, 166
Axis, Octocorallia, 77, 81

Balaenanemertes, 183
Balancers, 130, 131
Barrier reef, 117
Bath sponge, 4
Bdellonemertini, 189, 197
Beroida, 133
Bipalium, 147, 149, 155
Biradial symmetry, 30
Black corals, 83, 90, 94
Blastula, 98, 99, 104, 105, 170
Blood, Nemertea, 191, 193
Blue coral, 81
Bolinopsis, 139, 142
Boloceroides, 95
Bothrioplana, 155
Box jellies, 69, 93, 109
Brain, Nemertea, 180, 183, 187, 188,
    201
    Turbellaria, 153, 155, 156–159,
        158, 172, 173–175, 173
Brain coral, 88
Branching, monopodial, 42
    sympodial, 42
Branchiocerianthus, 43
Bunodeopsis, 81

Calcarea, 14, 17
    distribution, 22
Calliactis, 86
Callianira, 133, 134
Callicarpa, 44
Callyspongia, 3
Calycophorae, 56, 57, 92, 103, 104
Calyptoblastea, 92
Canal, circular, 44
    excurrent, 6
    incurrent, 6, 7, 8
    intracellular, 6, 7
    radial, Coelenterata, 29, 44, 45, 51,
        62, 65, 72
        Porifera, 6, 7, 8
    ring, 29, 45, 51, 65
Carnosa, 14
Carybdea, 66, 67, 70
Carybdeida, 68, 69
Cassiopea, 73, 74, 115
Caudal cirrus, 181, 182
Cell lineage, 170
Cell rosettes, 125, 128, 129

Cephalic grooves, Nemertea, 184
Cephalic lobes, Nemertea, 182
Cephalic slits, Nemertea, 184
Cephalothrix, development, 197, 198
Cerebral canal, Nemertea, 185, 186
Cerebral ganglia, Nemertea, 181, 187,
        188, 201
    Turbellaria, 156
Cerebral organs, Nemertea, 186
Cerebratulus, 181, 192
Ceriantharia, 83, 89, 91, 94
Cestida, 133
Cestoda, 144, 145, 164
Cestum, 132, 136
Challenger Expedition, 118
Chemoreceptors, Turbellaria, 152,
        153
Child, C. M., 169
Chironex, 69, 71
Chiropsalmus, 69
Chlorella, 34
Choanocytes, 4, 10, 11, 17, 21
Choanoflagellates, 11, 24
Chondrilla, 14
Chondrocladia, 2, 15, 22
Chondrocysts, 150
Chondrophorae, 60, 61, 63, 92
Choristida, 14
Chrysaora, 64
Chrysomitra, 103
Cinclides, 85
Circulatory system, Nemertea, 181,
        191, 192, 193
Classification, Coelenterata, 92–94
    Ctenophora, 132–133
    Nemertea, 196, 197
    Platyhelminthes, 164
    Porifera, 14, 15
Clava, 39
Clavularia, 82
Cleavage, radial holoblastic, 17, 98
    spiral, 169, 169, 170, 197
Cliona, 15
Clytia, 44
Cnidoblasts, 31, 34, 36
Cnidoglandular band, 75, 85
Cnidophores, 44, 45
Coelenterata, asexual reproduction,
        94–96, 95, 103, 105
    associations, 119–123, 121
    basic structure, 28
    behavior, 108–112
    classification, 92–94
    defensive mechanisms, 112
    digestion, 112, 113
    distribution, 115, 116
    ecology, 113, 115

excretion, 113
fossil, 26
histology, 31, 32, 33, 34–37
locomotion, 108–111
nematocysts, 26, 32, 34, 35, 36, 37,
    62, 76
nervous reactions, 107, 108
respiration, 107
sexual reproduction, 96–107, 97–
    106
skeleton, 27
    Alcyonaria, 76, 77, *80*, 81, 93
    Milleporina, 46–48, *46*, 92
    Stylasterina, 48–50, *48*, *49*, 92
    Zoantharia, 83, 87, 88, 90, 94
static organs, 51
swimming, 108
symmetry, 29, *30*, 60, 76–79, *78*,
    86, 89
Coelenteron, 27, 32, 40
Coeloblastula, 98, 99, 105, *197*, *198*
Coeloplana, *128*, *134*, 137, 143
Coenosarc, 39, 48
Coenosteum, 47, 48, 50
Coenothecalia, 81
Collar of actinian polyp, 85
Collar cell, 11
Collenchyme, 29, 34
Colloblasts, 125, *131*, 132, 142
Column, Anthozoa, 74, *75*
Comb jellies, 124
Commensalism, Coelenterata, 119,
    120
    Ctenophora, 143
    Nemertea, 204
    Porifera, 22, 23
Conaria larva, 103, *104*
Convoluta, 155
Corallimorpharia, 89, 94
Corals, 26, 88, 114
    growth, 88
    righting reaction, 110
Cordylophora, 43, 113
Cormidia, 57
Coronatae, 70, 72, 93
Cortex, 7, 15
Corymorpha, 43
Cotylea, 168, 171
Craniella, 14
Craspedacusta, 51, 52, *52*, 114
Craspedomonadidae, 11
Crenobia, 155
Crypthelia, *48*, 49
Ctenophora, aboral sensory organ,
    127, 130, *131*
    anal pores, 126
    asexual reproduction, 137

associations, 143
auricles, 133, *135*
balancers, 130, *131*
behavior, 141
body form, *134*, *135*
canal system, 126, *130*
cell rosettes, 125, *128*, 129
classification, 132
colloblasts, *131*, 132, 142
comb rows, 126, *127*
digestion, 141
distribution, 143
disymmetrical cleavage, 138
ecology, 142
general features, 125, 126, *127*,
    128, *131*
histology, 128–132, *129*, *131*
locomotion, 141, 142
luminescence, 142
nematocysts, 142
nervous reactions, 140, 141
nervous system, *129*, 130
oral lobes, 133
parasitic, 143
respiration, 140
sexual reproduction, 138–140, *139*
statocyst, 130
symmetry, 125, *127*
Ctenoplana, *134*, 136, 137
Cubomedusae, 27, 36, 68, 70, 71, 93
Cunina, *51*
Cuvier, Georges, 178
Cyanea, 60, 74, 108
Cyclosystem, *47*, *49*
Cydippid larva, 125, 133, *139*, 140
Cydippida, 132, 133, *134*
Cystonectae, 57
Cytochrome in Turbellaria, 173

Dactylometra, 73
Dactylopore, *47*, *49*
Dactylozooids, 41, *47*, *54*, 60
Daly, Reginald, 118
Dana, James D., 1
Darwin, Charles, 117
Delamination, 98, 99, 101
Demospongiae, 14, 15, 17
Dermal layer, 4, 9, 14, 24
Dermal ostia, 8
Desmophyes, *56*, 57
Desor's larva, 199, *200*
Development, Coelenterata, 96–107,
    97–106
    Ctenophora, 138–140, *139*
    Nemertea, 196–200, *196*, *198*, *199*
    Porifera, 17, *18*, *19*, *20*

Development (*continued*)
  Turbellaria, 169–171, *169, 172, 173, 177*
Digestion, Coelenterata, 112, 113
  Ctenophora, 141
  Nemertea, 202, 203
  Porifera, 20, 21
  Turbellaria, 176
Digestive system, Coelenterata, 27, *28, 29*
  Ctenophora, 126, *127*
  Nemertea, *181*, 193
  Turbellaria, 158–160, *158–160, 172, 173*
Diphyes, 103
Diphyopsis, 57
Discomedusae, 71
Dissogeny, 138
Distichopora, 48, 49
Distribution, Coelenterata, 115, 116
  Ctenophora, 143
  Nemertea, 203, 204
  Porifera, 21, 22
  Turbellaria, 176, 177
Disymmetrical cleavage, 138
Dougherty, E. C., 9
Dugesia, 145
Dynamene, 42

Ecology, Coelenterata, 113–115
  Ctenophora, 142, 143
  Nemertea, 203, 204
  Porifera, 21–23
  Turbellaria, 176, 177, 203
Eleutheria, 115
Ellis, John, 1, 25
Emplectonema, luminescence, 202
Eniwetok Atoll, geological core, 118
Enopla, 180, 196
Entolecithal eggs, Turbellaria, 169
Ephydatia, 15
Ephyra, 73, 94, 96, 103, 104, *105*
Epidermis, Coelenterata, 31, 33, 44, *65, 76*
  Ctenophora, *128*
  insunk, 148, *149*
  Nemertea, 184, *185, 195*
  Porifera, 7
  Turbellaria, 148, *149, 150, 151, 157*
Erythropodium, 79
Eucharis, 128
Eucheilota, 42
Eudoxids, 57, 109
Eudoxoides, 56
Euplectella, 3, 14

Euspongia, 5
Evolutionary aspects, Coelenterata, 26
  Ctenophora, 124
  Nemertea, 179
  Platyhelminthes, 145
  Porifera, 23, 24
Excretion, Coelenterata, 113
  Ctenophora, 125
  Nemertea, 200
  Porifera, 21
Excretory system, Nemertea, *192, 193, 194*
  Turbellaria, 160, *161, 162*
Exumbrella, 29, *65*
Eyes, Nemertea, 186
  Turbellaria, 154

Feeding, Coelenterata, 111
  Ctenophora, 141
  Nemertea, 202, 203
  Porifera, 20
  Turbellaria, 175, 176
Fertilization, Coelenterata, 98, 104, 105
  Ctenophora, 138
  Nemertea, 196
  Porifera, 10, 17
  Turbellaria, 163, 164
Filter-feeders, Porifera, 20
Flagella, action of, 20
Flagellated bands, 75, 85
Flagellated cells, Anthozoa, 76
Flagellated chambers, 4, 6, 7–9, 15
Flame bulbs, Nemertea, 193, *194*
  Turbellaria, 160, *161*
Flatworms, general features, 145, 146, *147*, 148
Float (*see* Pneumatophore)
Folia, 135
Food reserves, Nemertea, 203
  Porifera, 21
  Turbellaria, 176
Fosse, 75, 85
Fossils, Coelenterata, 26
  Nemertea, 179, *183*
  Porifera, 5
Fresh-water sponges, 16, 22
Fringing reef, 117
Fronds, 85
Frontal glands, Nemertea, 184, 186–189, *186, 187*
  Turbellaria, 150, *153*, 154, *158*
Frustules, 101
Funafuti Atoll, geological core, 118
Funnel, Siphonophora, 55
Funnels, subumbrellar, 62, 69

Gas gland, 55
Gastral layer, 4, *6*, 7, 9, 24
Gastric cavity, 29
Gastric filaments, 62, *65*, 72
Gastric pockets, 69
Gastric pouches, 51, 62, *65*
Gastrodermal lamella, 44
Gastrodermis, 27, 31, 32, 40, 76, 128
Gastropores, 47–49, *49*
Gastrovascular cavity, Anthozoa, 74
Gastrovascular system, Scyphozoa, 62
Gastrozooids, 41, *47*, 49, *54*, 60
Gastrula, 19, 24, 99, 104, 105
Gemmaria, *42*
Gemmules, *16*
Geodia, 14
Geological cores, 118
Geonemertes, *196*
Geoplana, *149*, *151*
Glial cells, Turbellaria, 156
Globuli cells, Nemertea, 188
Gonads, Actiniaria, 86, 87
    Alcyonaria, 79
    Antipatharia, 90
    Carybdeida, 69
    Ceriantharia, 89
    Coelenterata, 27
    Ctenophora, 125, 136, 137
    Hydra, 97, 98
    Nemertea, *181*, *183*, 184, *194*, *195*
    Scyphozoa, 62, *65*, 68
    Turbellaria, 160, 161, *162*, 165–167
Gonangium, 41
Gonionemus, 51, 101, 115
Gonodendra, *54*, 55, 60
Gonopalpon, 55, 60
Gonophores, 41, 44, *47*, 49, 55, *57*, 60
Gonothecae, 41
Gonozooids, 41
Goreau, T. F., 123
Gorgonacea, 76, 77, 81, *84*, 93
Gorgonia, *84*
Götte's larva, 171
Grant, R. E., 1
Grantia, stomoblastula, *18*
Gymnoblastea, 92

Hadromerina, 15
Halichondria, 15, 23
Halichondrina, 15
Haliclona, 15
Haliclystus, 67, 68
Halisarca, 14

Hamburger, V., 169
Haplosclerina, 15
Heterocoela, 14
Heteronemertini, *189*, 196
Hexactinellida, 3, 4, 8, 12, 14, 22
Hexacorallia, 77, 83
Hexasterophora, 14
Hippiospongia, 5
Hippopodius, 56
Hircinia, 15, 23
Histology, Coelenterata, 31, 32, 33, 34, 35, 36, 37, 44, 65, 67, 76
    Ctenophora, 128–130, *128*, *129*, 132
    Nemertea, 184, *185*, 186, *187*, 188, *189*, 193, *194*, *195*
    Porifera, 8, 9, *10*, 11
    Turbellaria, 148, *149*, *151*, 153, 154, *157*
Hofstenia, 155
Homocoela, 14
Hood, 65, 66
Hoplonemertini, *189*, 196
Hoploplana, 169
Horny corals, 74, 93
Hyalonema, 3, 14, 22
Hydra, 38, 94, 97, 98
Hydractinia, 41, 43, 121
Hydranth, 37, 38, 39, 40, *41*, *42*
Hydrichthys, 121
Hydrocaulus, 38, 39, 42
Hydrocorals, 47–49, 92
Hydroctena, 50, 53
Hydroid form, 37
Hydroidea, 92
Hydroids, 26
    athecate, 38, *40*, *41*, 44
    basic structure, 28
    colonial, 38, *40*–42, *44*
    fresh-water, 113
    growing point, *42*, 43, 99
    parasitic, 53, *121*
    solitary, 43
    thecate, 38, *41*, 44
Hydrolimax, *153*, 158
Hydromedusae, 44, *45*, 46
    asexual reproduction, 94, 95
Hydrorhiza, 38, 39, *40*, 42, 99
Hydrozoa, 26, 92
    anatomy, 38
    asexual reproduction, 94, 95
    life cycle, 99, *101–104*
    sexual reproduction, 96–103, *97–104*
    structure, 37–60, *38*, *40–42*, *45–54*, *56–59*, *61*, *63*
    symmetry, 30, 37

Hyman, L. H., 14, 145
Hypostome, 27, 38, 39

Inquilinism, 22
Insunk epidermis, 148, *149*
Inversion, Porifera, 19, 24
    Volvox, 19

Jellyfishes, 72, 92
    fresh-water, 51, 52, 92, 102

Kalyptorhynchia, proboscis, 165
Keratosa, 15

Lampetia, 133, *134*
Lappets, marginal, *51*
Lar, 39, *40, 44*
Larvae, actinula, *100-102*
    amphiblastula, 17, *18,* 19
    blastula, 98, 99, 104, 105, 170
    coeloblastula, 98, 99, 105, 197, *198*
    conaria, 103, *104*
    cydippid, 125, 133, *139,* 140
    Desor's, 199, 200
    ephyra, 73, 94, *96,* 103-105, *105*
    gastrula, *18,* 19, 24, 99, 104, 105
    Götte's, 171
    Müller's, 169, 171, *172, 173, 177*
    parenchymella, 17, *18,* 19, 20, 24
    pilidium, 198-200, *198, 199*
    planula, 24, 26, 96, 97, 99, 101,
        103-106
    rataria, 103, *104*
    scyphistoma, 104, *105*
    stereogastrula, 19, 99, 170, 197
    stomoblastula, 17, *18,* 19, 24
Lateral organ, Nemertea, *185,* 186
Lebrunia, 86
Leptomedusae, 44, *45,* 92
Leucandra, 2
Leuconia, water currents, 20
Leucosolenia, 14
Leucothea, 142
Life cycle, *Aglaura,* 101, *102*
    Anthozoa, 104, 105, *106,* 107
    Aurelia, 105
    Hydrozoa, 99, *101-104*
    Limnocnida, 102
    Obelia, 101
    Pelagia, 106
    Scyphozoa, 103, 104, *105, 106*
    Siphonophora, 103, *104*
    Trachylina, 100, 101, *102*

Tubularia, 99, 100
Velella, 101, *103, 104*
Limnocnida, 51, 52, 101, *102,* 114
Lineus, feeding and digestion, 202,
    203
    larva, 199
Linnaeus, C., 1
Linuche, 71
Lion's mane, 27
Liriope, 101
Lithostyle, *51*
Lobata, 132, 133, *135*
Locomotion, Coelenterata, 108-111
    Ctenophora, 141, 142
    Nemertea, 201
    Turbellaria, 175
Loggerhead sponge, 3
Lophocyte, 9, *10,* 14
Lucernaria, 67, 68
Luminescence, Ctenophora, 142
    Emplectonema, 202

Macrostomum, 159
Madreporaria, 83, 87, 88, 94
    nematocysts, 88
    septal filaments, 88
    skeleton, **87,** 88
    symmetry, 78, 87, 88
Maehrenthalia, 147
Malacobdella, development, 197, 198
Manubrium, 27, 29, 37, 39, 44, *45,*
    47, 51, 62
Medusa, 27
    acraspedote, 29
    basic structure, 28, 29
    craspedote, 29, 37
    Millepora, 47
    scyphozoan, 60
    sedentary, 110
Mesenteries, 29, 74
Mesogloea, 29, 30, 34, 65, 76, 77, 87
Mesolamella, 34
Mesostoma, 153
Metagenesis, 96, 103
Metazoa, Subkingdom, 5
Microciona, 15
Microhydra, 50, 52
Micropyle, 16
Microstomum, 150
Millepora, 46-48, *46, 47*
Milleporina, 46, 92
Minot, C., 144
Minyas, 110, 115
Mnemiopsis, 135
Monaxonida, 15
Monobrachium, 39, *40*

Monopodial growth, *42*, 94
Monostylifera, 196
Montastrea, 88
Moon-jelly, 74
Mouth arms, 62, *65*
Muggiaea, 60
Müller's larva, 169, 171, *172, 173,*
    177
Multipolar ingression, 98, 99
Murray, Sir John, 118
Musculature, Coelenterata, 31, 32,
    33, 44, 62, 66, 68, 75, 76, 86,
    87, 89
  Ctenophora, *129*
  Nemertea, *182, 185, 187, 188, 189,*
    192
  Turbellaria, *149, 151, 157, 157,*
    159
Mycale, 15
Myocytes, 9, *10,* 21
Myxospongida, 14

Narcomedusae, *50,* 52, 92
Nausithoe, 71, 72
Nectonemertes, 183
Nectophores, 55, *56,* 109
Nemathybomes, 85
Nematocysts, 26, 32, 34, *35, 36,* 62,
    76
  batteries, 27
  of Ctenophora, 142
  discharge, 36
  formation, 34
  function, 111
  of Madreporaria, 88
  of *Millepora,* 48
  in Turbellaria, 150
  of Zoantharia, 83
Nematocytes, 34
Nematophores, *41*
Nematotheca, *41*
Nemertea, asexual reproduction, 197
  associations, 204
  blood, 191, 193
  cephalic lobes, *182*
  circulatory system, *181,* 191, *192,*
    193
  classification, 196, 197
  digestion, 202, 203
  digestive system, *181,* 193
  distribution, 203, 204
  ecology, 203, 204
  evolution, 179, 190, 191
  excretory system, *192, 193, 194*
  eyes, 186
  feeding, 202, 203

fertilization, 196
form, 180, 182, *181–183*
frontal glands, 184, *186, 187, 188,*
    189
general features, 178–184
histology, 184, *185* 186, *187,* 188,
    189, 193, *194, 195*
locomotion, 201
metamorphosis of larvae, 199, 200
morphology, *181,* 184, *187,* 196
musculature, 182, *185, 187,* 188,
    189, 192
nervous reactions, 200–202
nervous system, *181,* 186–188, *186*
pigmentation, 180
proboscis, *187,* 189–191, *189, 192,*
    202
reproductive system, *181,* 194–196,
    195, 196
respiration, 200
sensory structures, 184, *185,* 186,
    187
sexual reproduction, *196,* 197–200,
    198, 199, 200
size, 180
Nemertopsis, 187
Nerve cells, Coelenterata, 32, 38, 40
  Ctenophora, 129, 130, *129, 130*
  Nemertea, 188
  Porifera, 9, *10,* 11
  Turbellaria, *153,* 156
Nerve net, 38, 107
Nerve plate, Tricladida, 166
Nerve reactions, Coelenterata, 108
  Ctenophora, 140–141
  Nemertea, 200–202
  Turbellaria, 174–175
Nervous system, Coelenterata, 66, 67,
    107
  Ctenophora, *129, 130*
  Nemertea, *181, 186,* 187, 188
  Turbellaria, 146, 148, *153,* 154,
    155, 156, *157, 158, 172,*
    173
Neurochord cells, Nemertea, 188
Neuroid transmission, 21
Neuronemertes, 188
Niobia, 95
Notoplana, 169
Nuda, 132
Nymphozoon, 147

Obelia, life cycle, *101*
Ocelli, Coelenterata, *65, 67,* 69, 108
  Nemertea, 186
  Turbellaria, *153,* 154

Octocorallia, 77–83, 93
  axis, 77, 81
  coenenchyme, 80
  colonial form, 82, *84*
  gonads, 79
  polyps, 77–80, *78, 79, 82*
  spicules, 80, *80*
  structure, *84*
  symmetry, *30,* 77–79, *78*
  water currents, 78
Ocyropsis, 142
Olindioides, 52
Olynthus, 2, 19
Operculum of nematocyst, 34, *35*
Oral arms, 62, *65*
Osculum, *4, 6,* 7, *8,* 21, 24
Osmoregulation, 174
Ostium, dermal, *7, 8*
  incurrent, *6, 7*
  internal, *6, 7, 8*
Otoporpa, *51*
Oulangia, 88

Packet glands, 184, *185*
Paleonemertini, *189,* 196
Palpons, 54
Parasitism, Coelenterata, *121*
  Ctenophora, 143
  Nemertea, 204
  Platyhelminthes, 144, 145, 164
Parazoa, Subkingdom, 5
Parenchyma, Turbellaria, 157
Parenchymella, 17, *18,* 19, *20,* 24
Pearse, A. S., 23
Pedal disc, 37, *75,* 83
Pedal laceration, 95
Pedalia, 66, *70, 71*
Pelagia, 73, 103, *106*
Pelagohydra, 110, 115
Pelagonemertes, 183, 195
Pennaria, 43
Pennatula, 84
Pennatulacea, 81, *84,* 93
Perisarc, 38, *39, 40*
Peronia, *51*
Phagocata, 145
Phallonemertes, 195
Pharynx, Turbellaria, *153, 155,* 158–
  160, *158, 159, 162, 172, 173*
Phylactocarp, *44*
Physalia, 53, 55, 109
  (*See also* Portuguese man-of-war)
Physiology, Coelenterata, 107–113
  Ctenophora, 140–142
  Nemertea, 200–203
  Porifera, 20, 21
  Turbellaria, 171, 173–176

Physonectae, *56,* 60, *61*
Physophorida, 92
Pilidium, 198–200, *198, 199*
Pinacocytes, 8, 9, *10,* 21
Pinnules, 78
Planocera, 155, 173
Planula, 24, 26, 96, 97, 99, 101, 103–
  106
Platyctenea, 132, *134,* 136, 137, 142,
  143
Platyelmia, 144
Platyhelminthes, classification, 165
  evolution, 145
  general features, 144, 145
Pleurobrachia, 133, 135
Plumularia, 44
Pneumatophore, 55, 56, 60, *61,* 63,
  109
Poecilosclerina, 15
Polar fields, *127,* 130
Polycelis, 145
Polycladida, *147,* 164, 167, 168
Polyp, basic structure, 27, 28, 29
Polypodium, 53
Polystylifera, 196
Porifera, asconoid structure, 5, 6, 7, 8,
  14
  asexual reproduction, 15–17, *16*
  associates, 3, 22, 23
  choanocytes, 4, 7, 8, *10*
  classification, 5, 14, 15
  color, 1
  dermal layer, 4
  digestion, 20, 21
  distribution, 21, 22
  ecology, 21–23
  enzymes, 21
  excretion, 21
  fertilization, *10,* 17
  filter feeding, 20
  form, 1, 2, 3, 4
  fresh-water, 22
  gastral layer, 4, *6,* 7
  histology, 8, 9, *10,* 11
  inversion of stomoblastula, *18,* 19
  leuconoid structure, 5, 6, 7, 8, 14
  nervous-type cells, 9, *10,* 11
  phylogeny, 23, 24
  physiology, 20, 21
  reaction to stimuli, 21
  respiration, 21
  sexual reproduction, 17, *18,* 19, 20
  skeleton, 4, 12, 14, 15
  spicules, 3, 4, 8, *10,* 12, *13, 16*
    (*See also* Spicules)
  syconoid structure, 5, 6, 7, 8, 14
  water current, 20

Porocytes, 7–9, *10*, 21
Porpema, 60, *61*
Porpita, 60, 109, 122
Portuguese man-of-war, 26, 36, *53*, 60
Praya, 57, *58*, 60
Proarmaueria, 183
Proboscidactyla, 44, *45*
Proboscis, Kalyptorhynchia, 165
  Nemertea, *187*, *189*, 190, 191, *192*, 202
Procarinina, 195
Prosopyle, 6–8
Protonephridium, Turbellaria, 160
Pseudoceros, *147*, 169
Pseudomanubrium, *50*, 51
Pseudoplexaura, *84*
Pseudotentacles, 85
Ptychodactiaria, 89

Radial canals, Coelenterata, 29, 44, *45*, 51, 62, *65*, 72
  Porifera, *6*, 7, 8,
Rataria, 103, *104*
Rathkea, *42*, 95
Reduction bodies, 16
Reefs, 116–118
Regeneration, Ctenophora, 137, 138
  Nemertea, 197
  Porifera, 15
  Turbellaria, 168, 169, 175
Reproductive system, Nemertea, *181*, 194–196, *195*, *196*
  Turbellaria, *147*, *158*, 160, *162*, 163
Respiration, Coelenterata, 107
  Ctenophora, 140
  Porifera, 21
  Nemertea, 200
  Turbellaria, 173
Reunition masses, 15
Rhabdites, *149*, 150
Rhabdocoela, *147*, 164–166
Rhabdoids, 150
Rhammites, 150
Rheoreceptors, Turbellaria, 152, *153*
Rhizostomae, 71–73, *73*, 93
Rhopalium, *65*, *66*, 72, 109
Rhopalonema, *50*
Rhynchocoel, *187*, 190, 191, *192*
Rhynchocoela, 179
Rhynchodaeum, 189
Ribbon worms, 178
Ring sinus, 62, 69
Rothschild, Lord, 14

Sargassum community, 114, 121, 177
Sarsia, *45*, 95
Schultze, Max, 179
Scleractinia (*see* Madreporaria)
Scleroblast, 9, 12, 14, 16, 77, 80
Scypha, 14
Scyphistoma, 29, 60, 72, 73, 94, 96, 103–105, *105*
Scyphozoa, 60, *62*, 66–74, *64–73*
  asexual reproduction, 94, 96
  form, *64*, *70–73*
  gastrovascular system, *62*, *65*
  life cycle, 103–104, *105*, *106*
  sexual reproduction, 103–104, *105*, *106*
  structure, *65–69*
  symmetry, 60
Sea anemones, 74, 81, 83, 85, 86, 94, 114
  avoidance reactions, 112
  burrowing, 83, 89
  locomotion, 110
Sea fans, 81, *84*
Sea gooseberry, *134*
Sea nettles, 26, 73
Sea pens, 74, *84*, 93
Sea wasps, 27, 68, 93
Semaeostomae, 71–73, *73*, 93
Sensory niche, 66
Sensory pits, 67
Septa, 29, 62, 68, 69, 74, 75, *76–79*, *78*, 86, *87*, 89
  complete, 29, 83
  Coronatae, 71
  formation, 105
  incomplete, 29
  perfect, 83
Septal filaments, 74, 75, 78, 79, 83, 85, 87–89, *87*
Sexual reproduction, Anthozoa, 104, 105, *106*, 107
  Coelenterata, 96–107, *97–106*
  Ctenophora, 138–140, *139*
  Hydrozoa, 96, *97–104*
  Nemertea, *196*, 197–200, *198*, *199*
  Porifera, 17, *18*, *19*, *20*
  Scyphozoa, 103–105, *105*, *106*
  Turbellaria, 169–173, *172*, *173*, 177
Siphonoglyph, 27, 74, 75, 78, 83, 107
Siphonophora, 53–57, *54*, *56–59*, 60, *61*, 92, 101, 102
Siphonozooids, 107
Soft corals, 74
Solenia, 79
Solmundella, 53

Sorocelis, 147
Spheciospongia, 3, 15, 23
Spicules, Octocorallia, 79–81, 84
    Porifera, 3, 4, 8, 10, 12, 13, 16
      amphidisc, 13, 14
      anchor, 3
      anisochela, 13
      aster, 13, 14
      desma, 13, 14
      discohexaster, 13
      floricome, 13
      formation of, 10, 14
      of gemmules, 16
      hexactinal, 12, 13
      hexasters, 13, 14
      megascleres, 12, 14, 15
      microscleres, 12, 14, 15
      monaxon, 12–15, 13
      oxea, 15
      oxyhexaster, 13
      pinulated pentact, 13
      polyaxon, 14
      scopula, 13
      sigma, 13
      spheraster, 13
      sphere, 14
      sterraster, 13
      tetraxon, 12, 13, 14
      triaene, 13, 14
      triaxon, 12, 13, 14
      triradiate, 12, 13
      tylostyle, 13, 15
Spinipora, 49
Spirocysts, 36
Sponges, associates of, 22, 23
    boring, 15
    as camouflage, 23
    chicken-liver, 14
    commercial, 4, 5
    fire, 15
    fresh-water, 9, 15, 16, 22
    horny, 15
    loggerhead, 15
    synthetic, 5
Spongia, 5, 15
Spongilla, 15
Spongillidae, 9, 15, 22
Spongin, 4, 5, 13, 14, 15
Spongioblast, 9, 14
Spongocoel, 6, 7, 8, 18, 19, 24
Starvation, in Nemertea, 203
Statocyst, Coelenterata, 51
    Ctenophora, 127, 130, 131
    Nemertea, 186
    Turbellaria, 154, 155
Stauromedusae, 67, 68, 68, 69, 93
Stem, of Siphonophora, 57, 58, 59

Stenostomum, 151
Stephanoscyphus, 71, 72
Stereogastrula, 19, 99, 170, 197
Stinging coral, 46, 47, 92
Stolon, 37, 81, 82
Stolonifera, 81, 82, 93
Stoma, 75, 85
Stomoblastula, 17, 18, 19, 24
Stomolophus, 74
Stony corals, 74, 83, 87, 88, 94
Strobila, 103, 105
Strobilation, 104
Stygiomedusa, 73
Stylasterina, 48, 49–50, 48, 49, 92
Style, 49
Stylets, 190, 192
Stylochus, 171
Suberites, 23
Subgenital pits, 62, 65
Subumbrella, 29, 44, 65
Subumbrellar funnels, 62, 69, 107
Suckers, Coelenterata, 51
    Turbellaria, 152
Suctorial mouths, 62, 72
Sulculus, 83
Sulcus, 74, 83
Sycon, 14, 18
Symbiosis, in Coelenterata, 119, 122,
    123
    in Porifera, 23
Symmetry, Actiniaria, 30, 78, 86
    Anthozoa, 30, 76–78, 78
    Ceriantharia, 78, 89
    Coelenterata, 29, 30, 60, 76–79,
      78, 86, 89
    Ctenophora, 125, 127
    Hydrozoa, 30, 37
    Octocorallia, 30, 77–79, 78
    Scleractinia, 78, 87, 88
    Scyphozoa, 60
    Zoantharia, 30, 77, 78, 86
    Zoanthidea, 89
Sympodial growth, 42, 94
Synaptic nervous system, 108

Tabulae, 47
Tangoreceptors, Turbellaria, 152
Tedania, 15
Telestacea, 81, 82, 93
Telesto, 82
Tenaculi, 85
Tentacles, adhesive, 52
    capitate, 38, 39
    filiform, 38, 39
Tentaculata, 132
Tentaculozooids, 41

Tentilla, 54, *58*, 59
Tethya, 21
Tetracelis, *149*
Tetractinellida, 14
Tetraplatia, 53
Theca, 87, 98
  gonotheca, *38*, 41
  hydrotheca, *41*
  nematotheca, *41*
Thimble jelly, 71
Thysanozoon, *169*, *172*
Toxicity, of Coelenterata, 26, 69, 71
  of Nemertea, 202
Trabecular net, 8
Trachylina, 50, 92, 101, *101*, *102*
Trachymedusae, 50–52, 92, 115
Trematoda, 144, 145, 164
Trembley, Abraham, 25
Tricladida, *147*, 164, 166, 167
Tubulanus, 186
Tubularia, *100*, 101
Tubulariidae, 99
Turbellaria, adhesive structures, 151,
    152, *153*
  asexual reproduction, *162*, 168,
    169, 171, 173
  cerebral eyes, *147*
  classification, 164–168
  digestion, 176
  digestive system, 158–160, *158–*
    160, *172*, *173*
  distribution, 176, 177
  ecology, 176, 177, 203
  epidermis, 148–150
  excretory system, 160, *161*, *162*
  feeding, 175, 176
  fertilization, 163, 164
  form, 146, *147*
  frontal glands, *153*, *154*, *158*
  general features, 145–148
  histology, 148, *149*, 150–152, *151*,
    153, *154*, *157*
  locomotion, 175
  Müller's larva, 169, 171, *172*, *173*,
    177
  musculature, *149*, *151*, *157*, *157*,
    159
  nervous reactions, 174, 175
  nervous system, 146, 148, 153–
    158, *153*, *155*, *158*, *172*, *173*
  osmoregulation, 174
  pharynx, *153*, *155*, 158–160, *158*,
    159, *162*, *172*, *173*
  physiology, 171, 173
  pigmentation, 158

receptors, 152, *153*, 154
regeneration, 168, 169, 175
reproductive system, *147*, *158*, 160,
    161, *162*, 163
respiration, 173
sexual reproduction, 169–171, *169*,
    172, *173*, 177
size, 146
spiral cleavage, *169*, *170*
statocyst, *147*
tentacles, *147*
Tuzet, Odette, 9

Umbrella, 29, 57, 60, *65*
Unipolar ingression, 98

Vallicula, 137
Vaughan, T. Wayland, 116
Velarium, 69, *70*, 71, 109
Velella, 60, *63*, 102, *103*, *104*, 109,
    122
Velum, 29, 37, 44, 50, *51*, 109
Ventral nerve plate, Turbellaria, 156
Venus' flower basket, 3
Venus' girdle, *135*, 136
Vermes, 144
Verongia, 15
Vesicles, 85
Vogt, C., 144
Vogtia, 56
Volvox, 19, 24

Warts, 85
Water currents, Coelenterata, 78, 107
  Porifera, 6, 20
Wilson, H. V., 15

Yungia, *172*

Zoantharia, 36, 77, 83, 93
  nematocysts, 83
  siphonoglyph, 83
  symmetry, 30, 77, 78, 86
Zoanthidea, 89, 90, 94, 114
Zoochlorellae, 23, 32
Zooids, 41
Zoophytes, sponges, 1
Zooxanthellae, 23, 32, *33*, 113, 122,
    123